Muslim Prisoner Litigation

Muslim Prisoner Litigation

AN UNSUNG AMERICAN TRADITION

SpearIt

UNIVERSITY OF CALIFORNIA PRESS

University of California Press
Oakland, California

© 2023 by SpearIt

Library of Congress Cataloging-in-Publication Data

Names: SpearIt, author.
Title: Muslim prisoner litigation : an unsung American tradition / SpearIt.
Description: Oakland, California : University of California Press, [2023] |
    Includes bibliographical references and index.
Identifiers: LCCN 2023002304 | ISBN 9780520384842 (hardback) |
    ISBN 9780520384859 (paperback) | ISBN 9780520384866 (epub)
Subjects: LCSH: Muslim prisoners—Legal status, laws, etc.—United
    States. | Muslim prisoners—Religious life. | Prisoners—Civil rights—
    United States.
Classification: LCC KF9731 .S69 2023 | DDC 344.7303/56—dc23/
    eng/20230524
LC record available at https://lccn.loc.gov/2023002304

Manufactured in the United States of America

32 31 30 29 28 27 26 25 24 23
10 9 8 7 6 5 4 3 2 1

Contents

Acknowledgments

This book is possible because of my unfailing support system, and I am grateful to have many behind me who have helped with this project. In terms of material support, I am indebted to the Pitt Momentum Fund, University of Pittsburgh School of Law, including Amy Wildermuth, Haider Ala-Hamoudi, Debbie Brake, Sheila Velez Martinez, Karen Shephard, Karen Knochel, Deb Geary, Cori Parise, LuAnn Driscoll, and Lynsey Gutzmer, my research assistant. I also would like to thank Maura Roessner and staff at the University of California Press, who had faith in the project and were patient with me in bringing it to fruition.

I started this book during troubled times. In the 2018–19 academic year, I visited at a law school under the impression that I would be auditioning for a permanent job. I moved across the country for this opportunity, but, by the time I arrived, there had been a change in management, and the newly installed dean derailed the possibility of any such audition. It was hard to learn as a single parent that I had uprooted my four children, rented my home, gotten a leave of absence from my home institution, and lost a year of retirement savings—all for nothing. However, I did not go quietly. I complained to the dean and the university president, who refused to organize a meeting that included the professor who recruited me with the misrepresentations. There was no fair procedure, and instead, my legitimate grievances were weaponized against me and used to suspend me "with pay." The administration said I created a "hostile work environment," which became its basis for forcing me to sit out teaching for the spring semester. As part of the suspension, I was mandated not to be in contact with any employee or student at the school.

So there I was, painted as the most dangerous man in a new town with hardly any friends and a growing sense of frustration from being mistreated and silenced by the school. It was in this moment of disruption that a book was born. It was a rare moment, free from teaching and service obligations, and with time to reflect on what had happened to me. My thoughts kept taking me to my work on prisons and cases about guards mistreating Muslims, who, in turn, complained and were made to suffer further for daring to complain. I began to look up other case law and research other sources. The initial investigations lured me away from my own problems, and I learned of tribulations that made my situation seem trivial by comparison. This experience primed me to want to talk about the guards, prisons, and courts, and the way they silenced people in prison. I unknowingly sought consolation in these stories of prison-heroes who dared to challenge their captors. I saw their struggles and was awed at the great risk some took to be heard. The research centered my thoughts and gave me focus when I was without recourse, and instead of giving into anger and hatred, I gave myself to this project, and it gave me therapy. My sincerest desire is for this work to benefit the reader as much as writing it has helped me.

SpearIt
Pittsburgh 2023

Abbreviations

AEDPA	Antiterrorism and Effective Death Penalty Act
AMS	Archive of Muhammad Speaks
BOP	Federal Bureau of Prisons
CAIR	Council on American-Islamic Relations
CMUs	communication management units
NGE	Nation of Gods and Earths
NOI	Nation of Islam
PLRA	Prison Litigation Reform Act
RFRA	Religious Freedom Restoration Act
RLUIPA	Religious Land Use and Institutionalized Person Act
Section 1983	Civil Rights Act of 1871

Introduction

The Black Muslims are undoubtedly the largest and most
organized group ever to reside in American prisons. Their
impact upon the field of corrections, particularly on
prisoners' rights litigation, has yet to be adequately addressed.

—James B. Jacobs, "Stratification and Conflict among
  Prison Inmates"

For most Americans, "prison jihad" may sound frightening and conjure
images of religious militants, bearded, turbaned, and under the spell of
foreign radical networks. After all, former US Congressman Peter King
spent several years in Congress on a crusade trying to convince lawmakers
and the American public that Muslims in prison had fallen under the sway
of Al-Qaeda and were heading toward extremist violence. He was not the
only one. Reporters, commentators, and even scholars found themselves
lured by the exciting prospect of prisons becoming a new frontier of the
American "war on terror." While this may be the immediate impression,
there is nothing like that happening in American prisons. However, there
has been a different type of jihad taking place, one that is real and identifi-
able. This is not the sensational jihad of headline media; rather, this jihad
is uneventful and quiet by comparison and has persisted since the 1960s
with hardly any public notice.

Despite little attention and recognition, Muslims in prison occupy a
unique spot in the history of prison litigation, which is partly indebted to
the influence of Islamic ideology. While the role of Muslims in this history
has yet to be adequately addressed in scholarship, even decades after the
dearth was recognized, less is known about how religion itself influenced

1

the course of prison law jurisprudence. This book attempts to remove some critical gaps in our understanding by chronicling a different type of prison jihad. In this jihad, the primary weapon is the ability to tell one's story to the world beyond, to narrate the pain, suffering, and unfairness that characterizes life for some behind prison walls. By situating Muslim efforts in their rightful place in the history of American prison law, the book takes the study of law and religion in new and unexpected directions and invites consideration of Muslims, not as villains who wish to harm the country, but as upholders of the most cherished principles that undergird American law and society.

While King was correct about the reality of prison jihad, he was wrong in propagating the idea that Muslims were under the sway of foreign terrorist operatives and embracing extremist violence. In time, his two main fears failed to manifest in any meaningful way, and he abandoned his campaign to paint Muslims as a unique threat to prison and national security. As mistaken as he was, King's crusades nonetheless caused unjustified antagonism and fomented Islamophobia. His crusade translated into real suffering in communities already reeling from the social and political backlash that followed the attacks of 9/11. His efforts have contributed to making the word "jihad" a dog whistle against Muslims and he is credited with causing much harm to Muslim communities.[1] King's misunderstandings about Islam in prison, as flawed as they were, were especially unfortunate because they overshadowed the righteous struggles that were taking place in court.

To describe this legal development in terms of "jihad" is no stretch of the imagination. The word jihad may best be understood as the duty to "struggle" or "sacrifice" in the path of God, to "make Allah's cause succeed," or to "strive" for the cause of Allah.[2] Sometimes passages in the Quran apply the term as authorization to fight in physical combat, however in other contexts, the concept is internal, with the believer struggling to overcome desire, temptation, and other forces that sway one from submission to Allah. Muslims have endured hardship, violence, and oppression by prisons and prison staff simply due to their faith. The Muslim response has not been physical combat or clandestine violence; rather, it has been to engage in various forms of struggle, including formal complaints, protests, and protracted litigation to resist their subjugation.

From this point of view, Muslims may be seen as caught in the middle of two struggles. On one hand, there is a genuine struggle with adversaries who have abused Muslims physically and psychologically and have deprived them of freedoms and rights. On the other, it is sometimes impossible to separate such struggles from the person since the very ability to succeed in personal struggle may be compromised by repression. Whether they are deprived of religious reading materials, access to religious leaders, or fellowship with other Muslims, these hardships bear directly on one's ability to succeed with internal struggles. Hence, Muslims in prison straddle both senses of jihad, the personal struggle of self and external struggle against an adversary.

By embracing normative channels to voice their grievances, Muslims in prison may be rightly seen as freedom fighters in a world where freedoms are scarce. It is a world where they are outmatched by the state at every turn—a modern-day David and Goliath story—where the victory is simply getting one's case heard before a court. However, in the post-9/11 era, Americans have viewed Islam as a fanatical religion. Muslims continue to be vilified by mainstream media and politicians and signaled out for differential treatment by the government. In the popular American imagination, Muslims remain untrustworthy, suspect, and ultimately, the most dangerous and despised religious group in the country.

Muslim Prisoner Litigation: An Unsung American Tradition recalibrates this imbalance and addresses gaps in scholarship that have been neglected far too long. One is to understand how religion influences litigation efforts at various levels of analysis; another is to recognize how litigation efforts advance and support the rule of law. Building on the work of scholars such as Edward E. Curtis IV, whose study of the Nation of Islam (NOI) explored how the religious community rooted its identity, political analysis, and cultural expression in Islamic thought and history, this work examines how these factors played out in the prison context. Simultaneously, the work supplements Garret Felber's central claims in *Those Who Know Don't Say* (2019). In that work, Felber theorized the prison litigation efforts of NOI members as a part of a multipronged strategy to resist the carceral state. As impressive and comprehensive as this account is, it speaks little about the significance of the community's political and religious ideas on those same efforts. In the pages that follow,

Muslim Prisoner Litigation offers a comprehensive analysis of this critical part of the puzzle.

The book describes how religion has influenced, and continues to influence, the course of prison litigation. One obvious way is when the legal claim itself centers on a religious issue. In some instances, the ability to practice religion or participate in religious activities may be the issue at stake. These instances represent a purely religious type of motivation behind the litigation, which may be broadly conceived as struggling on behalf of Islam or advocating for the cause of religion. Sometimes, litigation has been influenced by religious organizations on the outside and the organization of individuals and groups inside. In such conscious attempts to work together or file cases strategically, religion exerts influence through religious organizing. Examples include when Muslims in prison create templates and other documents to help others with court filings, or when modern groups like CAIR (Council on American-Islamic Relations) or Muslim Advocates orchestrate litigation efforts and represent individuals and class action plaintiffs in civil rights cases. At other times, religion influences litigation through religious ideology that motivates and authorizes an individual to take action in court, regardless of whether the case involves a religious claim. While initiating a court action might appear to the naked eye to be a secular or mundane affair, for some, the act of litigating can express the epitome of religious conviction, particularly when litigants understand their actions as a duty and ground their efforts within fundamental Islamic concepts of justice and equality.

These religious influences, however, do not exert their will toward political or military dominance. Instead, the litigation represents a civil struggle that relies on the law and courts to challenge prison conditions and abuse by guards. Recognizing the role of religion is imperative because this history of litigation challenges the Peter King–type narratives about Islam and undermines the persistent conflation of Muslims and violence. Examination of religion in this context tells a different story. In these confines, the force of religion transforms lawbreakers into lawmakers, who have helped to shape the prisoners' rights movement and who eschew violence as a means of resolving grievances.

In detailing these monumental efforts of Muslims in prison, this book sheds light on other interconnections between Islam and American prisons. Even in the shadows of scant scholarly treatment, the efforts of Muslims have been central to the prisoners' rights movement in America. People in prison of all persuasions have benefitted from cases litigated by Muslims, which, in turn, have had positive influences on prison culture and prison administration. As one scholar has noted, early cases involving Muslim litigants "began the process through which the Muslims' litigation would develop a legal legacy of enhanced, albeit limited, constitutional protections for all prisoners."[3] It is equally true that prisons occupy a special space in the annals of Islamic history in America. Conversion to Islam, for example, is prevalent in prison, particularly among African American males, and prison conversions contribute to the growth of Islam in America. It is also worth noting that Muslims are disproportionately represented in prison compared to their numbers on the outside. For example, nearly 10 percent of the federal prison population is Muslim, compared to an entire adult population of about 1 percent on the outside. These figures suggest not only that prisons house a relatively dense percentage of Muslims, but also that this figure represents a significant portion of the entire American Muslim population. Even more, this disproportionate population has an even greater disproportionate impact on litigation, representing some 30 percent of statutory religious rights claims brought in federal court.[4] This legacy distinguishes Muslims from their religious counterparts in prison, and the raw magnitude of lawsuits puts Muslims in a class all by themselves.

In addition to detailing the primary legal struggles that have produced this legacy, *Muslim Prisoner Litigation* focuses on factors that drive Muslims to turn to courts in the first place. Like Muslims outside of prison who use courts to get divorces, sue for injuries, or push for religious freedoms, those in prison have proved willing to use courts to settle their grievances with prison staff, rules, and regulations. In many cases, the turn to the law is not by accident but instead represents the fruit of strategic and conscious efforts by religious leaders to use the courts systematically. It is also significant that many of these lawsuits are initiated by individuals who convert to Islam. A convert's zeal for a newfound religion may make converts particularly sensitive to curbs and restrictions imposed on religious freedom, especially when restrictions confound one's ability to engage in traditional practices. From this perspective, the prevalence of conversion among Muslim litigants may be more causal than coincidental regarding factors influencing litigation efforts.

In detailing the actions brought by Muslims in prison, this book concentrates on one of the most underclass demographics in society and takes an "outsider" perspective to analyze litigation efforts. This "bottom-up" approach is a way to prioritize the views of those who endure oppression and discrimination. Analyzing this legal phenomenon through outsider jurisprudence offers a useful mode of interpreting religious repression by the state, and beyond, the response of filing a legal claim. Perhaps of all groups of people, Muslims in prison represent the most fringe of outsider identities. Intersectionally, they carry the identity of being Black, poor, a prisoner, criminal, gang member, and religious subvert. *Muslim Prisoner Litigation* relies on critical outsider perspectives to develop the notion that through litigation, Muslims engage in a type of spiritual activism that offers a means for marginal, outsider populations to resist oppression.

For those interested in religion and American Islam, this book will be fascinating, but it is equally a lesson in legal history. This story conveys that even the most destitute in society can rise collectively to challenge and change the law. Beyond these natural audiences, the book speaks to those interested in achieving a better understanding of the realities inside American prisons. As court opinions, documents, and other sources detail, the grievances litigated by Muslims dive deep into the miseries that Muslims have endured in prison for decades. For the reader, this excursion into the innards of the prison experience gives a voyeuristic look at a system that has taken state power and run wild. The research presented in this work offers stark documentation of state oppression from the view of those who have suffered it the most.

Data gathering on prison-based litigation produces several dominant motifs that are useful to the reader and the analysis of cases, court opinions, and individuals featured in this study. The motifs are also key for understanding the surveys and letters from Muslims in prison who have litigated cases. For this part of the research, commentary was obtained from individuals who were actively litigating or who had litigated a civil claim within the past five years. These voices are intended to complement the sentiments of litigants in the early decades of prison litigation. The surveys inquire into the motivations for litigation and allow for open-ended responses to questions about the influences of religion on the decision to litigate. While these themes may not be self-evident, they speak to unmistakable trends and provide important conceptual markers for this work.

NATION OF ISLAM FOLLOWERS SPARKED THE MOVEMENT

This work is consciously unbalanced when it comes to its focus. Indeed, much of the evidence and details concentrate on the NOI since the phenomenon of Muslim prison litigation is largely grounded in the efforts of NOI members. Early efforts by NOI members legitimized Islam behind bars, made the Quran standard in prison libraries, and paved the way for further litigation efforts. In the earliest lawsuits, converts from the NOI were the dominant force in creating space for Islam in prisons. Most early claims were made by adherents of this group, who, along with others, were collectively labeled "Black Muslims." It is safe to say that followers of this denomination sacrificed and suffered the most to make Islam a legitimate religion in prison.

In these early years, the face of a Muslim in court was almost always Black. However, in the post-9/11 era, this face has been changing rapidly. Muslim litigants are more diverse in terms of both race and religious denomination, particularly as Sunni, Shia, and other adherents have increasingly brought claims in court, including from members of the American Society of Muslims, Al-Islam, local mosques, and other African American–based organizations that have continued litigation efforts. Trends in immigration contribute to the diversity and denominations of Islam in America, with influxes of Muslims coming from African, South Asian, and Middle Eastern countries. With these social developments, the assumption that a Muslim litigant is a Black NOI member is not as likely as in previous decades.

The NOI is central to the origin story of Muslim prison litigation, which sets a critical tone for litigation as a matter of religious principle in a way that would resonate with later generations. Muslims of all persuasions would look to litigation in earnest and continue the NOI's work into the modern period. Even though the impact of the NOI has declined in recent decades, the group's pioneering efforts place it at the center of this study. The NOI's role is particularly remarkable because this group, often considered heterodox or even non-Muslim from the Muslim mainstream, made it possible for members of other denominations to have standing in court as Muslims. Members paved the way for later generations of Muslims of different denominations to benefit from the freedoms and rights that members of this organization struggled to obtain. All Muslims in prison continue to benefit from the groundwork laid by the cadre of NOI members determined to use courts in the struggle. Islam is taken for granted today by Muslims in prison and is viewed by prison administrations as a genuine religion, which is in large part due to the NOI and the hardships its members were willing to endure.

JUSTICE AND EQUALITY ARE CENTRAL TO ISLAMIC WORLDVIEWS

Muslims understand Islam through the prisms of justice and equality, which should be no surprise, considering the emphasis placed on these ideas in scripture and tradition. The Quran is replete with verses imploring followers to seek justice and provide it to others, as well as proclaiming racial equality among all humans. While it is true that other religious traditions place value and emphasis on these notions as well, Muslims in America have embraced these ideas fervently. Islamic history in American prisons has largely been characterized by racial and religious repression, which may be a part of the reason Muslims in this country have gravitated toward these ideals—they resonate loudly with their life experiences— unfair treatment by the criminal justice system, racism, and Islamophobia.

While it may be easy to think that Muslims in prison sue simply because they want greater religious freedoms or extra perks, this understanding hits only some of the mark. A more nuanced analysis will recognize that individuals are motivated by the specific messages inherent in Islam and have dovetailed these values into court action. Moreover, the notion of equality is particularly critical since it has layers of meaning for one in prison, including ever-elusive racial equality, equality among people in prison, and equality for people in prison compared to those people outside. Hence, multiple aspects of religious ideology may be relevant to these considerations due to traditional emphases on social and racial equality.

Under the leadership of Elijah Muhammad, the NOI incessantly stressed justice and equality for the Black man. For Muhammad, the question of racial justice was inextricable from his nationalistic interpretation of Islam. His writings indicate this orientation, as he extolls in the article, "justice for Muslims or Suffer the Consequences," justice is a divine principle that intersects race: "This teaching is . . . to show us that we have been deprived of justice by others (the white race) who are greater in power and knowledge of their own civilization. The white race refuses to give equal justice to us."[5] Appositionally, he describes the force of the devil: "[Satan] is an enemy and opposer of the freedom, justice, and equality that is given by the God of truth and justice." These attitudes were part and parcel of NOI consciousness, as exemplified in the group's weekly publication, *Muhammad Speaks*, which declared, "we believe in justice for all, whether in God or not; we believe as others, that we are due equal justice as human beings. We believe in equality—as a nation—of equals. We do not believe that we are equal with our slave masters in the status of 'freed slaves.'"

While Muhammad took Islam as an opportunity to speak to racial injustices and inherent racial differences, others, such as Malcolm X and Warith Deen Muhammad, would take Islam as a pathway to racial equality to stress the inherent unity in mankind. Having gone to Mecca and seen with his own eyes the diversity of the Islamic world, Malcolm X once famously described Islam as a cure for the cancer of racism.[6] Such views find support in passages of the Quran and Hadith, which proclaim the unity of humankind: "O people, We have created you male and female and made you into nations and tribes that you may know one another. Verily, the most noble of you to Allah is the most righteous of you."[7] "Among His signs is the creation of the heavens and the earth and the diversity of your languages and your colors. Verily, in that are signs for people with knowledge."[8] According to these statements, different skin colors and languages are a sign of creative power, which are all divine in Allah's creation as described in Hadith: "Verily, Allah Almighty created Adam from a handful which He took from the earth, so the children of Adam come in accordance with the earth. Some come with red skin, white skin, or black skin, and whatever is in between: thin, thick, dirty, and clean."[9] Moreover, the Prophet Muhammad himself is portrayed as one who sought to eliminate barriers that divided by tribe, clan, or caste, which he saw as subservient to one's identity as a Muslim: "O people, your Lord is one and your father Adam is one. There is no favor of an Arab over a foreigner, nor a foreigner over an Arab, and neither white skin over black skin, nor black skin over white skin, except by righteousness."[10]

CONVERSION FUELS THE PROCESS

Religious conversion is a force that builds on the strong emphasis on striving for justice and equality in the real world. As history has shown, the early stage of Muslim prison litigation was initiated by African Americans who had converted to the NOI and other religious organizations. With such numerical strength, converts effectively energized these movements and brought unparalleled determination and willingness to sacrifice themselves in the name of advancing the faith. One convert described Islam as a "lifeboat," and others described it as the key to becoming "free," as Malcolm X did in his autobiography. Under the zeal of conversion, some have shown a low tolerance for seeing their fellow believers treated harshly and denied the very religious liberties enjoyed by followers of other faiths. Their angst and grief were channeled into concrete actions that were sustained sometimes for decades. Converts are not "regular" religious adherents who were born into a religion or simply took it for granted. Instead, many often found Islam when they were at the end of hope, rock bottom, addicted, suicidal, and sometimes all at once. This potential was exemplified in the conversion of Malcolm X, which he proclaims "saved" him. After his conversion and release from prison, he would go on to work tireless hours on behalf of Muslims and go to great extremes to preserve and defend the faith.

In considering the Islamic emphasis on justice and equality, it is likely that some self-selection occurs among converts. Preaching efforts that emphasize these ideals are likely to be attractive to individuals who already harbor similar attitudes in their own outlook. Converts of this persuasion, attracted by these traditional values, often prove willing to work tirelessly to see justice done, reinforcing these very values. This sort of self-selection effectively fortifies the faith with individuals who are strong in their commitment to justice principles and willing to work to make these ideas a reality for themselves and others.

RELIGION IS ALL-PERVASIVE

Understanding the factors inculcated in Muslim prison litigation is a function of how well one grasps the religious influences. In addition to the influences just described, including religious values that inspire individuals to challenge prison officials and practices, not to speak of the fact that religious converts are the steam that pumps the litigation engine, there are other influences. Sometimes the religion of the guards in prison is a factor. Recent and past litigation has repeatedly shown that sometimes Christian guards view their religion as superior and see Islam as subversive. Guards have been known to ridicule Muslims by calling them names like "Mohammed" or "Al-Qaeda," or deride them by making fun of Islamic attire as "nightgowns." Similarly, prisons have shown favoritism to Christianity by instituting Christian-only wings and extending more services and resources to Christian groups. The religious influence on the prison staff is an important and overlooked aspect of institutional oppression.

Sometimes revulsion from Christianity is an impetus that informs a convert's worldview. From the perspective of one under incarceration, Christianity may be viewed as a part of the existential problem of being in prison. Beginning with the Christian justification of slavery and a prison system run by Christian actors, the situation creates the impression of a long lineage of Christian oppression against Blacks and Muslims. As one biographer described, "Imagine yourself beaten by guards of a foreign nation; imagine yourself torn away from the rest of the prison population; imagine yourself put in a segregated cell and told you can come back to the "normal" jail when you are ready to behave like the Christian guards want you to behave."[11] Malcolm X shared this revulsion and rebuked the Christian minister who attempted to preach to him. His antagonism toward Christianity was so pronounced, he became known as "Satan" in prison. After he was released, he used this invective to connect Christianity to these evils as a hook to recruit others to the faith: "I firmly believe that it was . . . the Judaic-Christian society . . . that created all of the factors that send so many so-called negroes to prison. . . ."[12]

A STUDY FILLED WITH COUNTERINTUITIVE FINDINGS

For many readers, the lessons of this study may strike against commonly held perceptions and ideas about the Muslim faith. Moreover, there are unique lessons about the law, its characteristics, and its function in society. In an age where some fear that Muslims are trying to supplant American law with sharia law, this study points in the opposite direction. Rather than show Muslims as antagonistic to legal structures, this study reveals Muslims literally put faith into the American legal system. Through the litigation, Muslims have proved willing to engage the system under the belief they will ultimately get their day in court. In this paradox, the consummate outsider, the "criminal," becomes the rule of law's greatest devotee. On the contrary, prisons and prison officials are shown to have great difficulty following the law and applying it equally. In some instances, even when Muslims obtain court victories, getting the prisons to follow the law is a different beast altogether. The litigation reveals the spectacle of Muslims trying to follow proper legal channels to hold prisons accountable and uphold the law. As counterintuitive as it may seem, the convict appears as the law-abiding citizen who plays by the rules, while prison officials may subvert the law to such a degree that sometimes they look like the criminal. This situation gives rise to the ironic specter of prison officials, who are supposed to be in the business of reforming and rehabilitating individuals, instead comporting themselves in ways that suggest they are the ones in need of reform. The findings challenge popular stereotypes about Muslims and alarmist narratives about the role of Muslims in prison.

Chapter 1, *At the Intersection of Religion and Punishment,* introduces the reader to the project and where it sits in historical context. In addition to familiarizing the reader with the problem examined in this project, the chapter discusses the nature of the research and the data that informs the study. The chapter introduces OutCrit jurisprudence as the primary hermeneutic for interpreting litigation efforts, as well as concepts employed in this study. The chapter also introduces the key religious studies terms, concepts, and practices. This discussion leads to the final part of the chapter, which provides a synopsis of what in the Muslim religion proves attractive to those behind bars who ultimately decide to litigate.

With a description of the project in place, chapter 2, *Islam in American Prisons,* traces the origins of the Muslim presence in prisons and details the phenomenon of conversion in prison. This chapter begins by discussing the prison as a sacred space for conversion to Islam. Relatedly, the chapter describes some of the challenges for converts and other adherents to practice religion in prison. For Muslims, the ability to practice religion is confounded by mistreatment by prison guards, which is also examined. Finally, with this synopsis in place, the chapter moves on to consider Islamic ideas about responding to such injustices and to fathom litigation as a way of responding to these wrongs within a religious framework.

At the dawning of Muslim prisoner litigation, the initial challenge is the subject of chapter 3, *The Struggle to be Recognized by Prisons.* For Muslims to sue in court, adherents first had to establish Islam as a genuine religion. In these earliest phases of litigation in the mid-1900s, Muslims were just a tiny fraction of the American population at large and, as such, were not well understood in the corrections context. This lack of knowledge led to unfortunate consequences, including instances where some Muslims—rather than being afforded religious rights—were instead targeted by the FBI and prison officials as troublemakers. Hence, even if Islam was established as a genuine religion, it hardly followed that believers were automatically granted the status of a sincere follower. It does show, however, that the battle to establish Islam in prison is only as useful as one can demonstrate that he is a sincere follower. One such individual is featured in this chapter, Martin Sostre, who embodies the ultimate litigator who was also renowned as a jailhouse lawyer. His profile embodies the sort of individual who is at the heart of this book, who sees litigation as the spiritual response to injustice. The chapter ends by situating these developments in prison within the broader context of the Civil Rights Movement and the US Supreme Court's expanding view of religion. These two developments provided an opportune moment for Muslims to begin looking to courts to establish religious freedom.

The initial struggles to establish Islam in prison gave Muslims the legal standing to challenge prison policies and sue for religious rights. Chapter 4, *Fighting for Religious Rights,* examines some prominent cases that helped shape jurisprudence in this area of prison law. Muslims sued prisons for an array of religious rights and secured victories to expand religious free exercise for all people in prison. Claims included the right to worship, groom themselves and dress according to religious tradition, and secure dietary rights, among other legal claims. As the cases reveal, when prisons treat Muslims differently from other religious groups, it may trigger equal protection claims; other times, the prison's treatment of other religions or religious groups can trigger establishment claims. The lawsuits demonstrate the specific challenges Muslims leveled when it came to religious rights and indicate that litigation has helped bring about concrete changes in prison and strengthened the ability of Muslims in prison to practice religion.

Chapter 5, *Holding Prisons Accountable,* examines Muslim litigation that generally centers on prisoners' rights. The chapter begins by outlining how prison staff have historically undermined the idea that "no one is above the law." The institutional actors who undermine this core legal principle force people in prison to learn that the institution and actors often place themselves above the law, sometimes by evading accountability, other times through their acts and omissions. The chapter moves on to detail how this sort of treatment and double standards intensified after the attacks of September 11, 2001. In the decade following the attacks, Muslims experienced a new wave of repression that mirrored earlier forms of oppression, albeit in an updated fashion. The chapter concludes by offering a composite of the most recent struggles that have occupied Muslims in court, including the ability to engage in hunger strikes, practice Ramadan, and wear hijabs.

Chapter 6, *Muslim Litigiosity,* circles back to the main proposition of this work to make concluding observations on the phenomenon of Muslim prisoner litigation. The Muslim proclivity for appropriating the legal system and the legacy it has left is an ongoing development that has been largely overlooked in the annals of American legal history and Islamic history. As one scholar has noted, the "collective lawsuits advanced by the NOI Muslim inmates are a missing chapter of Muslim-American jurisprudential history."[13] This history unveils religious influences that forces us to reimagine the role of religion on litigation. Simultaneously, lawsuits that are directly inspired by religious ideology have the effect of supporting and advancing the rule of law. When ideology, action, and the rule of law are aligned, this study deems that state of affairs "litigation praxis." As the term implies, when Muslims engage in litigation, they are not engaging in haphazard suits, but the suits are a direct result of Islamic ideology being implemented in the world, to make the world better.

Chapter 7, *Conclusions and Final Thoughts*, offers a final set of points gleaned from the preceding chapters. The first is recognition that examination of this legal history from the outsider perspective offers grave lessons in state dominance and religious repression. It is equally true that behind prison walls, there is something of a role-reversal that occurs between keeper and kept. The Muslim, a convicted criminal, is shown to be a law-abiding individual pursuing legal remedies while his keepers are engaging in heinous and unlawful conduct. Taken wholly, the lawsuits undermine various stereotypes about Muslims, including that Muslims in prison pose a unique challenge to prison or national security. Although some "experts" have touted prisons as "fertile grounds" for violent extremism or violent prison jihad, decades of litigation show Muslims as having positive, salutary impacts on prisons and rehabilitation efforts. This legal history makes a myth of such alarmist portrayals. Finally, the work concludes by looking forward and considering how justice in prison might be expanded and how the work of prison-based litigation might be supported to achieve more just outcomes.

1 At the Intersection of Religion and Punishment

American prisons have come a long way since first opening for business in the late 1700s. Then, like now, there were competing ideas about how prisons should operate and what goals were supposed to be achieved for society and those sentenced. Among early prison advocates were religionists known as Quakers, who advocated for punishment as a means of reform through solitary confinement. Quakers actively rejected the death penalty and instead embraced the Catholic system of penitence. They pushed for "penitentiaries," which prescribed solitary isolation for imprisonment. The idea was for the punished individual to use the time in isolation to pray and reflect on one's wrongs and to mend relations with God, literally to pay penitence. In these and other penal institutions, wards were often given only a Bible for reading, and it was assumed they were Christian.

At this point in American history, state penal institutions' conduct, such as handing out Bibles, hardly raised eyebrows about the separation of church and state. At that time, the First Amendment had yet to apply to the states, so the religious protections enshrined in its clauses offered little to state citizens until the 1940s.[1] By the same token, those incarcerated could not invoke the Eighth Amendment's prohibition against "cruel and unusual" punishment to challenge state punishment practices in federal court until the 1960s, when federal judges began to revolt and started intervening. In this era of federal awakening to the plight of those behind bars, Muslims began to embrace litigation to change the status quo. Over the next half-century, Muslims in prison would march to court in record numbers and help steer the course of prison law in America.

Today, prison is still a place of penitence, and its intended design of helping criminals find God continues, except that some old markers have changed. In the new economy, African Americans and Latinos make up a disproportionate number of those incarcerated in the United States. When it comes to religion, the Muslim religion is recognized as garnering the greatest number of converts per capita than other religions. Also, when it comes to the rights of those sentenced and obligations of the state, the US Constitution and federal courts now have much more to say. For instance, it is no longer safe to assume that one is a Christian, and the First Amendment would almost certainly prohibit prisons from giving out only the Bible. Moreover, states must conform to the Eighth Amendment's prohibition against cruel and unusual punishment practices. Shifts in the last half-century have been accompanied by litigation launched by Muslim converts, who have led an unceasing wave of lawsuits against the very institutions that incarcerate them.

This chapter provides an overview of the data and theoretical concepts that inform this book. The first section begins by giving a sense of the magnitude and importance of the Muslim contribution to prison law, policy, and culture. It is difficult to overstate how these contributions have collectively influenced law and life in prison, for as legal history demonstrates, when Muslims began filing lawsuits, "civil rights" was a distant concept for people in prison. However, these suits eventually opened federal courts to claims from people in prison, creating a new body of law broadly conceived as prison law jurisprudence. From then on, court cases would impact not simply the ability of one to file a court claim but also the very policies and regulations that govern prison. Through these developments, prison culture transformed as well, from litigation of issues ranging from dress, hygiene and grooming, and food to what items a ward can have in his possession. While these contributions by Muslim litigants remain something of an unsung achievement, they must be recognized as critical to the development of American law and our understanding of Islamic history in America.

The chapter also establishes the idea that in prison, religion catalyzes action. Whether it be greater involvement in religious programming, proselytization, protest, or full-blown litigation, religion is not some sedative that renders followers docile and domesticated. For some, religion is a spark that leads to a path of activism, of standing up for oneself and one's fellow beings. Here, the role of religious converts plays a pronounced role since, as will be discussed, religious converts are known to have strong determination and reservoirs of energy to dedicate to their newfound faith. The work of converts presents a clear example of how religion is not a quieting force, but quite the opposite: it gives individuals unwavering confidence, strength, and willpower to act against unfairness and injustice.

Finally, as this study of Muslim prisoner litigation involves religion and law as central themes, this chapter introduces OutCrit jurisprudence as the primary orientation for analyzing the sociolegal aspects of this phenomenon. The final section of this chapter is thus dedicated to equipping the reader with the main tenets of OutCrit philosophy and outlining those concepts that will be most useful for parsing Muslim litigation efforts. Rigorous treatment of the legal and religious dimensions affords the reader a dynamic account of what is happening in these cases beyond the mere black letter of the law. As this book posits, it is important also to recognize the position of litigants as social outsiders, whose marginal status makes their experience of the law unlike the way others experience it. This primer on OutCrit, along with the data and theoretical underpinnings of this work, provides a viable means of considering litigation efforts at multiple levels of analysis.

It is somewhat astonishing that despite the sheer volume of lawsuits brought by Muslims in prison, no work has examined this topic comprehensively. A much-needed study was published recently that focused on the patterns of free exercise of religion claims by incarcerated Muslims.[2] While this work represents an important empirical contribution, there has been little scholarship that pays attention to other types of claims by Muslim litigants, including Equal Protection, Due Process, and Cruel and Unusual punishment claims, not to speak of the dearth in research on the motivations of litigants.

By filling some of this academic void, this work also unveils some legends within African American cultural history. One is the legend of the convict-turned-Muslim, which has been a long-standing staple in African-Americana. Another is the legend of the jailhouse lawyer—the erudite inmate who studies the law and provides legal assistance to others incarcerated—sometimes possessing legal abilities that rival those of seasoned attorneys. Jailhouse lawyers are, in fact, a part of the Muslim contribution to prison culture. While it is true Muslims hold a pedigree of court activity, scholarship has been somewhat slow in understanding this unique aspect of Islam in America. Namely, incarcerated Muslims are among the most litigious Muslims in America and, in prison, the most litigious religious group of all.

In addition to analyzing state and federal civil lawsuits involving Muslim litigants in prison, including court opinions, documentaries, and archival materials, the data include statements from incarcerated Muslims. The research includes commentary from Muslims who have litigated a case within the last half decade.[3] Their voice complements the legal and archival materials with contemporary accounts of Muslim ideas and attitudes about litigation. Together, these sources will provide a comprehensive account of the early years of litigation as a comparative backdrop for considering attitudes in the present.

A LONG-STANDING LEGACY IN LAW, POLICY, AND PRISON CULTURE

There is much to say about the collective impact of Muslims on prison history in America. Broadly speaking, the litigation has been described as a "correctional law revolution, and the beginning of an evolving concern of the courts in correctional matters."[4] "Some researchers have credited the legal battles as the catalyst for creating recognized diversity within the inmate social system and changing the structure of the prison system."[5] "In fact," Kathleen Moore writes, "the area of law to which Muslims have made their most substantial contribution to date is the area of prisoners' rights litigation."[6] While litigants from various Muslim denominations comprised only a tiny minority of the prison population in the 1960s, they made significant and lasting imprints when it came to prison law.

Several markers and metrics further indicate the Islamic influences on prison law in general. Perhaps most significantly, *Cooper v. Pate* is widely viewed as the case that opened federal courts to people in prison. Featuring a Muslim petitioner, the case, for many in prison, was *the* watershed moment of judicial reckoning. In terse terms, the Supreme Court's opinion issued a forceful pushback against the "hands-off" philosophy, which had dominated court thinking for a century and a half.[7] This case was one of the earliest glimpses of how Muslims were treated at the time, but as the litigation trend continued in the new millennium, a growing body of cases gave a harsh account of the experiences of Muslims in prison. These early decades of litigation showed a willingness of Muslims to engage in long-term commitments of pursuing lawsuits. The efforts would situate Muslim efforts in court as central to the prisoners' rights movement.[8]

In recent decades, Muslims continue to look to courts to settle grievances. Such a bent is supported by findings of the US Commission on Civil Rights, which noted that between 2005 and 2007, it received the largest percentage of complaints from Muslims, which accounted for over 26 percent of all complaints.[9] Also, between 2001 and 2006, Muslims were the most common plaintiffs bringing forth Religious Land Use and Institutionalized Persons Act (RLUIPA) claims, accounting for approximately 30 percent of all claims.[10] These results are even more striking when compared to the percentage of Muslims in society. For example, at about this same time, Muslims represented 9 percent of the federal prison population and accounted for about 0.6 percent of adults aged eighteen and over nationally.[11] The figures demonstrate the disproportionate levels of Muslim involvement in litigation compared to their numbers in prison. The feat is magnified when considering that adult Muslims make up less than 1 percent of the adult American population.

The influence of Muslims and litigation efforts directly contribute to shaping prison culture behind bars. As will be discussed, there was a time when Muslims in prison had to fight just to establish Islam as a genuine religion. From these days, Muslims have become a highly visible part of the prison culture, a fixture that would influence how prisons operate and how its wards are treated. Nowadays, whether it be a film like Malcolm X or a television series like OZ, Muslims are depicted as inherent in the prison experience, almost as if Muslims must be featured to lend authenticity to the drama.

In real life, one need only consider the creation of "Black August" as a noteworthy influence of Muslims in prison. This holiday, created in the 1970s, lasted over the month of August. The holiday was initially observed by Blacks in prison who refused food and water before sundown, refused the canteen, drugs, and other illicit behaviors. However, this exertion of Black power and prison resistance deliberately dovetailed with Ramadan practices, demonstrating Islam's influence on Black prison protest, racial pride, and culture itself.[12] By adopting Muslim meditative practices, those who observed the holiday similarly sought to demonstrate self-control and discipline beyond what the institution required. They regulated themselves by imitating what they saw Muslims doing in the observance of Ramadan and daily practice. In doing so, followers of Black August showed that Muslims enforcing religious codes rubbed off on the general population to the extent that a new holiday would be modeled after the actions of Muslims.

RELIGION IN PRISON: FAR FROM OPIATE

> Islam is most impressive for prison inmates because of its
> simplicity, comprehensiveness, universal egalitarianism, and
> the brotherhood of its community. It has special appeal to
> those who are oppressed and are not tied to any privileged
> class.[13]

Religion is a theme that pervades this study. In this work, however, religion is not some tranquilizing force on the population, or as Karl Marx put it, "the sigh of the oppressed creature . . . the opium of the people."[14] For Muslims in prison, religion plays the exact opposite role and instead has been an activating agent to propel action, including legal action. Rather than being what the oppressed creature uses to soothe the oppression, religion proves to be a force that counters it. Religion is the inspiration to stand up and stand against subjugation.

As a study of law and religion, it is not enough to rehearse black letter law and the legal holding of a court opinion. There are religious aspects that must be examined to enhance our understanding about the motivations of Muslims who litigate. For example, what inspires individuals to go through the trouble of litigating? How does religious conviction factor in? How do religious tenets? What of the players in the justice system? How do their biases and phobias inculcate themselves in the treatment of Muslims in correctional systems? The answer to these and other questions requires a rigorous framework for considering the impetus for the legal actions brought by Muslims in prison. Collectively, the force of religion is a strong catalyst that helps to shape, change, and even abolish the law.

As an initial consideration, it is worth taking a moment to define what is meant by the term "Muslim." While it may be tempting to gloss the point, determining exactly who is a Muslim in America is not as straightforward as one might imagine. The United States plays home to various religious groups that identify as Muslim. In the same way, the term "Christian" gives only a general sense of identification; the same holds true for "Muslim." There is no litmus test to claim to be Muslim, and as there are many self-proclaimed Christians who hardly read the Bible or even attend church, such individuals may still consider themselves Christian. For academic study, this reality presents problems. Specifically, it admonishes the researcher to refrain from making value judgments about who is or is not a follower of the faith. This is a pitfall to be avoided, particularly because some Christians would withhold the status of "Christian" to several other groups who understand themselves as such. Indeed, Mormons, Seventh Day Adventists, and Jehovah's Witnesses are often denied this status by more mainstream followers. Lest the researcher takes sides in the labeling, a better approach must be sought.

In American Islam, a convoluted past makes this question more difficult. After the establishment of Muslim organizations within African American communities, the later arrival of mass Muslims from South Asia, Africa, and the Middle East increased the diversity. When these newcomers arrived at American shores, they derided the African American Muslims as inauthentic and divorced from "true" Islam. They often accused their Black predecessors of following false prophets and perverting the religion as they understood it. Although, in time, most Muslims in African American communities would eventually align themselves with Sunni Islam, some of their communities encountered suspicion and accusations of heterodoxy from their Sunni and Shia counterparts. In turn, in Five Percent Nation of Islam circles, it is a saying that "Sunni" Muslim stands for "soon to be" Muslim.[15] As such, this internal wrangling cautions against the temptation of making normative claims about what constitutes Islam or being Muslim.

Instead, a prudent researcher should consider a Muslim as anyone who claims to be one or claims to follow Islam. Rather than defining Muslims through essentialist strategies or simply comparing newer groups to more traditional ones, it has been suggested that "the student of Islam should not even insist on using a person's identification with the Quran as a kind of minimal definition of what it means to be a Muslim. Instead, wherever and whenever a person calls himself or herself Muslim, scholars should include this person's voice in their understanding of what constitutes Islam."[16] This strategy has been lauded for pointing scholarship "in the right direction" when it comes to the question of whether a person is Muslim.[17] This approach is similar to Harry Dammer, whose conversion study identifies a "religious inmate as someone who proclaims to practice and believe in one of the formal and accepted denominations within the prison."[18] Here it is worth remembering that NOI followers pushed to have Islam recognized as a genuine religion in prison as a matter of law. To exclude this group from the realm of what constitutes a Muslim would paradoxically undo the history that legitimated Islam in prison in the first place.

There are other issues worth bearing in mind when trying to understand who is Muslim and who is not. The litigation reveals that Muslims in prison have been historically feared and hated and that there is very little benefit to identifying oneself as a Muslim. For many incarcerated, claiming to be a Muslim is rarely a ticket to preferred treatment and perks and more likely results in a harder time in prison. The situation was exacerbated under the Trump Administration, which fostered a renaissance in Islamophobia that did not stop at the prison gates.[19] In the outside cultural economy, invective against Islam is common; Muslims have been killed, mosques burnt, and even non-Muslims mistaken for Muslims have been killed. The claim of being a Muslim, then, is not without costs. These costs should be considered when assessing whom to include in what constitutes Islam or who is a Muslim.

THE ROLE OF RELIGIOUS CONVERSION

> The emergence of NOI converts as a force behind bars was
> conditioned in part by the imprisonment of its leadership
> and key members during the Second World War.[20]

How religious conversion fits into litigation efforts is complex, so it is worth examining some key characteristics. As this quote intimates, however, there is a clear connection to Elijah Muhammad and Muhammad Ali, who were both conscientious objectors to war. The former spent time in prison for his refusal to enlist in the military, and Ali was essentially stripped of his livelihood during the years it took for his lawsuit to be decided, which culminated in a Supreme Court victory for Ali. These individuals and their heroic deeds inspired many and set the stage for conversions and activism that were rooted in religion.

In some ways, the phenomenon of conversion relates closely to the original intention of "penitentiary" as a form of imprisonment. In the early years of American prisons, those who advocated for the penitent model of imprisonment were hoping for a type of conversion as well. Their idea was that true penitence, where an individual has genuine remorse for the crime committed and the harm caused, is a path to mending ways with God. They hoped for individual transformations, such that the wrongdoer would learn to obey God's law, and by default, would obey man's law. The process of conversion to Islam in prison mirrors such a transformation and supports that penitence is alive and well behind bars.

Conversion represents an important means by which Islam in America has spread. In prison, many have turned to Islam to help them through troubled times. Whether one finds Islam inside or outside of prison, being a convert is a common denominator among many who take the plunge into litigation. Being a religious convert is not something that can be divorced from litigation, but instead, it is intimately connected. A convert may understand the teachings of Islam as directly supportive of efforts to seek justice in court by litigating. For such an individual, the task becomes an act of spiritual significance.

As a general concept, "conversion" implies a secular or religious transformation. It is as sensible to talk about political conversion as it is religious conversion, and sometimes an individual can have overlapping experiences of the two. Several litigants featured in this work have lives marked by profound shifts in their political and religious thinking. For some, the very act of bringing a lawsuit for religious rights may constitute a political act. This is especially true for individuals who have demonstrated very little care about the law—former criminals who now are on the opposite side of the law. As one litigant described, during his era, "the purchasing of a Quran was seen as a political act, one that drew a line in the sand between guards and prisoners." Lawsuits brought by Muslims may thus be rightly seen as a religious exercise, a political exercise, or a mixture of the two.

The word "conversion" derives from the Latin *con* + *vertere*, which conveys the act of "turning," "turning around," "revolving," or "revolution." In the religious context, it indicates a turn away from a previous lifestyle toward a new worldview. This twofold act may include embracing the mannerisms of a tradition, adopting new lands as new spiritual motherlands, adopting a spiritual name, and revamping clothing, grooming, and dietary habits. Such wholesale change can appear radical to friends and relatives, even though these are common occurrences among converts.

William James's *The Varieties of Religious Experience* (1902) and Rudolf Otto's *The Idea of the Holy* (1923) are among the early scholarly commentaries on conversion. These pioneering works are relevant to understanding conversion in the prison context, including the timing of conversion and how fear, trauma, and crisis factor into the process. From their view, such physical and emotional pains did seem to play a role in religious conversion, as antecedent factors such as trauma or desperation were a common theme among subjects of study. Such deeply painful experiences were triggers to search for deeper meaning. The idea that crisis or trauma is a sufficient condition for religious conversion is important because it may help explain why a significant number of individuals in prison convert. These early views accord with one study that tied the prevalence of conversion to the severity of the detention, showing individuals are more likely to convert in the harsher and more dangerous maximum-security institutions than in medium- or minimum-security facilities.[21]

From this perspective, both the prospect of going to prison and prison life itself could be sufficient triggers for the sort of pains these scholars saw as setting the psychological stage for conversion. Their insights support the notion that the prevalence of conversion is in part a reflection of the place itself, which is a sacred space for people experiencing some of the most frightening and stressful times of their lives. In other words, some of the prevalence of conversion has to do with the nature of what the prison represents—perhaps the hardest times an individual has ever faced.

William James's writings on conversion offer compelling observations about the nature of religious conversion. James observed that converts had different timings when it came to conversion—some took months and years, while for others, it can be like a lightning strike, where emotional interests "may shift before one almost as rapidly as the sparks that run through burnt-up paper . . . if the change be a religious one, we call it a conversion, especially if it be by crisis, or sudden."[22] James's description emphasizes that crisis may be an antecedent of conversion, which maps well onto this study and suggests a connection between the phenomenon of religious conversion and its prevalence in prison. According to James's logic, the traumatic and terrifying aspects of prison can set in motion the necessary conditions for transformation: "To say that a man is 'converted' means, in these terms, that religious ideas, previously peripheral in his consciousness, now take a central place, and that religious aims form the habitual centre of energy." Religion becomes the center of a convert's universe, and other matters that occupy this space move to the periphery; the convert's mind becomes absorbed in something more than fears about incarceration, surveillance, and violence.

Adding to these ideas was Rudolph Otto's notion of "*mysterium tremendum*," or "terrible mystery." This term aimed to convey the frightening, wholly other, and most powerful moments of religious experience and experiences. For converts, these are the awe-inspiring aspects of religion, those moments that produce life-changing, spiritual awakenings and moments of sheer spiritual ecstasy. Otto describes the manifestation of these intense feelings as "a gentle tide, pervading the mind with a tranquil mood of deepest worship. It may pass over into more set and lasting attitude of the soul, continuing, as it were, thrillingly vibrant and resonant, until at last it dies away and the soul resumes to 'profane', non-religious mood of everyday experience."[23] These emotions, however, take starker forms as well: "It has its wild and demonic forms and can sink to an almost grisly horror and shuddering. It has its crude, barbaric antecedents . . . It may become hushed, trembling, and speechless humility of the creature in the presence of—whom or what? In the presence of that which is a mystery inexpressible and above all creatures."[24]

Otto describes these feelings and physical sensations as reactions to the overpowering and wholly other nature of religious experience. The experiences are more than simply cerebral but capture the body itself. The physical aspects of experience are very real. "We say: 'my blood ran ice cold', and 'my flesh crept'. The 'cold blood' feeling may be a symptom of the ordinary, natural fear, but there is something non-natural or supernatural about the symptom of 'creeping flesh'. And anyone who is capable of more precise introspection must recognize that the distinction between such a 'dread' and natural fear is not simply one of degree and intensity. The awe or dread may indeed be so overwhelmingly great that it seems to penetrate to the very marrow, making the man's hair bristle and his limbs quake." These emotionally charged experiences often reflect the dual characteristics of repulsion and attraction. Attraction may be characterized by feelings of union, peace, familiarity, and ecstasy; repulsion can be rooted in awe, fear, terror, or the quality of complete alterity.

James and Otto's ideas underscore why the prison is an ideal locus for religious conversion. The ideas also suggest that when it comes to discussions of those who convert in prison, it may be somewhat inaccurate to speak of "prison convert," as if everything occurred in prison. For some, this portrayal may be accurate, but for others, the conversion process may have initiated long before arriving at the prison gates. Their works emphasize that people in prison are often in a state of personal crisis before the experience of conversion. Crisis may functionally begin at arrest and only worsen the further one gets entangled in the criminal justice system, including being jailed, facing trial, sentencing, and prison itself. Hence, with the prospect of deprivation of liberty, goods, services, sexual relations, and security staring an individual in the face, the crisis starts long before imprisonment.

From the perspective of one headed to prison, there may be an overlapping of shock, dread, and fear compounded by machinations of prison life. This aspect of suffering models the findings of one researcher who noted that "pain was necessary to break down the old, to efface the deformed likeness, so that the new one could be formed in its place."[25] Such looming threats might push a believer to cling tighter to previously held beliefs, or it may cause him to reach out for something new. From a deprivation perspective, the logic is clear: prison life takes many tolls, and religion offers a "variety of ways to help endure the stressors often associated with the prison environment." Similarly, one study found that "acute personal crises and in some cases mental breakdowns" were motivating factors for conversion: "Prison is also experienced as a survival challenge. The first time a person enters, he encounters an alien society over which he has almost no say. The message is 'Do what you can to survive this experience.' There may be a feeling of shock or dread—or basic fear—that the newly admitted inmate feels upon finding himself facing a sentence of imprisonment."[26] Facing a prison sentence may help set the conditions to find meaning in the crisis. It is a process that may ultimately end up with an individual embracing religion in prison, even though the quest was triggered long before passing through the prison gates.

Malcolm X exhibited these characteristics in his prison conversion. He experienced beatings and the punishing madness of solitary confinement. However, during these profound times of change, he also had mystical, life-changing experiences that further strengthened his faith. In one instance, he came face to face with what seemed to be an answer to his feverish prayers for Allah to reveal himself. In this account, he witnesses an apparition of Master W. D. Farad in an experience that harkens to the *mysterium tremendum;* only this episode takes place in a prison cell.[27] Malcolm X's narrative makes the ideas advanced by James and Otto credible. Severe stressors and hardships characterized his path of transformation, and, at the same time, he experienced moments that, above all, signified spiritually that he was on the right path.

The characteristics of conversion provide a poignant sense of why Muslims are willing to engage in the long and arduous litigation process. According to researchers, "these challenges were nearly always initiated by NOI converts and pursued with minimal outside assistance. In the instances when the NOI provided legal representation, it was usually after these pro se petitions had wound their way through the lower courts and showed some promise of success on appeal."[28] Hence, in many cases, the raw dedication and religious devotion sustained the lawsuits. Understanding how conversion can catalyze individuals who were down and out, essentially like the living dead, underscores the power of converts, collectively. When one is given his life back by God and experiences this sort of rebirth, he is ready to give that life to the cause of his newfound faith. Religious conversion is a key factor that energizes litigation efforts and reinforces that religion is an activating and mobilizing force that has quite the opposite effect of what Marx had in mind.

OUTCRIT JURISPRUDENCE TO UNDERSTAND LAW FROM THE OUTSIDE

> Muslims have one thing in common—their religious identity races them as outsiders to American society. Irrespective of how they interpret Islamic doctrine or practice, American mainstream society homogenizes them as a suspicious fifth column.[29]

The narratives found in this book proclaim one overarching truth about prison law—that is, the "law" can look very different depending on who is looking. For most Americans, the thought of imprisonment or the death penalty is a far-removed threat, a remote possibility that rarely interferes with one's goals or aspirations. From this vantage, the law looks like a tool rather than a threat; prison is for bad guys and those who have chosen to break the rules, end of the story. In middle-class America, such aspects of the criminal justice system hardly register as a cause for concern, whether it be prisons or the police. However, that same legal system appears drastically different when one is poor; not only is the probability of contact with police magnified due to indigency, but the indigent are the least capable of defending themselves against the criminal system. Skin color can also affect how the law looks because racial minorities are prosecuted and imprisoned at disproportionate rates, not to mention that those in prison generally live in a world largely run by White males. Layer on being Muslim, and the law sometimes seems unrecognizable. From this viewpoint, the law appears to support two entirely different systems.

Imagine, for example, what the law looks like behind bars for Muslims compared to Christians. While some groups enjoy the full panoply of constitutional freedoms and protections, Muslims have had to fight to obtain rights that others take for granted. The treatment of each under the law may also be different. Christians are not treated as a religious monolith. They do not have to plead their case for programming, services, or holidays. They need not attend religious services to be counted as a Christian. As many lawsuits demonstrate, the system can appear harsh and unforgiving or fair and just. Accordingly, many of the Muslim struggles examined are not only about advancing the rights of Muslims but also about claims that seek greater rights and better treatment for all who are in the misery of lock and key.

Given the different faces of law, this book orients its vision toward understanding the law from the perspective of those whose social position makes them least able to fend for themselves. To provide this perspective, this work employs OutCrit jurisprudence as an interpretive tool for approaching and analyzing Muslim prison litigation. While history may be written from the point of the victors, this work aims to tell the story of the losers. After all, in most of the stories, Muslims are the ones who are denied rights, forced to endure suffering, and forced to exhaust all legal channels, only to end up in court, where statistically, they are likely to lose their case. The outsider perspective helps convey how the law impacts some groups over others and seeks "to inform the discourse on legal issues from the perspectives of those outside the dominant culture, thereby hoping to create changes in both legal dialogue and interpretation. The objective of altering legal theory is pursued by supplying stories that are missing."[30]

As a philosophic approach to the law, OutCrit jurisprudence, also known as "critical jurisprudence" or simply "outsider jurisprudence," was both an extension and critique of the critical legal studies, a movement that voiced skepticism of law as a science, questioned whether a text contains one right meaning, and distrusted the law's neutral and objective façade.[31] With empiricism by its side, this critical branch of legal scholarship became the launching pad for several other theoretical movements and critical perspectives of the law,[32] including Critical Race Theory, LatCrit, ClassCrits, Feminist Theory, and others whose scholarship primarily concerned itself with the oppression of marginalized groups by the dominant group and remedies.[33]

Outsider is something of an umbrella term for these various schools of thought. OutCrit is a way of describing both the perspective and the philosophical goal, which "denotes the social position (outsider) and the analytical stance (critical) of diverse formation vis-à-vis law and culture. OutCrit jurisprudence reacts to and critiques the exclusion and marginalization of outsiders from society's social, cultural, and economic mainstreams ..."[34] This approach employs transformative techniques to address these marginalized and vulnerable groups. Scholars associated with this approach envision a post-subordination world, where traditionally subordinated groups are free of social disdain and can access justice in a meaningful way.[35] In this vision, a transformation of socio-legal conditions is needed to provide security for marginalized groups traditionally relegated to outsider status.

This study begins with the proposition that Muslims in prison are positioned at the very fringe of outsider America, which makes the application of OutCrit philosophy particularly useful for understanding litigation efforts. As a mode of approaching the law that takes the "outsider" perspective, this lens squares with the lived experiences of Muslims in prison—who are outsiders *par excellence*. One need only recall the intersectional identities that put them near the very bottom of the American social totem pole. These include race, class, status as a convict, and perhaps gangster. On top of these stigmatizing and disadvantaging markers is the fact of being Muslim itself, which today is undoubtedly the most feared and persecuted religion. These characteristics together sketch a portrait of Muslims in prison as perhaps one of the most feared characters in the American psyche: all at once, he is Black, criminal, gangster, poor, and terrorist.

The OutCrit focus provides insight into how the most marginalized and unlikely demographic can become staunch purveyors of the Rule of Law. As one historian notes, while historians of the civil rights movement challenged traditional narratives, "incarcerated people, Black Nationalists, and Muslims rarely appear as leading figures," yet these leaders understood that "courtrooms, police precincts, solitary confinement cells and other spaces of white rule were places to lay claims on the state and challenge its legitimacy."[36] As such, the OutCrit focus highlights how a religious group that makes up a relatively small fraction of American society was able to have such a significant impact through litigation. As Muslims both in and outside of prison face layers of state surveillance, subordination, and discrimination, this perspective is beneficial to account for the

difficult existence of life behind bars for Muslims, and why filing grievances and ultimately litigating is viewed, in most instances, as the appropriate response. The perspective is geared toward analyzing what Garrett
Felber described as the "emerging web of state surveillance (that) monitored Muslim rituals and attempted to construct a religioracial formation
to justify the suppression of Islam in prisons."[37]

The use of narrative is at the heart of this study; after all, the core of a
case is about petitioners telling their stories to the court to persuade the
court of their plight. In this context, narrative affords voiceless individuals
the opportunity to be heard and provides "a way to introduce experiences
and points of view that are otherwise ignored in the dominant legal discourse."[38] There is power in storytelling, whether through court filings,
affidavits, depositions, testimony, or other procedures. The narrative is a
means by which individuals in prison can express their pain, frustrations,
and powerlessness at the hands of their keepers; it has the "power to shape
reality by means of the language, to suspend the disbelief of the listeners
to the story, to influence and persuade."[39] The narrative is the content that
feeds litigation and is the force that allows marginalized people to make
the outside world aware of what happens behind locked gates.

Litigants' reliance on narrative often arises from intersocial conflict,
which this book describes as "culture war." Culture war may be viewed as
a struggle over the elements that define a culture—values, beliefs, arti-
facts, and practices, among others; after all, as has been noted, "the power
of culture is first and foremost symbolic. It's the power to name things; it's
to define reality, to frame debate."[40] In the struggle to control these powers, tactics of war may be discursive or may manifest into physical action.
A key point to understand is that it is not a new phenomenon. In broad
strokes, Edward Said's *Orientalism* developed a historical framework for
understanding the Western world's contempt for the East, the Orient. The
work was a remarkable critique of Western scholarship on Eastern subjects, which claimed that these works were far from objective, neutral
undertakings. Instead, the scholarship was essentially political and subservient to Western culture's imperialist attitudes and agendas. While he
might not have framed it as such, these scholars were engaged in their
culture war centuries ago because the works reinforced Western dominance and were political instruments of domination.

Inherent in culture war are various sites of contention. While no over-arching issue or division can define culture war, there are indeed culture wars that revolve around specific issues. While one may consider formal pronouncements by the government, such as the "war on poverty," "war on drugs," or "war on terror," this work concentrates on two aspects of culture—race and religion—as the dominant issues that impact Muslims in prison. Indeed, there are struggles that have plagued Muslims that are distinctly religious, including Providentialism and Islamophobia. Still, it is equally true that because Islam is predominantly practiced by African Americans, racism and xenophobia are equally inculcated. The two ele-ments may operate independently and distinctly from one another, or they can share overlapping space. The term "Black Muslim" perhaps offers the best example of how both attitudes work together to create an objec-tified, othered identity, or in the words of Sahar Aziz, a "racialized Muslim" that represents a double-layered cultural enemy.

These long-standing attitudes were nothing strange in the American colonies. Of course, it hardly needs to be mentioned that African slaves were considered inferior to Whites but the latter also inherited many pre-dispositions toward Islam from their European ancestors. One scholar employed the term "islamicism" to articulate these perceptions among Americans in the colonial period through the nineteenth century.[41] This concept included a domestic variety, "which 'othered' Islam as the ideal-ized antithesis of domestic American situations . . . Islam was initially constructed as a cultural enemy, one that was despotic, anti-Christian, and morally corrupt, whereas America was imagined as democratic, Christian and virtuous."[42] These attitudes had real-life consequences since "the fear and hatred of Islam in Europe (which was almost as old as Islam itself) were inherited by European American descendants and so made it impossible for Muslim slaves to perpetuate their faith."[43] Culture war, then, taken to its logical conclusion, can effectively wipe out religion.

In post-9/11 America, attitudes and treatment of Muslims illustrate the modern mechanics of culture war. Campaigns such as anti-sharia legisla-tion, "no Muslim zones," mosque burnings, critiques of women wearing hijabs, and attempts to prevent mosques from being built are sites of con-tention that pit American rage against all things Islamic. For example, leg-islators have enacted anti-sharia bills, constructing sharia as "foreign" or "international" and, ultimately, un-American.[44] These bills discriminated against Muslim Americans, appealing to public ignorance about Islam and the immediate fear of terrorism, nowhere mentioning anything related to the Jewish or Christian faith. Even before these struggles, Muslims experienced cultural opposition in prison. They experienced multiple layers of culture war because Muslims in prison overwhelmingly tend to be Black, yet their keepers are usually not and are usually Christian. The cleavage between these groups was wide and resulted in Muslims being constructed as "others" by guards who thought of themselves as superior not simply for not being imprisoned, but sometimes because they were White or Christian. Richard Delgado writes, "the dominant group creates its own stories as well. The stories of narratives told by the ingroup remind it of its identity in relation to outgroups, and provide it with a form of shared reality in which its own superior position is seen as natural."[45]

These hallmark analytical devices of OutCrit jurisprudence allow for the critique of the ways prisons have controlled narrative within a context of a culture war, which has produced an effective means of denying substantive equality to incarcerated Muslims. From this perspective, the litigation manifests as a critique of the government, expressed by the lowest in society working within a system stacked against them. Moreover, by appropriating courts and the law, Muslim litigants regained some narrative control by litigating and exposing the state's wrongdoing. These conceptual markers are central to many of the cases that will be explored and underscore how different the law can look from the outside.

2 Islam in American Prisons

Islam in the United States is still in its infancy compared to other parts of the world, yet there has been a greening over the last century. Over this time, the Muslim presence has gone from scattered pockets of communities to a thriving Islamic religious scape. Even in the face of widespread Islamophobia, Muslim bans, anti-sharia law movements, Muslim-focused Countering Violent Extremism programming, and other adversities, the Muslim population continues to wax. It is on track to becoming the second-largest religious minority by 2040.[1] Today, there are likely more Muslims in the country than there have ever been, with various organizations, mosques, preachers, and religious leaders offering a marketplace of competing interpretations of Islam.

Although Islam's history in America is shorter than in other places, it is one of the most unique habitats for Islam to develop. The ascent of American Islam gave rise to two of the most popular and high-profile Muslims of all time—Malcolm X and Muhammad Ali. Their lives offer a gateway to understanding how the country has come to host such a diverse and complex Muslim population. For many, it may be hard to fathom that two *Americans* rank among the most famous Muslims ever since the founding of Islam by the Prophet Muhammad some fourteen hundred years ago. However, in the years following their rise to fame in the 1960s, these two celebrities were the face of Islam—black faces for America and other parts of the world.

Immense in popularity and worldwide notoriety, they shared many experiences, including converting to the NOI, and both were entangled in the criminal justice system. More directly, Malcolm X was a mentor to Ali and influenced Ali's embrace of the NOI. They likewise shared an exodus from the organization and embraced Sunni Islam. Their biographies offer a glimpse of a progressively complex scene that happened decades ago. They also provide a starting point for understanding how prisons occupy such a critical space in the history and growth of Islam in America.

Malcolm X's conversion begins the saga of conversion to Islam in prison, yet as mentioned previously, his predecessor, Elijah Muhammad, also experienced incarceration. This time of imprisonment shaped his attitudes toward prisons and gave him insights into his preaching efforts toward the men inside, such as Malcolm X. Muhammad's years incarcerated "definitely made him more sympathetic to the plight of incarcerated members of the race and permanently reserved for them a place in his heart."[2] His detention also showed him "that prisons were fertile recruitment grounds ... For simply showing compassion and concern for their well-being, the movement would eventually succeed in transforming hundreds of converts into loyal and sometimes lifelong dues-paying members."[3] So despite not being a prison convert per se, the prison experience exposed him to new ideas and more modern ways of running his organization.[4]

Case in point is Malcolm X, whose conversion took place in Charleston State Prison in Massachusetts, where he served an eight-to-ten-year sentence. His entry into prison in 1946 was for multiple crimes, including larceny and breaking and entering. It was here he first encountered Elijah Muhammad's teachings on Islam and his kindness. His remarkable conversion story is documented in the celebrated *Autobiography of Malcolm X*, which devotes three chapters to his turn to Islam in prison. Through this gripping account, the reader learns of his brutal treatment by prison guards, his withdrawal from narcotics, and his experiences in solitary confinement, including mental breakdowns and a descent into mania. In this confinement, his conversion begins and is a climactic moment in the autobiography. Where he had once feared the prison and the guards, conversion had put the fear of God into him, and now he feared nothing else.

While incarcerated, Malcolm would undergo various transformations, including abandoning his criminal lifestyle. Indeed, after he exited prison, his life would turn 180 degrees; whereas prior, he was a lawbreaker, as a free man, he would encourage and assist several individuals in prison in filing their petitions in court.[5] He would also agitate the prison for better conditions, "impelled by the requirements of his faith. He and other Muslims not only insisted on changes in their food and on the rules governing typhoid inoculations; they asked to be moved into cells that faced east, so they could pray more easily toward Mecca. When the warden rejected their requests, Malcom threatened to take their grievances to the Egyptian consul's office, at which point the warden backed down."[6] From transgressor, he transformed into a law-abiding citizen who modeled that even radical Muslims were willing to protest within existing civil and legal structures.

Malcolm X portrays prison as a saving space, a sacred space that fostered his remarkable transformation. Although he would enter the prison semi-literate, his encounter with the NOI doctrine stimulated his intellectual curiosity and inspired him to spend his days absorbed in learning and studying. As he describes, "months passed without my even thinking about being imprisoned. In fact, up to then, I never had been so truly free in my life."[7] During this humbling journey, the prison was privy to all his struggles with faith, including his intense shame at not being able to kneel in prayer. He writes, "I had to force myself to bend my knees. And waves of shame and embarrassment would force me back up."[8] In another instance, Malcolm X shows how other mystical experiences paralleled these changes. One includes him watching his brother's demise and believing it was the result of Allah's chastisement, because he believed his brother had done wrong; he believed that he personally witnessed a curse come upon his brother.

These and other episodes have classical markings of the *mysterium tremendum*, as moments of deep spiritual significance, embodying aspects of attraction and fear. For Malcolm X and the countless number of converts who would follow in his footsteps, the fear of prison can vanish under the sway of religion. Perceptions of the prison can transform from viewing it as a degraded and violent place to seeing it as a house of redemption and revival. The prison can hold a special space in the convert's mind, as that place where he encountered the Divine. For such individuals, the penal place of "corrections" gets displaced by the religious transformation, as Malcolm X exemplifies. His conversion transformed the central problem of his life, imprisonment, and made it almost invisible, to the point he hardly even remembered he was there on punishment. For him, the space became *dar ul islam*, the territory guided by Islamic scripture and eschatology. As one scholar describes, by "staking out an Islamic space and filling it with a universe of alternative sensations, names, and even a different alphabet, the prison jama'a establishes the conditions of the most dreaded aspect of detention—the duration of one's sentence, the 'terror of time.'"[9]

As Malcolm X experienced the terror of time on the inside, Muhammad Ali experienced it on the outside. As history tells, Malcolm X had to go to prison to experience a radical transformation in his life, but for Ali, the situation was reversed—he experienced a radical transformation that made him a potential candidate for prison. Like Malcolm X, he was fearless in his quest for justice to the point of risking incarceration.

Ali's troubles began soon after he refused to be drafted for service in the US Army in 1966. He was following the NOI's general opposition to Blacks joining the military, decrying, "War is against the teachings of the Quran. I'm not trying to dodge the draft. We are not supposed to take part in no wars unless declared by Allah or The Messenger . . . We don't take part in Christian wars or wars of any unbelievers."[10] "We are not to be the aggressor but we will defend ourselves if attacked," he said, famously stating: "Man, I ain't got no quarrel with them Viet Cong." Ali elaborated, "Why should they ask me to put on a uniform and go ten thousand miles from home and drop bombs and bullets on brown people in Vietnam while so-called Negro people in Louisville are treated like dogs and denied simple human rights?"

Prior to Muhammad Ali's resistance, Elijah Muhammad and others laid groundwork for a cultural battle to avoid serving in the military. They would ultimately spend time in prison for refusing to enlist in an American war, so Ali's refusal fell in line with his own leader's conduct. From the NOI's perspective, the war itself was racially unjust because a disproportionate number of Blacks were deployed in war, and more critically, a disproportionate number was killed. Moreover, the hypocrisy was unbearable—at home, dogs were being used to attack Blacks, and Blacks, in turn, were being forced to attack Vietnamese. The hypocrisy extended, with Blacks told to be nonviolent at home while the country was engaged in atrocities abroad. The Muslims wanted nothing to do with a military draft that would force them to kill for a society that hounded Blacks with police, the KKK, and vigilante civilians.

During the war efforts, *Muhammad Speaks* was particularly critical of the country's role in Vietnam and defensive of members who refused to join. In practically every newspaper of that era were gruesome and heart-breaking images of slaughtered civilians, Vietnamese toddlers smoking American cigarettes, and stories of rampant sexual violence committed against civilians. In addition, several articles directly defended Ali's decision to object to enlisting, and a number suggested the government wanted Ali for political purposes. After all, he was the most famous member of the organization and an important figure for recruitment efforts, not to mention he contributed generously to NOI projects. Above all, were his personal efforts in preaching and proselytizing. Ali spent significant time traveling and speaking on behalf of the organization. Thus, it was not a sham for him to claim conscientious objector status because he was really a minister for the movement—perhaps the greatest loudspeaker the movement ever had. Yet like Muslims in prison, he was treated differently. While White Christian ministers were exempted from the draft, he was forced to fight.

Soon after officially refusing to enlist, he was tried and convicted by a jury in federal court for violating the Selective Service laws, which the Fifth Circuit Court of Appeals upheld. Ali considered himself a conscientious objector and argued that "the Holy Quran and the teachings of the Honorable Elijah Muhammad tell us and it is that we are not to participate in wars on the side of nobody who—on the side of nonbelievers, and this is a Christian country and this is not a Muslim country."[11] The Supreme Court took up Ali's appeal and eventually overturned his conviction, producing a momentous victory. Although Ali was not jailed for most of the nearly five years it took for his case to be decided, he was stripped of his championship titles, and state boxing commissions refused to allow him to box professionally in their jurisdictions. Instead, he spent these years not only forsaking his prime years in his professional livelihood but also dealing with the stress of a potential prison sentence. In hindsight, it is apparent Ali was undaunted in his willingness to litigate his case until the end, which, in turn, helped propel him into superstardom. His case was one of the country's most high-profile court cases ever witnessed, and in the eyes of many, Muslim and non-Muslim alike, the Supreme Court victory made his legend rise to fulfill his moniker as "the greatest."

Although the NOI is where Ali started in Islam, it would not be where he ended up. Ali would eventually disavow the NOI and relinquish its racialist ideals. His abandonment of the organization came after 1975, when Elijah Muhammad's son, Wallace Muhammad, split from the organization to orient followers around Sunni Islam. Ali would follow Wallace Muhammad's lead, marking his life with two distinct transitions in faith, first to the NOI and later to Sunni Islam. Even more remarkable is that in his later years, Ali developed some affinity for Sufism, what is often described as the mystical or esoteric orders of Islam. His history illustrates the complexity of Islam in America and showcases how one can migrate through different denominations over the course of one's lifetime. Such a feat is a toast to the diversity of Islam in America. Denominational options are available for those interested in the faith. Ali spanned three different traditions, and, by all accounts, he is remembered as a devout Muslim.

A SACRED SPACE FOR CONVERSION

> [Elijah] Muhammad's time in prison . . . convinced him that
> the conversion of the "living dead" inside America's penal
> system was of paramount importance to the overall aim of
> liberating African Americans from their white oppressors.[12]

Conversion to Islam in jails and prisons is a unique phenomenon in American corrections. Correctional systems, in general, are a special space for the spread of Islam. In Black culture, the legend of a Black man going to prison and converting to Islam is a slice of a common trope, one that simultaneously influences Muslim prison litigation. As far back as the early 1960s, it was noted that the legend was no accident because "the regeneration of criminals and other fallen persons is a prime concern of the Black Muslims, and they have an enviable record of success."[13] While the present work looks at those "fallen" souls who go on to litigate cases, there are significant numbers of individuals who convert inside the prison's confines and can be called prison converts in a genuine sense of the term. One Baltimore minister described his witness of conversions: "The progress and change in the inmates of these institutions after they hear the teachings of the honorable Elijah Muhammad is almost unbelievable. Men who have never prayed or even thought about going to church—who have never given a thought to accepting any religion—are now facing the East in recognition of the God that Messenger Muhammad tells about, Almighty Allah. These men are now standing guard at their posts just as if there were Mosques in prison, without any fear whatsoever."[14]

While many are attracted to Islam's messages of social justice and racial equality, there is also an attraction to Islam due to cultural factors that add layered meaning to one's conversion. For example, it is common among African Americans and Latinos to refer to themselves as a "revert" to convey it is not just a turn but a *return* to one's religion. It is a path to discovering the African and Iberian connections to Islam and recognizing Islam as a part of their cultural ancestry. The notion of "reversion" links the believer to a glorious past as a descendant of Muslims, to a time before Christians entered the picture and imposed Christianity on them. The impact that such ideas have on one's will to litigate is uncertain. However, conceiving of one's religious identity in this way indicates something more powerful and transformative is occurring than a generic conversion. A cultural conversion also occurs, where racial identity transforms from a marker of shame and disgrace into one of beauty, pride, and self-esteem.

It may not be a surprise that the popularity of Islam in prison is part and parcel a result of the early African American new religious movements. After some of these groups were founded, it would not take long before they started to make prison-preaching a staple of their ministries, as one intellectual notes, "there are scholars who have observed that the history to establish Islam in American penal institutions dates back to the 1930s."[15] Some of these efforts were directly inspired by the words of Elijah Muhammad. One NOI member described in an article, "The Devil Shall Cast Some of You into Prison," writing: "The prisons and jails are filled with followers and non-followers of Messenger Muhammad, and the devils (white race) are constantly trying to convict more Black people to long sentences in prison ... Messenger Muhammad wrote, '[t]he so-called prisoners are fast becoming converts to Islam. This is Allah's doings that the scriptures may be fulfilled wherein it says; '[w]hich executes Judgement for the oppressed, which give the food to the hungry. The Lord looseth the prisoners.'"[16]

By the time Malcolm X converted to the NOI between 1946 and 1952, the NOI and other groups were already proselytizing behind bars, including his family members who would visit and write letters. He also had a spiritual mentor in prison who played a major factor in his turn to faith. Other groups contributed to these efforts to make Muslim outreach in prison an ongoing focus. Prisons, in turn, would become a central locus for the expansion of Islam in underclass America. It is difficult to overstate the prison's centrality as a place of proselytizing. In recent decades, the shift to relying on prisons for the mass incarceration of offenders has contributed by providing a massive and literally captive audience for preaching efforts, particularly an audience of disillusioned individuals who have felt the sting of the poverty, racism, and injustices of American law and the justice system.

There are no reliable statistics compiled for the number of Muslims in all American penal institutions, particularly because religion is not recorded for an individual who enters or exits prison. However, there have been various estimates, if dated. One suggests 15 percent of the US prison population is Muslim,[17] which elsewhere has been estimated as between 300,000[18] and 350,000 prisoners.[19] At the federal level, in 2014, the Office of the Inspector General reported that approximately 6 percent of the 150,000 federal inmates seek Islamic services.[20] Hasan estimated in 1991 that thirty-five thousand incarcerated individuals converted annually to Islam.[21] In contrast, Nyang estimated in 1999 that one out of every ten conversions among African Americans takes place in the prison setting,[22] with more recent commentary suggesting that conversion to Islam in all city, state, and federal institutions is between thirty thousand and forty thousand annually.[23]

Even if these figures may not be as current or accurate as one may hope, they give a sense of the importance of prison conversion and offer a prelude to recognizing conversion as a well-known narrative in Black culture in America. Malcolm X's history illustrates how his work exemplifies the

African American Muslim community's "first-hand experience with the prison setting."[24] From his time to the prison conversion of the boxer Mike Tyson in the 1990s, to the present, the prison holds a strong, almost mystical space in Black consciousness.

Several early literary works illustrate the point. One is James Baldwin's critically acclaimed *The Fire Next Time,* which proclaims: "Elijah Muhammad has been able to do what generations of welfare workers and committees and resolutions and reports and housing projects and playgrounds have failed to do: to heal and redeem drunkards and junkies, to convert people who have come out of prison and keep them out, to make men chaste and women virtuous, and to invest both the male and female with pride and serenity that hang about them like an unfailing light."[25] Three years later, Claude Brown's 1965 autobiography, *Manchild in the Promised Land,* raises the issue of conversion rather seriously, asking, "damn . . . what the hell is going on in the jails here? It seems that everybody who comes out is a Muslim." Eldridge Cleaver's *Soul on Ice* gave further indications of how Islam grew in influence in the 1960s: "Every black inmate was exposed to the Black Muslims' teachings . . . it was not a rare sight to see several Muslims walking around the yard, each with a potential convert." These depictions would be echoed in scholarship that explained preaching on behalf of Muslims: "The Muslims were also unique among prisoner groups in their vigorous recruitment of membership . . . they preached their doctrine on the recreation yards on the industrial assignments, and inside the cell houses."[26] Some three decades later, Nathan McCall's autobiography, *Makes me Wanna Holler!,* told a similar story about Muslim outreach behind bars, describing, "No African-American spends much time in prison without being exposed to the doctrines of Black Muslims. . . . Brothers respected the Muslims for being disciplined, religious people, and at the same time, warriors. The Muslims did not believe in that stuff about turning the other cheek. Nobody messed with them because many of them were hard-nosed cats who were eager to throw down for a righteous cause."[27]

Even in hip-hop culture, the notion of prison conversion to Islam is a notable trope. One such example is in Tupac Shakur's "I Ain't Mad at Cha," which details the transformation of one of his trusted homies, who gets incarcerated and turns to the faith:

Member when you had a jheri curl didn't quite learn
On the block, witcha glock, trippin off sherm
Collect calls to the till, sayin' how ya changed
Oh you a Muslim now, no more dope game
Heard you might be comin' home, just got bail
Wanna go to the Mosque, don't wanna chase tail
Seems I lost my little homie he's a changed man
Hit the pen and now no sinnin' is the game plan[28]

As the lyrics detail, Tupac's former comrade lived a life on the street, pack-ing a gun, doing drugs, and selling them too. In addition, the line about the Jheri curl is telling because it indicates a revolution in consciousness, one that transforms ideas about racial inferiority. Indeed, this is the same sort of consciousness that had Malcolm X giving himself konks—it was an attempt to shed his natural, physical attributes to chase White ideals of beauty. Just like Malcolm X, Tupac's homie changed after time spent in jail. No longer was he interested in chasing women, a life of hustling and crime, or a White appearance; instead, he was ready to live a clean life as a Muslim. Perhaps the most telling aspect of the song is that such religious transformations are understood in Black culture. There is no apostasy for a Black man to find Islam in prison, which is the point of the song, "I ain't mad at cha," almost as if conversion to Islam in prison is an inevitable rite of passage for some.

For those who experience conversion in the prison setting, an individu-al's change in views can result in a change in the way he perceives the prison itself. For some converts, the prison undergoes a type of conversion as well. Malcolm X is an exemplification, for not only did he recognize his old ways of thinking slid away from him "like snow from a roof," the prison transformed as well. What was once a dreaded place became a spiritual, sacred space that housed his personal, emotional, and sometimes trau-matic experiences. For him and others, the prison plays witness to the *mysterium tremendum,* and watches individuals in their most vulnerable moments. Men who were once terrified of the prospects of "doing time," now find themselves unafraid. Under such a worldview, the prison re-manifests as a postmodern *umma* that purifies the profane. In one swoop, the most base, filthy, and forgotten place in America becomes another's Mecca. In this scenario, the bondage of imprisonment paradoxically bestows the gift of freedom. As one convert describes, echoing the words of Malcolm X half a century before, "that was a turning point in my life and I don't regret . . . going and experiencing some of the things I experienced in that confinement, that restricted area; because in that area I became a man, and a free man."[29]

SPECIAL CHALLENGES FOR PRACTICING RELIGION

> The NOI offered hostility to the prison and . . . offered a
> political explanation for black imprisonment as well as a
> personal code for responding to confinement.[30]

There are some important points to note about Islam's appeal regarding prison conversion. In early research, C. Eric Lincoln's study on the NOI noted clear bonds between the organization and prison, including the racial appeal for prisoners, positing that the NOI operated "on the premise that 'knowledge of self' and the truth about the White man—when tied in with a constructive program, such as building the black nation—is sufficient to reclaim the corrigible."[31] Hence, the work of Muslim outreach is a prime factor, as is the fact Muslims are overrepresented in state prisons in general. According to one report, "Muslims are overrepresented in state prisons by a factor of eight relative to the general population. In some state systems, Muslims are overrepresented by a factor of closer to eighteen, with more than 20 percent of prisoners identifying as Muslim."[32]

One of the early studies of conversion to Islam was Robert Dannin's *Black Pilgrimage to Islam,* a pioneering study that still stands as the most authoritative text on the subject. As Dannin describes, "Islam's attraction for prisoners lies in its power to transcend the material and often brutally inhumane conditions of prison. Although it may seem to some just another jailhouse mirage, the Muslim prisoner sees entry into that space as a miracle of rebirth . . ."[33] There is no singular dimension to the influence, but instead, the impact operates at various levels of being: "on the one hand, the regime upholds Quaranic injunctions and encourages the sublimation of desire into a rigorous program of study and prayer. On the other, and more subtly, a man's adherence to these injunctions illustrates counter disciplinary resistance to the more overt dominant hierarchies encountered in prison life." Adopting new religious ideas and expressions steers the convert to reinterpret the world through an empowered frame. Adherence to a strict regime itself resists deviant prison subcultures, including drug and alcohol use, sexual promiscuity, and gang activities. Beyond, it resists the prison administration as well, as demonstrated in the litigation. In addition to such outward expressions of resistance, there is inward resistance against prisons, one that abides by a different legal code, because "the community ethos remains more or less impermeable to the prison administration, the sharia helps define and reproduce an alternative social space where the inmates' behavior can be monitored and judged according to Islamic rules."[34]

Here, it is correct to observe that many of these positive impacts are possible in other religions, so what, then, makes Islam so exceptional in American prisons? Writing about Stateville prison in the early 1960s, Jacobs observed that "Muslims offered legitimacy and significance to the frustration, bitterness, and egotism of some of Stateville's most recalcitrant inmates."[35] Another study noted the NOI worldview offered a powerful conversion narrative, "an insider account of the 'true' history of race and the structure of the United States, a set of codes and mores that invited people to make themselves anew for a higher spiritual purpose, a sense of superiority in an institution that continually told them they were inferior."[36] Some success may be inherent in the religious practices. It has also been described that religious movements are successful only "to the extent that they sustain strong internal attachments, while remaining an open social network, able to maintain and form ties to outsiders."[37] As applied to the prison context, this idea reveals two aspects about Islamic practice and beliefs. First is the strong emphasis on communal prayer (jamaat) that, in the words of the study, helps "sustain strong internal attachments." The emphasis on communal prayer is exemplified in the cases that detail the inability of Muslims to congregate and worship, which remains a contentious area of law. It may also be the case that communal-based worship, as one scholar notes, has natural advantages over other practices in the incarcerated environment: "Historically, Christian prison reformers envisioned conversion as cloistered reflection or silent prayer. Islamic teaching, however, changes self-image and social relationships primarily through communal prayer ... the greater the capacity of the prison jamaat to establish the privilege of congregational prayer, the greater the potential effect on the Muslim."[38]

Scholars posit other reasons to account for Islam's growth in prison. Some suggest the process of adopting a new religion may be a distancing mechanism and way of expressing the erosion of one's social context and its religious authorities. Conversion is a way to disassociate oneself from the dominant Christian culture because conversion may offer a "symbolic challenge to Christian hegemony." As racial minorities have fallen victim to Christian oppression through slavery, colonialism, and missionary work, Islam offers a path to reclaiming a history of kings and conquerors. This attitude is evident in one individual who described his "Christian guards" were starving him and letting his injured leg rot.[39] Others suggest that Islam has a special appeal to those who are oppressed and unprivileged. These ideas support Dannin's contention that for converts, Islam functions as a "grammar of dissent." It provides the language and idiom to critique the existing reality; rather than believing one's situation is the result of merit alone, the individual begins to understand that greater systemic forces are at play.

The appeal of Islam as a vehicle of justice is synonymous with its use as a tool to fight oppression. This bent is seen early on in letters written to *Muhammad Speaks* from behind bars. In one letter, an individual describes how Islam helped him when everything else failed: "Like so many black people in America, I was made a scapegoat and sent to prison for a crime I had not committed . . . During the first four years of my incarceration, I engaged in futile prayer, hoping Jesus would use his mysterious power to grant me justice. I even turned to the prison authorities, but they all failed to help."[40] For this individual who experienced injustice at the hands of the system, the turn to Islam was life-changing: "I am forever thankful to Allah (God) . . . for having delivered me from feelings of inferiority, for granting me the drive and determination to keep on pushing the Message of the Honorable Elijah Muhammad."

Sometimes one's conversion impacts the very people who witness the transformation. According to veteran prison-preacher Imam Muhammad Abdullah, who founded Taif Tul Islam in Los Angeles, genuine conversion can inspire conversion: "The discipline that Islam requires, charity, and cleanliness, are really admired by people . . . this begins a conversion of many because they are living with either their former crime partner(s) and the knowledge of his past, and to see that person or people change right before their very eyes is enough for some." This point was underscored by research on conversion: "When people say they feel peace or that they have found freedom within their imprisonment, any listener cannot help but be swayed by the obvious emotion with which they speak."[41]

This foray into Islam in American society and prisons aims to serve as a historical and spiritual backdrop for considering the cases and data in the chapters that follow. Most importantly, it is an outline of some of the primary factors of conversion and a blueprint for tracing how individuals can turn into a savior in a place that many would consider hell. Converts are known for putting religion at the center of their lives, in the hot spots of the brain, when it comes to serving God and religion. Consequently, some of their energies are used to express dissent against prison policies and regulations. These insights convey some of the lived experiences and religious persecution that animate the Muslim will to litigate ongoing legal issues.

A HOUSE OF PAIN AND RELIGIOUS PERSECUTION

Hardship defines prison life, yet Muslims also endure mistreatment due to religious biases. Mistreatment of Muslims by prison officials occurs through two primary means. One is through direct conduct—both illicit and through the enactment of policies, rules, and regulations. The other is through omission, when officials fail to carry out their legal responsibilities, or worse, turn a blind eye to abuse by both staff and other wards.[42] The acts and omissions of prison staff can create an oppressive mix of domination and subjugation, where staff engage in abusive and repressive treatment of those they have been entrusted to care for or, more critically, rehabilitate. This dual aspect of staff conduct is the foundation for understanding litigation efforts since both forms of mistreatment become the basis for complaints and grievances that would spawn court action.

Cooper is one of the earliest and most illustrious examples of how staff treatment and conditions in prison create oppressive conditions for Muslims.[43] As that case unfolded, it was determined that Cooper, a con-

vert to the NOI, was sent to solitary confinement and given other penalties for claiming to be a Muslim. In solitary, he was alone nearly constantly,
with a blanket and one meal a day, and he could shower and shave once a
week and was allowed a half-hour of exercise daily in a small pen.[44]
Writing in 1967, the Seventh Circuit Appeals Court seemed dismayed
that Cooper's decade in segregation was "almost of record length."[45] This
pioneering case opened the saga of prison litigation with a stark sense of
what Muslims were experiencing in prison.

Later, litigation would involve different manifestations of the same
issues Cooper dealt with in the 1960s and new problems too. Muslims
would continue to struggle against the use of solitary confinement, newly
created Communication Management Units, excessive use of force,
restrictions on access to courts and libraries, inadequate nutrition, and
lack of medical care, access to visitors, canteen, work detail, recreation,
and programming. These issues merely hint at the range of issues over
which prison officials exercise control in such a totalized environment.
However, they give a clear indication that repressive measures collectively
can add up to make a person's life in prison miserable.

Hardships for Muslims sometimes are the product of religious bias,
which can take multiple forms, including favoring one's religion or disfa-
voring another's. In the apex of bias, the two manifest simultaneously. Such
has been shown in research, writings, and other testimonials that describe
guards using extralegal violence, harassment, sacrilegious epithets and
other antagonizing language, and confiscating worship items, including
incense, oils, beads, and foodstuffs.[46] One individual describes how
Muslims face discrimination because of prejudices and misconceptions:

> For instance, if I'm praying and a prison guard walks pass [sic] he'd kick the
> door calling me while I'm in the middle of salat. If I don't answer I'd get
> written up for refusing to obey an order even though no order was given. Or
> if we're in the yard and salat comes in Muslims aren't permitted to pray in
> the yard, however if Christians want to hold hands in a circle and recite the
> serenity prayer, this is allowed. It's the unfair treatment Muslims receive
> from staff who are ex-military and don't like Muslims that fuel the fire for
> religious injustices.[47]

This description sounds similar to one individual, who identified as
Albanian and was incarcerated in federal prison in New York State: "They

have no respect while we are praying, walking in [the] room and inter-rupting our prayer."[48] This individual went on to describe why he choose the path of litigation: "The main reason that I filed the lawsuits is because they violate our religious rights and they think they can get away with it, which they do because judges side with them. It is a totally corrupt injus-tice system. I filed the lawsuits because they denied my rights to pray Eid-al-Adha prayer for 2 consecutive years; they were throwing the Qur'an on the floor, desecrating it so they can humiliate."

One of the more sobering aspects of prison is when prison staff retaliates against a ward who has complained to the prison administration or filed a claim in court. In both instances, the person may be targeted as a retaliatory measure for filing grievances despite following the prison's protocol. Some retaliatory measures are more benign than others; for example, an individ-ual in Georgia state prison wrote, "If you can, please supply some S.A.S.E. They are retaliating on my indigent legal supplies @ times b/c of litigation upon prison officials."[49] More starkly, some actions can turn a person's world upside down, starting literally when guards "shakedown" a cell. As wards have no privacy right in their cells, guards can turn a cell upside down and inside out, which is essentially the unfettered ability to ransack a cell. In addition, guards can confiscate material possessions. In one such case, the prisoner-petitioner claimed he had personal belongings confiscated from his cell for filing a complaint that stated officers filed false charges against him.[50] The court sided with the Muslim petitioner, who persuaded the court to let the case proceed. This victory, however vindicating, hardly meant that petitioner's long-term living conditions improved. After all, court docu-ments alleged that even other corrections officers warned the official there would be grievances filed against him because of his conduct, to which he replied, "I don't care about [a] fucking grievance because I kill Muslims."[51]

With the existential threat of retaliation in the ether, the sheer number of Muslims willing to take cases to court seems to convey the bravery required to do so. The reality of retaliation makes complaining or litigat-ing a dangerous business and puts the petitioner in harm's way for simply attempting to seek redress of a problem. Perhaps one of the most blatant and harmful means of retaliation is when a prison transfers a ward to a different facility, defeating litigation efforts and creating untold havoc in that person's life.

UNMASKING THE MUSLIM WILL TO LITIGATE

Justice is an attribute of Allah (God) Himself.[52]

Messenger Muhammad has taken up the cause for justice of
the black man in America.[53]

What connects the large number of Muslim litigants to religion itself? And
why do Muslims go through such a painstaking process of suing in court?
The answers are crucial when considering the already unsavory living conditions behind bars. It is not easy to exist, with illness, violence, and reduced
life expectancy characterizing prison life. In this extreme existence, against
such stacked odds, it is a wonder what sustains this long-standing struggle
between Muslims and prisons. One might even be tempted to say that
Muslims sue "religiously," yet this proposition would not be entirely false.
This idea must be taken seriously because several factors internal to the
Muslim faith support this proposition. As we will see, some of the inspiration that motivates litigation comes directly from religious scripture, tradition, and practices. From the lessons and edicts found in Muslim tradition,
there is much that stresses the duty to seek justice, which offers a path to
understanding litigation within a theological frame. When one considers
the above quote from a follower of Elijah Muhammad, it underscores a
religious movement premised on seeking justice, which brings this point
full circle—justice is both a cause and effect of the NOI's existence.

Islamic traditions place a premium on the pursuit of worldly justice
and equality.[54] There are prominent themes of social and racial justice
found in Islamic traditions, which convey a strong message that the pursuit of justice is part of one's duty as a Muslim. As NOI members catalyzed
prison litigation efforts, their messaging at this time shows a clear willingness to look to litigation as a means of righting wrongs. Teachings in Islam
about justice and equality provide a theological frame for understanding
attitudes in the prison context.

The Quran abounds with references to justice that emphasize its place
in a variety of human settings, including within the family, community,
and even people in prison, as in the mandate to be "kind to . . . those bond-
speople in your possession."[55] Other verses emphasize social justice and
extol that, alongside the worship of God, one should show kindness toward
these disenfranchised groups.[56] This exhortation is strong, urging one to

stand for justice even against other Muslims: "O ye who believe stand out firmly for justice as witnesses to Allah, even as against yourselves."[57] When it comes to oppression and tyranny, the Quran is unequivocal about resisting tyranny and looking out for the safety and sanctity of one's fellow humans. Those who stand up to oppressors are likened to saviors sent by the grace of God: "And what is it with you? You do not fight in the cause of Allah and for oppressed men, women, and children who cry out, 'Our Lord! Deliver us from this land of oppressors! Appoint for us a savior; appoint for us a helper—all by your grace.' Believers fight for the cause of Allah, whereas disbelievers fight for the cause of the Devil. So fight against Satan's forces . . ."[58] As the statements propound, standing up for justice and standing against subordination is God's work, for as described in the Quran, "Allah commands justice, the doing of good . . ."[59] On the contrary, the Quran lays out over two hundred admonitions against injustice.[60]

The Quran and other traditional sources offer additional insights into Islamic teachings on racial equality. Islam was conceived on the idea that humans are equal from the beginning, including the notion that "everyone is born a Muslim."[61] Already discussed were passages likening skin color to the colors of clay in the earth and others describing that no race is above another, yet others reinforce the point: "Among His signs is the creation of the heavens and the earth and the diversity of your languages and your colors. Verily, in that are signs for people with knowledge."[62] From these perspectives, different skin colors and languages are a sign of creative power, all of which are divine in Allah's creation.

Scholars and commentators indicate the value placed on justice and its different dimensions in Islamic tradition.[63] "One of the principles which underlie the Islamic worldview is justice. Justice also is the real goal of religion. It was the mission of every prophet. It is the message of every scripture."[64] Describing justice as the "foundation of Islamic theology," one scholar describes social justice as "anchored in the Qur'anic concept of spiritual justice through which humanity is tasked with serving as God's appointed custodian [khalifa] on Earth and judging fairly between people and upholding the rights of all creation."[65] Another describes the practical dimensions, including that "Muslims are strongly encouraged to pursue and demand fair treatment for themselves, and even more importantly for others, through a range of reasonable means . . . e.g. arbitration, a legal process, advocacy, etc."[66] The theme of acting on behalf of non-Muslims is pervasive, as another commentator explains: "Social justice is a religious act, one could say and a religious act which ironically transcends the boundaries of religion or even ideology when it comes to who its beneficiaries are."[67] Muslims of different denominations have embraced these messages while engaging in the "legal process" and "advocacy," including criminal defense and human rights work. One individual who has litigated several cases from prison described his understanding: "For every Muslim, enjoining what is right and forbidding what is wrong is the key to fight for truth and justice. It is an Islamic concept and practice [that] permeates the soul of every true believer. It doesn't have to be an Islamic matter, but any injustice, and we are commanded to fight oppression until no more oppression exists. Not in a violent manner, but in a peaceful way."[68]

Outside prison, Muslims express similar sentiments about their duty to act. For example, Sahar Aziz has written that Muslims claim "Islam inspires them to advocate for human and civil rights. Some have memorized the Qur'an while others are recent converts whose knowledge of Islam grows exponentially each day."[69] Aziz describes a famous hadith that is repeatedly referenced by Muslim justice advocates and organizations in the United States: "Whosoever of you sees an evil, let him change it with his hand; and if he is not able to do so, then [let him change it] with his tongue; and if he is not able to do so, then with his heart—and that is the weakest of faith."[70] As the passage indicates, there are levels of protest inherent in advocating against evil, the most basic of which is human thought; at a bare minimum, seeing evil should illicit protest in the mind, which is equated with the weakest form of faith. Higher than this is protesting with one's words and voice. Beyond, if one is able, one should try to change the situation with action—to stand up and do something about it. This maxim to oppose evil "is frequently interpreted as mandate against injustice and oppression, and it inspires many Muslims in the United States to defend civil and human rights at the local, state, national, and international level."[71] In addition, Muslim Student Associations across the country invoke this saying in their calls on members to defend certain causes, including joining the campaign against sexual assault on campus. Their testimony supports that advocacy is not something that arises spontaneously but is distilled from Islamic teachings.

The NOI's founding intertwined with themes centered on racial and religious justice. Elijah Muhammad merged these issues by championing justice and equality for the Black man, and he "believed in a sense of divine judgment that was tied to human agency."[72] Perhaps the movement's most prominent expressions appear in its early newspaper, *Muhammad Speaks,* which regarded itself in various ways, including as "A Militant Monthly Dedicated to Justice for the Black Man" and adopted slogans such as "Justice and Equality of the so-called Negro, The Earth Belongs to Allah."[73]

In the days of Elijah Muhammad, racial justice was a distant concept, and poverty was the status quo for many Blacks in America who were denied justice and constantly made second-class citizens. The NOI and other groups took White oppression against Blacks as an opportunity to superordinate Blackness, making such treatment the dividing line of its nationalist views. This point is evident in a letter to *Muhammad Speaks* from an individual in Soledad Prison in California, who, having survived being shot in prison, felt his Islamic beliefs and his desire for racial justice begin to grow: "I respect everyone I come in contact with but this is not going to stop me from speaking the truth, because I don't care nothing about falsehood and those representing falsehood. I am only concerned with Black truth, Black peace." In the closing of his letter, he asks, "will you stand up with me for Black truth? All you soldiers on the battlefield—keep the faith!"[74]

Other entries strike at the heart of what justice means to followers. Consider "The ABC of Divine Knowledge," which situates justice as a divine attribute:

J is for justice.
Justice is equality.
Justice is freedom and peace.
Justice is part of the Muslim's divine faith.
Every Muslim believes in justice.
Justice is an attribute of Allah (God) Himself.
Allah is the most justice.
Justice is Good.
Without justice, nothing can be good.
The devil knows no justice.
The devil is the enemy of justice.
That is why there is no good in the devil.

I do not like the devil.
I do not like those who do not believe in justice.[75]

The poem identifies Allah with justice, which is the enemy of the Devil. The very last sentence closes with a rebuke to "those who do not believe in justice," drawing cosmic battle lines that legitimize the taking of earthly action. In this struggle, justice is the central tenet, as described in "Up You Mighty Nation":

Rise up and shine you mighty sons,
For gods you were born and will die;
The Muslim cry is Justice
For Allah we live—we die.[76]

As this brief survey of sources reveals, it is not difficult to find support in the Quran or in Muslim traditions that authorizes struggling for justice. Islam endorses action against oppression, and there is a spiritual benefit in doing so. Tradition advocates using the "hand" to stop oppression, and Muslims in prison have done just that—by researching the law, handwriting documents, and typing out complaints, briefs, and other legal documents. Engaging in such a struggle is a powerful experience that provides an alternate reference point for one's identity. One need only consider a person incarcerated, discarded by society, and existing in a world of crime and violence—that same person, under the sway of Islam, may undergo a remarkable transformation. Instead of a common criminal, he can rise to the status of "savior" and attain the sublime "grace of God." It is perhaps no accident that when Malcolm X described his conversion in prison, he described the transformation as one that began at "Satan" and ultimately brought him to "Savior." He explains that in prison, he made a concrete decision: "to devote the rest of my life to telling the white man about himself—or die."[77] At the end of the chapter tellingly entitled "Savior," he recalls a preaching moment where he describes his newfound commitment to racial justice: "I have sat at our Messenger's feet, hearing the truth from his own mouth! I have pledged on my knees to Allah to tell the white man about his crimes and the Black man the true teachings of our Honorable Elijah Muhammad. I don't care if it costs my life."[78]

3 The Struggle to Be Recognized by Prisons

> It is impossible to understand the vehemence and the determination with which the prison resisted every Muslim demand, no matter how insignificant, except by understanding that what seemed to be at stake was the very survival of the authoritarian regime. Permitting Muslims to possess a copy of the Quran did not on its face threaten prison security, but recognition of the Muslims as a bona fide religious group . . . was perceived as a grave threat to the moral order of the prison.
>
> —James B. Jacobs, *Stateville: The Penitentiary in Mass Society*

The infamous prison described, Stateville Correctional Center, is a spectacle for the type of double vision that prison officials have in their treatment of Muslims. On the one hand, Muslims historically have been the focus of a heavy gaze, of surveillance, spying, and eavesdropping under an aura of suspicion and mistrust. Some have been designated as a security threat group and given harsher punishment as a result. On the other hand, Muslims have been somewhat invisible to prison officials and have struggled to be recognized as genuine faith adherents. These situations offer clear examples of what Asma Uddin describes in her book *When Islam is not a Religion*, which highlights non-Muslim constructions of Islam as something other than a genuine religion. Whether it is Muslims in the 1960s facing solitary confinement for being Muslim or demanding Qurans, or groups in the 2020s still trying to shake off the gang or security threat group branding, prison officials have a long and sordid history of disenfranchising Muslims of religious rights. Muslims have uneasily existed in the middle of this contradiction, where they are unique and distinguishable enough to surveil but fall outside of what constitutes a religion.

Stateville, known in its heyday as the "world's toughest prison," is the prison that housed Thomas Cooper, whose case would become the cornerstone of the prisoners' rights movement. Cooper encountered the NOI and Elijah Muhammad's teachings in these confines, which came when he hit rock bottom. When he started his foray into the teachings of Muhammad, the transition was remarkable—it breathed new life into his hopeless situation. He soon began to walk a religious path, and embedded in this newfound faith was a willingness and determination to take his troubles as far as he could in court. Cooper launched a protracted campaign to challenge Stateville's prison conditions, which ushered in the dawning of a civil rights movement in prison that grew in the shadows of a Jim Crow civil society.[1]

How Cooper ended up in Stateville is quite a dramatic sequence. Like Malcolm X, he was involved in a small street criminal enterprise. Cooper's crew, however, was far more vicious than the burglarizing and fencing that landed Malcolm X in prison. From the criminal side of things, Cooper was in for far more serious crimes; for him, it was murder. Several of Cooper's associates were involved in at least twelve tavern robberies around the time of the murder.[2] Among these, he and another from the group committed two of them, each resulting in a barkeep being killed. Shortly after one of the killings, one of Cooper's companions was wounded in a gun battle with a security guard, which left the companion "hopelessly paralyzed."[3] Although this individual would get probation for his misdeeds, Cooper pled guilty and was sentenced to two consecutive one-hundred-year sentences.

This sentence may seem drastic, but this sentence of life was certainly not a sentence of death, which was a looming possibility because Illinois at the time was a death penalty state. When this two-century sentence was handed down to him, Cooper was twenty years old. Based on the penal laws of Illinois, it would be over thirty years before Cooper would ever be eligible for parole.

Of course, he still received a death sentence in being spared capital punishment because it seemed likely he would spend his death in prison. This point is especially true because life expectancy is generally lower for people in prison, with evidence suggesting every year in prison reduces one's life by two years.[4] Things looked bleak for Cooper. Having escaped death itself and now staring at a humanly impossible prison sentence, Cooper's life fell into disarray. After a pretrial and a trial period of stressing about the case and whether he would receive the death penalty, he would go from a free man to being essentially sentenced to death by imprisonment. The point here is not to muster sympathy for his plight but to consider the strain this caused on his body and psyche. For most humans, the plight of a potential death sentence can make the hairs go grey quickly, and Cooper was in this state for the five-to-six-month interlude between his arrest and sentencing, where he learned he would spend the rest of his life behind bars.

After his sentencing, Cooper must have harbored a mixed bag of emotions. In one sense, he was relieved, even ecstatic, at the prospect of not having to face the death penalty or having to live on death row. In another, he was devastated that he would undoubtedly spend the rest of his breathing days behind bars. With so much to manage in his own life, he had no clue of what life had in store, nor could he have imagined he would rise from these ashes and go from lawbreaker to lawmaker.

According to court records, Cooper converted to Islam while serving this sentence. Behind bars, followers of the NOI introduced him to Elijah Muhammad's writings, and by 1957, he wrote to Elijah Muhammad and formally requested to become a disciple. Muhammad consented, and Cooper took on the name "Thomas X. Cooper." Taking on a new name is common for converts like Cooper, and it simultaneously acts as a mark to indicate a rebirth or evolution of the person or even that the former person is dead.

By the time Cooper was at Stateville, it was a massive prison complex that held a population of about forty-five hundred. Only fifty-eight documented Muslims were then being held, yet despite the minuscule figures, the prison warden believed Muslims posed a tremendous threat to institutional security. In particular, he paid close attention to those Muslims, and even resorted to eavesdropping and solitary confinement to keep dominion over them, including Cooper.

The time in solitary was harsh. From Cooper's view, his extra punishment was the result of simply being a Muslim and fighting to be recognized as an adherent of a legitimate religion. From the prison's perspective, Cooper and his companions were violent troublemakers. As one scholar describes, it was a hostile situation: "Cooper would remain in Segregation, for more than a year. There, prison guards kept him in a cell by himself with only a blanket and a ration of just one meal a day. As per regulations, he was only able to get a bath and a shave once a week as well as one haircut and one visitor per month. Rather than going to the yard to exercise, officials only allowed Cooper to walk around a small pen enclosed by a twenty-foot wall for thirty minutes, three to five times a week."[5] Despite the hardships, Cooper and the other Muslims in segregation found ways to subvert the prison. Research into the prison records details several ways this occurred, "including that Cooper and congregation continued to worship together by communicating from cell-to-cell, often by taking the water out of their toilets and using the sewage pipes as a crude means of communication. They also joined each other in initiating hunger strikes and other disturbances."[6]

This draconian treatment of Cooper, however, backfired. Even though prison officials tried to break him with their zero-tolerance policies, the extralegal punishment seemingly served to strengthen his resolve. One prison documentary that explores Stateville underscores the point: "For the next decade, that is where he would remain. But instead of neutralizing Cooper, the isolation radicalized him."[7] The unfair and harsh punishment created a being who became bent on resistance and pressing his grievances in court. It was here, in solitary, that he waged a long and arduous legal struggle that would ultimately become a groundbreaking legal decision. It reverberated nationwide and stood for the proposition that civil rights were not simply abandoned at the prison gates.

COOPER V. PATE: A NEW BEGINNING BEHIND BARS

> The shift from a "hands-off" to "hands-on" philosophy in
> the courts can be traced to one case, Cooper v. Pate . . .
> Cooper opened the door to other issues that inmates faced
> as consequences of their incarceration . . . [and] Despite
> being a prisoner, one does not surrender the constitutional
> protections guaranteed to citizens.[8]

Cooper is widely regarded as something of a ground-zero for the civil rights movement in prison. Cooper's turn to federal court began in 1962, when he filed a civil rights suit in the US District Court for the Northern District of Illinois against his warden and the Illinois Director of Public Safety, alleging their violation of his rights under the Fourteenth, Eighth, and Fourth Amendments. Cooper argued he was denied permission to obtain and read certain publications, consult with ministers of his faith, and attend religious services solely because of his denomination of Muslim religious beliefs. Cooper also alleged he was placed in solitary confinement because of his religion. The court dismissed his petition for failure to state a claim; after all, at that time, there was hardly a civil rights claim that a person in prison could stake. Undeterred, Cooper appealed to the Seventh Circuit Court of Appeals, which affirmed the dismissal on November 5, 1963. On June 22, 1964, the Supreme Court reversed and, without commentary, held: "taking as true the allegations of the complaint, as they must be on a motion to dismiss, the complaint stated a cause of action and it was error to dismiss it."[9]

In this terse opinion, the Court handed down its first modern prisoner civil rights lawsuit and made courts more relevant than ever for people in prison. *Cooper* was remarkable on many counts, including that it opened an avenue for people in state prison to seek redress in federal court.

When the case went back on remand, the District Court held a trial, and on July 23, 1965, the court issued an opinion and order enjoining prison officials from (1) refusing to allow Plaintiff and other followers of Elijah Muhammad to purchase copies of the Holy Quran; (2) categorically refusing to allow followers of Elijah Muhammad to communicate by mail and visit with ministers of their faith; and (3) categorically refusing to allow followers of Elijah Muhammad to attend religious services. The court also held Cooper's religion did not entitle him to access special newspapers and language books. Both sides appealed different aspects of the judgment, but the judgments were affirmed in 1967.

At the time, litigating such a case was no easy task. Part of the reason is that prison administrators were quite antagonistic toward Muslims. As one individual incarcerated in Washington, DC, noted at the time, unfairness pervaded the justice system on the inside and out, particularly how Black life was devalued; as he writes, "I came into Islam as nothing:

rejected and despised by the society that had made it possible for thousands of young black men such as myself, to be reduced to nothing."[10] If things were rigged to trap Blacks in prison, he found during his conversion in prison that such injustices continued behind bars, especially for Muslims: "During this time there was all-out opposition to Islam by the officials. The Muslim inmates were really treated badly to put fear into those who might accept. Their favorite plan was to harass and lock-up or get rid of by any other means, those inmates who were acting as our spiritual guides."

A litigant like Cooper likely faced multiple difficulties, including xenophobia, racism, and courts that were somewhat incompetent in their knowledge of American Islam. This was evident through some of the court's statements in Cooper's appellate decision. For example, the appeals court referred to his desire to purchase religious reading materials from "the Black Muslim Movement." This characterization is misleading because there is no such group by that name, and as the court records attest, he was seeking materials from the NOI. Yet, rather than challenge the use of such a term, the court adopts this menacing raced-based nomenclature. There are several reasons that the term "Black Muslim" came into vogue as a reference to the NOI and other adherents, and most critically, the influence of C. Eric Lincoln's *Black Muslims in America* on scholarship, law enforcement, and prison personnel who used the term as well.[11] However, the NOI itself resisted this label and made attempts to shed the moniker, as Malcolm X explained: "From Mr. Muhammad on down, the name 'Black Muslims' distressed everyone in the Nation of Islam. I tried for at least two years to kill off that 'Black Muslims.' Every newspaper and magazine writer and microphone I got close to: 'No! We are black people here in America. Our religion is Islam. We are properly called "Muslims"!' But that 'Black Muslims' name never got dislodged." In the opinion, the court never once saw the inflammatory nature of the terms it used.

Perhaps never had the court racialized a religion as such. The court's language situated Muslims as one united Black front, a movement, despite the fact that African American–oriented Muslim groups faced external and internal strife since they came into existence. Moreover, the opinion seems bereft of a basic understanding of Islam. For example, in the opinion, the court explains that Cooper's "principle complaint seems to be that he was placed in solitary confinement because he insisted upon obtaining a Muslim bible, termed by him 'Quran.'"[12] Here, the three appellate court judges seem a bit clueless about the religious aspects of the case before them. They seem to think that Cooper has coined the word, Quran, and instead choose to ignore this and designate it a "Muslim bible."

By the time the court handed down the second appellate decision, the court took a more nuanced approach. For example, in a footnote, the court described Cooper as a "follower of the sect of Muslims led by Elijah Muhammad," which it further clarifies in the footnote: "This group is sometimes referred to as 'Black Muslims'; we will refer to it in this opinion as the Elijah Muhammad Muslims."[13] This is quite a shift from the earlier Seventh Circuit opinion, which unabashedly adopted the phrase "Black Muslim Movement" without ever verifying whether such a thing existed. The same with the holy book, which the court takes for granted, stating Cooper sought "permission to purchase and read the Koran."

When Cooper began litigating his claims from his solitary cell in 1962, he probably could have never imagined that his case would turn into the watershed it did, described by some scholars as the *Brown v. Board of Education* of the prisoners' rights movement.[14] The decision changed the course of prison law, gave rise to civil rights in prison, and contributed to the growing trend of courts abandoning the "hands off" approach to prisons, where "the prisoner was shut off from the courts and placed outside the protection of the rule of law."[15] Until the 1960s, courts hardly ever interfered with prison life, and what prisons did with prisoners was the state's business; and as *Ruffin v. Commonwealth* had stated in the late 1800s, prisoners were "slaves of the state." The Seventh Circuit explained this position just a few years prior, in 1956, when it wrote, "it is not the function of the courts to superintend the treatment and discipline of prisoners in penitentiaries." It was prison officials then, not courts, who handled claims from wards, as Kathleen Moore notes, a distinctive feature of the 1900s–1960s was confidence "placed in the discretionary authority of public officials to understand and cure each 'deviant,' and to respond to the needs presented by each, on a case-by-case approach. Thus, prisoners were isolated from the rest of society by virtue of incarceration, and prison programs and practices were developed by prison officials who were given a great deal of latitude in corrections."[16]

Even though his case got sent back to the court to hear his claims, some of which he lost, his Supreme Court case was noteworthy. Cooper's case set a major precedent and stood for the proposition that people in prison have standing to present a legal claim. This case paved the way for other litigants to bring a range of other claims.[17] Although the holding was narrow, "for the prisoners' movement it was not the breadth of the decision that mattered, but the Supreme Court's determination that prisoners have constitutional rights; prison officials were not free to do with prisoners as they pleased."[18] By acknowledging that Cooper had a claim, the Court supported the conclusion that Muslims could sue for religious rights. In one swoop, imprisoned people had gone from a state of "civil death" to a place where civil rights had become a living reality. As cases go, it represented the first time that the Court sanctioned the use of Section 1983 of the Civil Rights Act for anyone in a prison cell.[19]

While the case had the outward appearance of a full-blown victory, it hardly meant it was the end of the story. Cooper would have to return to court to pursue his claims, which would not be settled until two years later: "When the appellate court ordered New York officials time to develop entirely new prison regulations that would have effectively recognized the NOI, they repeatedly resisted efforts to do so . . . it would not be until May 1966 that a new set of regulations would be implemented, but even this new policy would be the subject of another four years of litigation as [prison officials] continued to identify Muslim believers as a group distinct from all other prisoners."[20] The timeline gives a sense of the many obstacles faced by Cooper and the more unnerving situation where prison officials refuse to follow the new rules. The case reflected the clear distinction between getting the law to change versus getting prisons to follow the law. It also underscored the differential treatment of Muslims based on jurisdiction, as it would not be until 1970 that a federal district court in California would order San Quentin State Prison to extend religious rights to NOI followers.

Despite its struggles, the *Cooper* decision stands as a landmark that would have long-lasting impacts. One effect was to break up the power trust of prisons. As one scholar put it, "before Cooper, all power in prison had flowed from the wardens. Now, it flowed from the court . . . Almost overnight, the formerly hostile federal bench turned friendly. Inmates filed suits by the thousands in response."[21] It was a case that breached the walls that separated people in prison from civil rights, and his case would be followed by others who pressed for redress in court. By the end of the 1960s, federal courts decided more than two thousand Section 1983 lawsuits a year, which would rise to over thirty-nine thousand by 1995.[22] Considering the sheer number of civil rights claims brought under Section 1983, Cooper indeed left an important mark in the history of prisoners' rights. He helped lay a foundation for Islam as a genuine religion where Muslims could lay legal claims to religious liberty. His story is a remarkable introduction to the struggle to establish Islam as a religion and establish oneself as a sincere follower.

ESTABLISHING ISLAM AS A GENUINE RELIGION

Prison officials justify restriction placed solely upon Black Muslim prisoners on two basic grounds: First, they argue that the inflammatory doctrines of the Muslims are an incitement to violence and a threat to discipline within the prison. Second, they assert that the Black Muslim movement is a social and political, rather than a religious organization.[23]

The presence in our institutions of a small group of inmates who adhere to quasi-religious doctrines referred to as "Muslem," [sic] or who are members of the nation organization "Nation of Islam," has presented a management problem.[24]

In the 1960s, the efforts of Muslims in prison built on the previous decade's outreach efforts. When this statement was made in the 1950s by the California Department of Corrections, Muslims in New York were organizing in prison. Historian Garrett Felber describes how the Muslim Brotherhood was thriving in New York prisons: "Because they were not given a formal space to hold services within the prison, informal prayers . . . often took place on the prison yard. Men relied on an oral tradition of memorized prayer, and *surahs* passed from prisoner to prisoner . . . Many of these lessons were based on editorials by Elijah Muhammad and Malcolm X published in Black newspapers in the late 1950s."[25] As this account details, Muslims in prison essentially cobbled together whatever means they could to learn more about the faith and practice. Felber underscores the point with a letter from a Muslim in prison who wrote to Malcolm X, "Most of us have never seen the inside of a Temple ... We had to make up our own lessons from articles appearing in the Los Angeles Herald Dispatch." Piecing together the religion was made more difficult because many prisons censored or monitored such newspapers, or in some cases, banned Muslim materials altogether.

The reputation of Muslims was thoroughly tarnished in some prison systems, which made establishing Islam more difficult. Prison officials were concerned about the NOI attitudes regarding American society and World War II, which caused some to believe that prison security would be compromised by allowing Islamic practices within the prison.[26] Such attitudes were visible in the American Correctional Association's resolution in 1962, which denounced Muslims as a "race hatred group." The resolution stood as a bold declaration that what Muslims in prison were doing was something other than practicing religion. The statement offers a sense of the correctional milieu where Cooper's case was decided. For Muslims behind bars, religious freedoms were not simply handed over; they had to prove their legitimacy repeatedly. As Jacobs describes, one prison administration "implemented the decision on its very narrowest form, thereby necessitating years more litigation on related issues of the right of Muslims to the publication *Muhammad Speaks,* religious medallions, and pork free diets."[27] Such a result, in hindsight, minimized the size of the victory.

These events evince a long-standing tradition of casting Muslims as a particular threat in prison, a particular narrative that may be rightly seen as early instances of American Islamophobia. Such fearful and fearmonger attitudes toward Muslims manifested long before the events of September 11, 2001, and even before the bombing of the World Trade Center in 1993. Even before Malcolm X became infamous in America, prison officials harbored intense apprehension about dealing with Muslims in prison. Being marginalized in this way had consequences legally speaking because "when otherwise legally cognizable claims accrue for outsiders, the conflict between their stories and the stories of the dominant, insider culture places their rights and remedies at risk."[28] This process played out true to form as Muslims began to press for religious rights;

often, the courts sided with prison officials' accounts of events that led to the disenfranchisement, or worse, punishment of Muslims seeking to practice their religion.

In the year before the Association's resolution was passed, there was a remarkable case that heralded the *Cooper* decision. *Pierce v. La Vallee* featured a group of Muslims who sued under Section 1983 for their grievances, including the right to purchase and possess the Quran, the right to contact a spiritual advisor, and because they were subject to punishment solely for their religious beliefs. At trial, the court limited the issues to those about purchasing the Quran on the ground that other problems raised by the complaint concerned prison matters that were reviewable in state court. A year later, the Second Circuit heard the appeal and reversed the district court's decision. In a shocking opinion, the court held that the complaint raised by the prisoner-plaintiff raised issues distinguishable from state law questions involving physical abuse or restrictions on liberties.

Through the opinion, the court issued a serious blow to the great wall between federal courts and state prisons. Its words intimated the wall was beginning to crumble: "so we feel constrained to hold .. that the present complaints, with their charges of religious persecution, state a claim under the Civil Rights Act, which the district court should entertain."[29] Although the lower court found that the Muslims were not punished because of their beliefs, the case represented something far greater for Muslims at large and those in prison specifically. As the same court described, the issues pertaining to the Quran became moot because the Commissioner of Correction issued a directive to wardens of the state to approve purchases of several translations of the text, including the one the plaintiff sought.

There were prior cases that hold a place in the history of establishing Islam in prison. For example, in the year before the Association's resolution came *In Re Furguson,* where ten Muslims sought a writ of habeas corpus to remove the restrictions placed upon their religious activities in prison. Although, in the annals of legal scholarship, this case is not considered much of a landmark decision, it is an important case regarding the history of prisoners' rights in which a court shied away from insulating prison officials from their conduct and signaled a willingness to subject prison officials to judicial scrutiny. Ferguson was a member of the NOI who alleged that the prison denied Muslims the free exercise of religion.

In defense, the Director of Corrections argued that Muslims constituted a "quasi-religion," which posed a threat to the prison, staff, and those serving time. Due to the biased orientation of prison officials, Muslims were denied the right to a place of worship, the ability to gather to practice their religion, the right to obtain and possess religious literature, and to meet with religious leaders. The court upheld the restrictions imposed by the prison. However, by entertaining the case, the court signaled in California, people imprisoned may make claims based on issues beyond contesting the fact of confinement. Even though the court could have toed the historical line, as one researcher notes, "the significance of the decision is due partly to the court's willingness to hear the case in the first place; despite ruling against the prisoner-plaintiffs, the *Ferguson* court chose not to invoke the hands-off doctrine, and instead ruled on the merits."[30]

Although the case signaled an awakening of the federal judiciary to the plight of those behind bars, the court's treatment of the religion left a lot to be desired. In this case, the director filed documents highlighting the group as anti-White, anti-authoritarian, "quasi-religion," and as early as 1958, he marked Muslims as a "management problem." He pointed to these characteristics as a basis for denying them religious status and restricting their practices, measures he believed would reduce the potential threat of Muslims to "conflict with the health, safety, welfare and morals of the prison." This characterization of Islamic beliefs and practices was based on a narrow view of the NOI. "It was a view that mirrored depictions of the movement by federal and state governmental agencies, local police departments, national media outlets, and local papers ... The overall effect of these representations of the Nation of Islam was the perpetuation of the belief the NOI was not legitimately religious, it was not a legitimate Islamic Organization, and it was a radical politico-militant movement driven by a fanatical anti-white doctrine of hate and aggression."[31]

The court agreed with the defendant, deferring to the director's professional decision and essentially relying on a hands-off logic that ultimately handed down a defeat. However, the greater point was that the court chose to rule on the case's merits rather than dispense with it outright under the prevailing hands-off regime. It was a move away from precedent, but as one researcher notes, it was "incomplete" because "in its final determination, the court adhered to the underlying reasoning of the hands-off doctrine."[32] As such, the case was something of a state precursor to the sentiments that would be later moved to federal courts in the name of establishing Islam in prison.

Another early case, *Sewell v. Pegelow*, showed the tide for free exercise protections was beginning to change. According to the suit, Muslims at this Virginia facility were not simply denied certain rights, but individuals were punished for being Muslim.[33] One report notes in this case, "the court's language in describing the prisoners evinced a lack of familiarity with Muslim history in the United States."[34] In the opinion, the court describes the prisoners as "Negroes professing Islam and are known as Muslims."[35] However, the court notes the Muslims claimed their discrimination and deprivations were due to religion rather than race. The court summarized the complaint:

> They charge that all the Muslims in the institution, of who there were thirty-eight at the time, were put in isolation and deprived of institutional privileges, including medical attention. The complainants allege that they violated no disciplinary rules or regulations, and that for no reason other than their religion they were kept for 90 days in isolation . . . where they were provided only "one teaspoon of food for eating (and) slice of bread at each meal three times per day." . . . complainants were permitted to have a blanket and mattress only between the hours of 10:00 p.m. and 5:30 a.m. This mistreatment, the complainants repeat, was due solely to the hostility entertained by the prison officials toward persons of the Muslim faith.[36]

These individuals were also stripped of religious paraphernalia, and the prison officials suppressed their mail to other state officials. The court held that a district court has the power to grant relief where there has been a deprivation of civil rights. Even though incarcerated individuals made the claims, the courts were not proponents of keeping a wall between prisons and courts; as the *Sewell* court noted, "it has never been held that upon entering a prison one is entirely bereft of all of his civil rights and forfeits every protection of the law."[37] The court did not go as far as to adjudicate the extent of the prisoners' rights, but it believed that the complaints deserved a hearing.

The following year, *Fulwood v. Clemmer* involved a jail convert who helped establish the right for Muslims to practice behind bars.[38] In this case, a group of Muslims sought permission to hold religious services at

Lorton Reformatory in Virginia. The director denied their request, citing the decision not to allow Muslims to hold religious services was based primarily upon "his belief that the Muslims teach racial hatred, that such teaching is inflammatory and likely to create a disturbance or disorder, and hence would not promote the welfare of the prison population."[39] Nonetheless, the court recognized what they were primarily after was the ability to practice their religion; as the opinion describes, the "concept of religion is met by the Muslims in that they believe in Allah, as a supreme being and as the one true god. It follows, therefore, that the Muslim faith is a religion."[40]

By 1970, litigation was proceeding at a steady stream. In that year, NOI members in California prisons sued in federal court because they could not receive copies of the newspaper, *Muhammad Speaks,* and could not get a copy of the Quran translated by Abdullah Usuf Ali. Although this version was one of the most widely known and used translations in the English-speaking world, they could not obtain a copy for the prison library. Not only was the newspaper made unavailable, but copies were confiscated and individuals were punished if found to be in possession of this contraband. The district court frowned on the prison's conduct and ordered prison officials to allow the newspaper to be received on a regular basis and to make copies of the Quran available to other prisons. This victory was somewhat inevitable considering the previous cases examined, and it put a capstone on the process of getting the very basics of Islam established behind bars.

Through these and other cases, Muslims laid a foundation that later generations of Muslims and non-Muslims would build upon in future litigation. Not only would Muslims sue for rights that others in prison could enjoy, but they began building a jurisprudence that was useful to members of other religious groups. Such was evident in 1972 when the Supreme Court cited *Cooper* in allowing a religious discrimination claim by a Buddhist individual in prison to continue.[41] The precedent set in *Cooper* began to bear fruit for adherents of other religious groups. Supporting the point, one academic study noted these lawsuits are deliberate workings of the NOI, which launched strategic initiatives from the 1930s to the 1970s centered on litigation.[42] According to this study, "one of the simplest ways that the NOI could justify using the courts to protect their rights of its members was its consistent support for law and order," and "by the early 1960s, the NOI had clearly demonstrated a willingness to use the courts and competent legal counsel in a bid to protect the civil liberties of its membership."[43]

ESTABLISHING ONESELF AS A GENUINE FOLLOWER

One should not be befuddled into believing Cooper's victory handed Muslims in prison a one-way ticket to religious freedom. Even if the prison administration recognized Muslims were a legitimate religious group and could make religious accommodation claims, prisons could still divest individuals of their religious liberties. One way was for the prison to determine a person was not a genuine follower of the religion—the person was not a true believer but was simply using religion as a pretext for other ends. Courts, in turn, developed the "sincerity doctrine" as a tool for screening claims and used it to dispense with a free-exercise claim by finding a religious belief was not sincerely held. More critically, prison officials determined some groups constitute a gang, and any follower of the group is necessarily not religious. The first way looks at the individual and whether one is sincere about the faith, and the other looks at the religious group itself to determine whether it is legitimate. Both are ways to suppress Muslims in prison because either, the individual or the group, can be designated as something other than sincere or religious. For Muslims, these designations and doctrines represented additional hurdles to religious accommodation claims. One individual explains the enduring nature of these attitudes: "I am a Sunni Muslim. I have affiliations with no group or organization. My only oath is to Allah when I took my shahada. When I entered the prison system and told them I was Sunni Muslim, the prison said that this was a gang. Two decades later, prison officials still have and possess this ignorant disposition. Therefore they discriminate against Muslims like myself because they think it's a gang. Islam is not a gang."[44]

In the early 1960s, when Muslims in prison began to establish Islam behind bars, the NOI continued to inspire the formation of other groups. One of these, the Nation of Gods and Earths (NGE), most well known as The Five Percent Nation of Islam or simply "Five Percenters," was organized in 1963. The leader, Clarence 13X, was called "Allah the Father" by his followers. Despite his religious background and theological reasons for parting with the NOI, a 1965 FBI investigation branded his followers as a "Negro youth street gang," and, ever since, followers have struggled to shake this identification. The adoption of the "Gods and Earths" name itself is an attempt to distance themselves from the Five Percenter identity, which was associated with thuggery and gang life. In prison, this labeling has been problematic because some institutions have rubber-stamped the FBI's assessment that the group is a gang, as opposed to a religious group entitled to First Amendment protections.

Since these early times, individuals aligned with this NOI splinter struggled to obtain religious rights in prison. Note the issue is not whether the group constitutes a genuine branch of Islam but, more basically, whether it constitutes a religion at all. For some, it does not, and as a result, these followers are denied rights and protections. More ominously, rather than simply being denied these rights, followers may suffer harsher treatment by their status as a security threat, including solitary confinement. The FBI's initial designation of such groups as a "gang" was a cornerstone idea that state and federal institutions would follow for generations. Unfortunately, ignorance and fear were at the helm of this designation, and consequently, for some, religious rights behind bars were still something to be achieved.

It may very well be the case that C. Eric Lincoln's influential study described earlier contributed to these attitudes. Prison authorities had an appetite for the book, and they saw it as an objective portrait of the organization. Garrett Felber describes that as "the NOI became a greater topic of conversation in race relations and as its presence in prisons grew, the state attempted to develop a consistent logic to justify suppression of Islam among prisoners"; some of the strategy would derive from Lincoln's study, which "was widely read and distributed among criminologists and prison officials."[45] His book would eventually find its way to police departments and the Georgia Bureau of Investigation, and he would be invited to speak at gatherings held by the American Association of Correctional Psychologists, American Correctional Association, and other groups whose attitudes toward the NOI were often unfavorable or openly hostile.

While his study provided an air of legitimacy for the NOI's claim to religion, it also may have contributed to some attitudes that disenfranchised

Muslims under the "gang" banner. For example, Lincoln's work character-izes the NOI as a movement driven primarily by political goals and a racially charged philosophy: "In this context, although the Black Muslims call their Movement a religion, religious values are of secondary impor-tance, except to the extent that they foster and strengthen the sense of group solidarity."[46] The characterization of the group in terms of prioritiz-ing group solidarity overall lends itself to interpreting their behavior as based more on gang, rather than religious, codes. For Lincoln, the group afforded certain benefits, including being a part of a like-minded commu-nity actively fighting racism and feelings of helplessness and inferiority. It was a boost to group solidarity driven by a desire to overcome White oppression. In essence, Lincoln's position was that Muslims were political, if not criminal in nature, which was ideal for diminishing their status as adherents of genuine religion.

The move to define a clearly religious group as a gang dates back as far as the research tells, and the struggle continues. For example, in *Coward v. Robinson,* a federal judge in Virginia issued a Memorandum Opinion that Virginia prisons cease from continuing to classify the same group as a security threat rather than a religion. Under this policy, adherents were forbidden from "owning, creating, possessing, or passing to other indi-viduals any correspondence, documents, photographs, drawing, jewelry, symbols, or property of any type that contains or indicates gang identifi-ers, language, or information."[47] This policy essentially meant all their reli-gious paraphernalia. More critically, records from Virginia prisons indi-cate just how wanton the designation was because adherents were assigned more than one gang affiliation; that is, one could be designated as a "Five Percenter/Blood" or a "Five Percenter Crip." According to the court, this group appears to be the only "gang" that Virginia corrections lists with cross affiliation. Such contradictory treatment reaches a zenith when taken to the logical conclusion: members of the same gang could be on opposite sides of gang warfare. As this case shows, adherents have struggled against being defined out of existence by prison officials. The sentiment persists according to a survey sent out to all state correctional departments to determine the status of the Five Percenters, of which thirty-three states responded, with thirteen not recognizing the group as a legitimate religion. Thus, despite evolving ideas about what the Supreme

Court thought qualified as a "religion," this case indicates that even considering such victories, it did not mean individuals who identify as Muslims would be automatically free to practice freely.

MARTIN SOSTRE—JAILHOUSE LAWYER AND ACTIVIST EXTRAORDINAIRE

> His resistance was an act of war, and he identified his
> personal war as one with the forces of the third world . . .
> Sostre's ability to resist physical punishment was a
> requirement to his stance of noncooperation. He claimed
> that spiritual strength empowered him to continue
> resistance.[48]

La Vallee was important on its own merits in the history of Muslim litigation, but one of the plaintiffs would become one of the most influential prison activists of the 1970s. One journalist describes: "His name has been lost to history, but in the 1970s, prisoners, wardens and prison guards across the U.S. knew of Martin Sostre. He was a fearless prison activist at the dawn of the age of mass incarceration, an inmate willing to risk months in solitary confinement to fight for prisoners' rights."[49] Described as a moving force behind this litigation, "Sostre played an integral role in attracting other prisoners to Islam and filing litigation against New York officials."[50]

Sostre served two different prison sentences that took him to various correctional facilities. The first began with a short stint at Sing Sing in 1952, where he was transferred to Attica Correctional Facility and then to Clinton State Prison. During his time at Clinton, he embraced the NOI philosophy and began a serious quest in education, which led him to study nationalism, internationalism, and anarchism. There, Sostre met Teddy Anderson, a Muslim of the Ahmadiyya faith. It was this encounter that drew Sostre to Islam. Anderson loaned him a copy of the Quran, which at the time was the only copy at the prison. This friendship, coupled with his previous experience with Black nationalism in Harlem, led him to convert to the NOI, which, behind bars, was known as the Muslim Brotherhood. As one biographer described, Islam was the best formulation available for his mode of resistance, and at some point early in his first sentence, "Martin began to seek a means of declaring war on the ills of white-dominated society. And Islam itself at that time seemed to be such a declaration of war."[51] His interest in Islam encountered a roadblock. At the time, Muslims were denied access to the Quran and to basic religious rights, the very same rights that individuals of other faiths exercised. This clash, his growing interest in religion, and the lack of religious opportunity became the ground zero for his resistance against prisons and his willingness to endure immense suffering to advance the standing of people in prison. In terms of recognizing personalities in this culture war, Sostre may be regarded as a general who organized and led forces along prison battle lines.

As he tried to deepen his knowledge of the NOI tradition, he began to experience institutional roadblocks and began complaining to prison officials, particularly about the double standard in the treatment of Muslims. The events in Sostre's life illustrate a cycle that would repeat itself countless times in the 1950s and ensuing decades with others in prison. It typically began with Muslims at an institution recognizing the double standard that subordinates Muslims to Christians in prison. Muslims, in turn, complain and issue grievances to the administration. Rather than address the mistreatment of Muslims, the administration inflames their mistreatment by clamping down and punishing them further. As a result of being subject to additional punishments, Muslim followers are branded as troublemakers, with their placement in solitary confinement and other disciplinary actions used by the administration to prove the religion's negative impact on the prison environment. This cycle allows prison officials to dig into the religious beliefs as further evidence of the Muslim affinity to racism and hatred. While early scholarship on this point was somewhat ambivalent, this was the process that Muslims repeatedly claim they have had to overcome at prison facilities. It is seen in countless court opinions that detail the actions of prison administrators.[52] Lincoln noted Muslims' frequent involvement in prison agitations contributed to the "aura of menace with which many white American's view the movement. Undoubtedly, White harassment . . . contributes to the self-fulfillment of a somber prophecy."[53]

Accordingly, like other complainants in this book, officials labeled Sostre as an agitator for trying to establish his religious rights—in his case, for requesting to buy his own copy of the Quran and to be allowed visits from NOI ministers. In trying to obtain these freedoms, Sostre was branded a troublemaker and was punished by solitary confinement. This labeling was the beginning of the quest for Muslims to have rights in prison. Still, it also laid a foundation for prison officials and politicians to associate Muslims with troublemaking and even gang activity, despite that Muslims were, in fact, being treated unfairly. Sostre, however, turned the table against them and organized Muslims to fill solitary units. Rather than try to avoid the harsh punishment, he embraced it, reasoning that when "the box ceases to work, the entire disciplinary and security system breaks down."[54]

While some of the unfair treatment was punishment in solitary confinement, it should be noted the solitary confinement of the 1950s and 1960s was not the solitary of today. When Sostre spent time in solitary, the conditions of confinement were extreme and unsanitary, considering today's sanitized standards and protocols. In those days, prisons operated in an era of little to no government oversight, and solitary was its own universe, as Sostre describes: "I slept on a concrete floor with no bed and no mattress. All I had was a blanket which they gave me at night and took away early the next morning. The floor was so hard and cold that I could sleep only 10 minutes in one position . . . There was no light, no running water, no toilet."[55] The four years he spent in solitary was a radicalizing experience for Sostre as it was for Cooper, for it was here he began drafting petitions and filing legal complaints against prison officials, the beginnings of a decorated legal career.

During his first incarceration, Sostre used his time to study the law and develop his writing skills. He became an effective writ-writer and drafted templates for a burgeoning prison litigation movement, which used his drafts to submit various complaints. Although he was a high school dropout, he would go on to write remarkable petitions that demonstrated his erudition and deep understanding of the law—he was a true legal mind stuck behind bars. "His greatest achievement at that time was as plaintiff in the landmark case, *Sostre v. McGinnis,* which complained that Muslims in Attica prison were denied right to practice their faith, including to worship together congregationally, communicate with ministers of their faith, and obtain various religious publications."[56] In its opinion, the court recognized the NOI as a religion but said "the activities of the group are not exclusively religious," which was still short of recognizing it as full-fledged religion. This view was due in part to the court's focus on the group's teaching that the Christian religion was loathsome, as well as its focus on the group's ideas as being divergent from "orthodox Islam." Ultimately, the court reversed the dismissal of Sostre's claims of religious persecution, a holding that was described as "a major contribution to the Nation of Islam's struggle for recognition and to the emerging prisoners' rights movement."[57] As Sostre described, the results were far more lack-luster: "It took six years of suffering and litigation to get [this] ruling in 1964. I personally spent five years in solitary confinement struggling, and had my sentence not expired in September 1964, while in Attica solitary confinement, I probably would have spent many more years under torture . . . Thus the struggle to exercise a First Amendment 'preferred' right took from 1958 till 1971, thirteen years of torture, suffering and death."[58] Sostre became the paramount jailhouse lawyer who did more than simply represent his own interests. He helped countless individuals with their legal cases and was known for preparing templates and instructions for others filing claims, which "made it possible for NOI converts to coordinate their litigation."[59]

One of his towering cases was *Sostre v. Rockefeller*, which centered on issues related to his solitary confinement. The record of this case indicates that Sostre was familiar with solitary confinement by the time the litigation arose. Based on the facts of the case, prior to trial, the judge in the case ordered Sostre immediately released from solitary. Even more remarkably, the following year the judge issued a ruling that railed against the prison for its conditions of confinement and mistreatment of those confined. Even though appellate rulings would not uphold the amount of damages requested by Sostre, the court did award him twenty-five dollars a day for every day held in punitive segregation (372 days), plus an additional punitive award of an additional ten dollars a day for a total of $13,020.

Because the sum was considerable for the time and because, to date, there had not been such an award given to an individual in prison for time in solitary; the victory was momentous. It made all take notice, especially wardens across the country, who would be forced to pay attention to the ruling, which "is still relevant in the current debate over the use of solitary confinement."[60] For Sostre, the victories must have been relishing because, previously, he was punished with solitary for violating a prison rule that forbade him from practicing law.

Sostre also acted as legal counsel for others in prison, which came at a price. When he was transferred to the Green Haven Correctional facility, he was put into a special housing facility for alleged infractions, including practicing law without a license for mailing a legal certificate to his co-defendant. In this opinion, *Sostre v. Rockefeller,* the judge who wrote the opinion was the same who ruled on solitary issues the year before, the famed Constance Baker Motley. Already familiar with Sostre's treatment in the New York prison system, she seemingly pays him a nod of respect for his remarkable achievements, despite his incarcerated status: "Mr. Sostre . . . is also no stranger to the federal courts with his civil rights complaints against New York prison officials. He secured for Black Muslim prisoners their rights to certain unrestricted religious liberties during his prior incarceration. *Pierce, Sostre, Sa Marion v. La Vallee* (1961) and *Sostre v. McGinnis* (1964). His earlier legal activity also resulted in the elimination of some of the more outrageously inhumane aspects of solitary confinement in some of the state's prisons."[61]

One of his later cases, *Sostre v. Otis,* involved the censorship of literature.[62] In this litigation, Sostre sought to enjoin the prison from withholding certain literature he ordered in the mail, including the NOI publication, *Muhammad Speaks.* The court found the procedure for screening literature was deficient and ordered officials to allow Sostre to receive his publications. The court also ordered the prison back to the drawing board to modify existing procedures to ensure they complied with constitutional requirements. Sostre saw these victories as "a resounding defeat for the establishment who will now find it exceedingly difficult to torture with impunity the thousands of captive black (and white) political prisoners illegally held in their concentration camps."[63]

Sostre's influence on the development of prison law is noteworthy on multiple counts. For one, he participated in major cases that further established civil rights in prison and was involved in other litigation that successfully challenged conditions of confinement. He also embodied just how effective a jailhouse lawyer can be and left a blueprint for future generations in prison to follow. These achievements made significant contributions to the development of prisoners' rights, and according to Felber, "no single figure played a greater role in securing legal rights for prisoners in the history of the U.S. than Martin Sostre."[64] Sostre marks a glowing example of the determination and fortitude of a convert who put his mind and efforts into using courts to advance justice and to help those around him. Summing up his selfless mode, one author writes: "Rare is the man who can defend his own faith. But rarer still is the prisoner, deprived of lawyers, advocates, friends, and influence, living under inhuman conditions of solitary confinement who will laboriously pen a brief to a federal court for the right to practice his religion and the similar right of all his fellow prisoners in his own prison and throughout the United States."[65]

THE CIVIL RIGHTS MOVEMENT AND SUPREME COURT'S EXPANDING VIEW OF RELIGION

> Both black numerical superiority inside the prison and the
> example of black civil rights activity on the streets were
> factors facilitating the rise of black nationalism and Black
> Muslims, whose activities directly challenged the traditional
> relationship between keeper and kept.[66]

The struggles for civil rights that took place during the 1950s and 1960s are generally considered the work of lawyers and activists in America who began to challenge the status quo. In those years, there was growing public and political support for expanding civil rights in several areas of life, from voting rights to religious rights to women's rights and more. The push was generally known as the Civil Rights Movement. It was an era that saw the Court deliver groundbreaking rulings like *Brown v. Board of Education*, dismantling school segregation, and *Loving v. Virginia*, which struck down anti-miscegenation laws.[67] While some leaders became widely known for their efforts in pushing for civil rights on the outside, it was not individuals like Martin Luther King and the civil rights movement that effected the most significant legal change for people in prison, but the NOI.[68]

When Sostre's first federal case was decided, advocates for civil rights outside were already in full swing, and the country was changing, including federal judges who seemed ready to entertain the notion of a civil rights complaint by a person in prison. At this time, the country was undergoing an era of expanded rights, which also became an opportune moment to open a new frontier in prisoner litigation. As one scholar notes, "the civil rights movement contributed directly to politicizing inmates at Stateville," which is where Cooper was housed.[69] In his case, the movements on the outside seem to have catalyzed those on the inside.

As the press for civil rights progressed, other developments occurred in the judiciary, including the Court's ideological expansion of what constituted a "religion." By the time these cases burst through in the early 1960s, the Court was in a constant state of revising its view of religion and expanding what constituted a religion under the First Amendment. While the push toward civil rights was one of the background forces that helped to mobilize Muslims to seek justice in court, determining how much the Court's evolving definition helped Muslim litigants is less certain and more debatable.

The Court's broader reading of the term significantly impacts religious groups on the outside, including numerous new religious movements. By all appearances, the budding prisoners' rights movement seemed poised to benefit from the Court's evolution of thought from the 1940s to the 1960s. Prior to this, at the beginning of the century, the Court explained, "the term 'religion' has reference to one's views of his relations to his Creator, and to the obligations they impose of reverence for his being and character and obedience to his will."[70] In subsequent rulings, the Court added to this understanding with nationalistic and Christian themes: "we are a religious people," a "Christian Nation," with one Supreme Court justice characterizing the essence of religion as "belief in a relation to God involving duties superior to those arising from any other human relation."[71]

As such descriptions may allude, in the early twentieth century, First Amendment religion cases required a belief in a Supreme Being, which was, strictly speaking, a theistic definition of religion.[72] However, in the decades that followed, courts began to move away from this posture and include other life and death doctrines that did not require a deity.[73] This more functional understanding of religion included those "sincere beliefs" held by individuals that parallel the role of God in other people's lives. A practical outcome of expansion came in 1943 when the Second Circuit announced a broader concept of religion when interpreting the phrase "religious training and belief" as found in the Selective Service Act of 1940.[74] The next year, the Court characterized religion as a matter of a person's sincerity in beliefs and "the right to maintain theories of life and death and of the hereafter which are rank heresies to other faiths."[75] As evidence of its shifting course, in 1961, the Court would invalidate a provision that required all public officials in Maryland to profess a belief in God.[76] By 1965, the Court did a full reversal that moved away from focusing on the content of an individual's beliefs toward an "ultimate concern" test to define religion.[77]

The evolution in thought would lay the groundwork for the religious rights of non-Christians in prison. Implementing a broad, ecumenical definition of religion gave the appearance of a helpful gesture to Muslims trying to establish their religion and establish themselves as followers, despite prison administrations and the courts themselves knowing little about Islam in general. However, the Court's expanding view did not easily translate into the recognition of the NOI or Islam more broadly as worthy of constitutional protections. Even though, by the Court's language, they should have easily fit within its fluid definition of religion, there was nothing inevitable about the Court's recognition of them as legitimate.

The point is obvious in district and appellate courts, where many of these cases were decided. For example, in one case in 1967, a district court was willing to acknowledge the NOI as a "cult or a sect," but was not willing to allow members to congregate based on narratives that had been constructed about the organization and its beliefs. At trial, the defendants offered the testimony of currently incarcerated individuals who stated that "dangerous situations could result if Muslim principles were given broader circulation."[78] The statements demonstrate the difficulty for Muslims to control the discussion surrounding their beliefs and principles. Instead, the court adopted cherry-picked ideas that assigned explicit value judgments to the group, which offer a sense of the culture war— demoting a religion because of disagreement with the other's beliefs.

These court decisions were disjunctive and failed to recognize claims in a uniform manner, which left the status of Muslims far more uncertain than the Court's broadening definition of religion might have promised. Even well into the 1980s, federal appellate courts in various circuits, as well as state courts, continued to strike down constitutional challenges to prison policies on the premise that Islam fell outside of religion's scope. Even in cases where courts did recognize Islam as legitimate, First Amendment claims by Muslims were struck down due to the Court's deference to the discretion of prison administrations and dog-whistles about institutional security. *O'lone v. Shabazz* offers a prime example of how Muslims, while affirmatively recognized by the institution as a religious group, were disenfranchised from the free exercise of religion. Although adherents of other religions did not have to forsake this same right, Muslims lost essentially because their Friday congregation interfered with the weekday work schedules.

Hence, while the Court's opinions gave a robust, seemingly opened-ended concept of what religion could entail, it was not a foregone conclusion that Muslims would benefit from these holdings. Instead, Muslims would continue to struggle at the grassroots level across the various states and federal circuits to be included in what constituted religion. Even when Islam was found to fit the description, the Court did not hesitate to subvert essential religious practices to the whims of prison administrators. While the Court may have theorized religion in lofty court opinions, as the cases that follow demonstrate, it was Muslim litigants on the ground who had to scratch and claw their way to legal protections that would provide basic rights.

By outlining the legal origins of Islam in prison and positioning them against the relevant laws implicated, the study considers other issues that have inspired litigation. Despite the onerous hurdles inherent in a court action, Muslims in prison have been undeterred in seeking redress. Often, individuals take enormous risks and endure great pains to seek justice and hold prisons accountable to the law.

4 Fighting for Religious Rights

Cut the mustaches and leave the beard.

—Jami' at-Tirmidhi, *Book of Tafsir of the Quran*

Q: What exactly did you say . . .?
A: I said I was at war with him.
Q: Okay. What does that mean to say that you're at war with him?
A: I did not intend that as a threat, that was not a threat, it was spoken in the heat of anger, I was upset at my beard being shaved off—nearly all the way off after I told the man three times that I had a court order allowing me to grow a half inch beard, to trim it down to a half inch, and he tried to shave the whole thing off.

—Cross examination of the Plaintiff Muhammad,
　　Holt v. Hobbs

For much of the Muslim world, the guidance from the *hadith* tradition to "leave the beard" is a critical marker that has made Muslim males as distinct as women donning the iconic hijab. It is one of several mandates of faith that some Muslim groups worldwide have taken as an injunction for centuries. There have been numerous lawsuits at the state and federal level on this issue. However, it was *Holt v. Hobbs* that made it all the way to the Supreme Court in 2014. *Holt* centered on an Arkansas prison policy that held: "no inmates will be permitted to wear facial hair other than a neatly trimmed mustache that does not extend beyond the corner of the mouth or over the lip." The irony that mustaches were permitted, while beards were not, was not lost on Muslims, some of whom decided to sue in court, including the prisoner-plaintiff, Gregory Houston Holt, aka Abdul Maalik Muhammad. Muhammad, held in the Arkansas State prison system is doing "life plus [forty]" and is a follower of Sunni Islam, had all the markings of a devout follower: attending religious services, fasting during Ramadan, and associating with other Muslims. Muhammad confounded cultural stereotypes as well; as a white man incarcerated in a system that incarcerates Blacks at a rate four times that of Whites, he was nothing like the "Black Muslim" courts were used to seeing. *Holt* became a great victory for Muslims and individuals of other faiths who benefitted from his willingness to take this struggle to the high court. His case is exemplary for understanding just how long and hard Muslims have had to fight for religious rights, and in this case, for the right to maintain a half-inch beard.[1]

Muhammad initially sought permission to grow a beard through his prison's grievance process, but the request was rejected due to prison policy forbidding the wearing of beards. This rule, however, was not absolute because the prison granted exceptions for medical purposes. Muhammad's request was not to grow a full beard as tradition seemed to require, but a more moderate compromise—permission to grow a half-inch beard. Muhammad pointed to a 2001 federal district court decision, *Mayweathers v. Terhune*, another Muslim case that found California's prison policy of not permitting individuals to keep any facial hair was a violation of the Religious Land Use and Institutionalized Persons Act (RLUIPA).[2] Although California ran a much larger prison system, it did not encounter security problems after that case from permitting individuals to keep half-inch beards. In fact, in recent years, California prisons have lifted practically all hair and facial hair restrictions.[3] Despite being presented with this and other examples, Arkansas prison officials rejected Muhammad's request. The warden punctuated the point by warning Muhammad, "you will abide by ADC policies and if you choose to disobey, you can suffer the consequences."

Muhammad exhausted all administrative procedures and recourses for state court remedy; then he filed a complaint based on RLUIPA in federal court. He moved for a temporary restraining order so that he could wear the short beard until the court decided the case. The district court granted the request and sent the case to a magistrate for a hearing. Because of the injunction, Muhammad showed up at the hearing wearing a half-inch beard. His appearance drew a reaction of near disbelief from the magistrate judge who commented, "I look at your particular circumstance and I say, you know, it's almost preposterous to think that you could hide contraband in your beard."[4] Even after displaying such skepticism, the judge ultimately deferred to prison authorities and held the prison had demonstrated a compelling interest and employed the least restrictive means of achieving that goal. The district court adopted the judge's assessment and dismissed the case, which was upheld on appeal.

With no other legal options, Muhammad looked to the Supreme Court. The Court took the case, finding that, under RLUIPA, Holt met the requirements to trigger the statute's protection. Moreover, the Court pointed out that the district court made some mistakes in its analysis, including thinking his religious rights were being sufficiently accommodated by providing Muhammad with a prayer rug and religious books. The Court clarified RLUIPA was a law of protection, not accommodation. Hence, whether the Arkansas policy is a "substantial burden" is not about determining whether Muhammad has "enough" religious exercise, but whether he was stripped of religious exercise. The Court further reproached the lower court for considering the notion that not all Muslims agree one must grow a beard. Citing precedent that the Free Exercise clause is not limited to beliefs shared by all members of a religious group, the Court shut down this argument and stated Muhammad's belief "is by no means idiosyncratic."

In a 9–0 unanimous decision, the Court held the policy violated Muhammad's First Amendment rights. The Court rejected the prison's argument that applying its grooming policy to Holt was a security risk for contraband and inmate identification. The Court thought it was absurd to assume one could realistically hide dangerous contraband in a half-inch beard, mainly when there were so many other roomier spaces where contraband could be hidden. Moreover, the Court offered that a simple and obvious solution would be for the prison to photograph individuals with and without hair so that no identification concerns could be breached. Such a simple photograph system was used in California's massive prison system and other high-security prisons. The Court believed Arkansas could adopt a similar process. The Court also clarified how deference should apply in RLUIPA cases, which was different from before. "After

Holt, courts should first require prison officials to adduce some evidence that their policies are actually necessary to achieve the prison's asserted compelling interest, and only upon such a showing should the court grant deference to the official's justification."[5] There is no longer "unquestioning deference" to prisons. Instead, the institution must prove the denial is the least restrictive means of furthering a compelling government interest where "least" and "compelling" mean something.

Muhammad's victory of a half-inch beard may seem small in the grand scheme of problems people face in prison, but this was no ordinary win. It was not just a victory, but an instance of a little guy standing up to one of the most oppressive prison systems in the United States. Arkansas's history of prison brutality is legendary and rife with scandal. This was the state where rumors of bodies being dumped on the prison grounds set in motion a 1968 excavation by prison officials with media present. They unearthed three skeletons believed to be murder victims who were sentenced to prison. This discovery, "Bodiesburg" as it became known, revealed a scandal that gave a sense of what life might have been like, to witness first-hand how expendable these lives were. It is the same prison system that police investigation unveiled systematic brutality and institutional corruption. Among the extralegal punishments discovered was the dreaded "Tucker Telephone," a torture device that sent electric shocks through the victim's genitals. These findings would inspire the film *Brubaker,* which further exposed Arkansas as home to the worst of American prisons. Even this case illustrated how far prison staff was willing to go to have complete domination over individuals in prison, as described in a declaration made by Muhammad's cellmate: "I have seen numerous instances of people refusing to shave being placed in punitive isolation for this act. Also, I have witnessed staff members deny inmates chow call, library, visitation, recreation and other such activities due to not being clean shaved."[6]

More broadly speaking, this is the same state that was ground zero for other cultural battles, which was home to ongoing anti-Muslim controversies and varieties of Islamophobia. One spectacle included a gun-shooting range owner who created a "Muslim-free" shooting range that proudly declined services to Muslim customers. On the political front, Arkansas senator Tom Cotton weighed in on immigration debates by speculating publicly that ISIS and Mexican drug cartels could combine to attack

Arkansas. In such a xenophobic environment, Muhammad's victory stood as a comeuppance of sorts for Arkansas polity and the pointed bigotry Muslims have suffered as a result, both in and out of prison.

The case became another footnote in the heroic saga of Muslim prison litigation. Following this case, state prisons nationwide would need a genuine reason for impinging religious exercise. Simultaneously, the decision cautioned courts from yielding too much deference to prison authorities, and that courts should be particularly attentive when prison officials invoke "security" as the primary garb for restricting rights. This fight may have yielded to Muslims only a half-inch, but it was a milestone for Muslim rights in prison. Hence, more than anything, *Holt* was a wake-up call for all prison officials in all jurisdictions. It put prisons on notice that accommodating religious inmates should be taken seriously.

THE RIGHT TO WORSHIP

> The Black Muslims have been largely responsible for
> establishing prisoners' constitutional rights to worship.
> Prison officials perceive a threat to their authority in the
> close unity of Muslims. Accordingly, officials in most prisons,
> at one time or another, banned the practice of Islam or
> imposed tight restrictions on Muslims but not on other
> religious denominations.[7]

In the history of prison-law jurisprudence, Muslims have been at the center of litigation in the name of free exercise of religion.[8] As Kathleen M. Moore notes, "African-American Muslim inmates have been responsible in large part for establishing prisoners' constitutional rights to worship."[9] In the vast majority of instances, they continue to lose cases under various issues, including upholding denial of halal meats and other foods and preventing the performance of Khutba religious sermons during Friday prayer, the participation in Jumu'ah services, and the reciting of religious texts in Arabic. Other cases have shown Muslims as being forced to choose between access to Islamic services or access to the law library. In addition, cases have shown inmates being denied access to an Islamic chaplain or being penalized for attending Muslim services. Despite obstacles and setbacks, Muslims have plowed their way to ensuring a range of religious rights. Yet, they have suffered countless more defeats, including in some of the most high-profile cases in prison law jurisprudence.

O'Lone v. Estate of Shabazz is another landmark Supreme Court case, which endures as the prevailing standard for constitutional free-exercise claims by prisoner-petitioners. This case, which amounted to a loss for the Muslim plaintiffs, nonetheless was an important decision for determining when prison regulations violate rights bestowed by the US Constitution. In this case, the Court reviewed prison work regulations that prevented some Muslims from attending Friday Jumu'ah services. In its opinion, the Court sided with the prison policy, finding no First Amendment violation of the Muslims' free exercise of religion. The Court was convinced that Muslims did not have their constitutional rights violated because they were not deprived of all forms of religious practice. This opinion saw the court decline to take a stand on behalf of religious rights and instead resort to a hands-off sensibility.

Although the importance of this case diminished over time with the passing of legislation like RLUIPA and the Religious Freedom Restoration Act (RFRA), the case shows the persistence of Muslim litigants. The *Shabazz* opinion may have implemented a low bar for the standard of review for prison regulations that impede one's constitutional rights, but so long as there were other ways to practice religion, there would be deference to matters of institutional administration. To be sure, even before this case was handed down, many courts were already applying the deferential standard of review mandated by *Shabazz*.[10] Despite the setback, the case would inspire further litigation to ensure Muslims can attend Friday services. However, in addition to relying on the US Constitution, Muslims would use these new laws to reissue challenges. A range of cases show that post-*Shabazz*, Muslims in prison continued to push for attending Jumu'ah and other services.

Even with the RFRA, challenges by Muslims have succumbed to stingy interpretations of the statute by courts. In *Woods v. Evatt*, Muslims in a South Carolina prison claimed under RFRA that Christians received superior accommodation for their worship.[11] Whereas Christians could use the prison's visiting room to conduct services, which permitted worship with family and friends, Muslims were not permitted to use the room on Fridays for Jumu'ah services. Muslims also claimed that Christians were permitted gifts on Christian holidays, but Muslims were not for Muslim holidays. The district court rejected the claims and found the claim failed to demonstrate a substantial burden because religious accommodations did not have to be equal for all religious groups. The visitation room claim failed as well by the court's reasoning because allowing Muslims to use the visiting room on Fridays would disrupt visitation hours, while the Christian services on Sunday presented no visitation conflicts. Of course, underlying this tension is that the prison work and visitation schedule were constructed around Sundays and in deference to Christian sensibilities. As the prison regime is built around Christian influence, this case demonstrates how Christians have an advantage when it comes to securing the ability to partake in religion on the holy days compared to Muslims who traditionally congregate on Fridays.

Aside from these types of cases, there is a different kind of impingement on the right to worship. Sometimes the issue centers on a Muslim's right to worship, free from the presence of followers of different Muslim sects. In such situations, there is a battle to control the narrative about the religion, which is sometimes exacerbated by the administration treating Muslims as a monolith or, in the worst-case scenarios, having to determine what is and is not Islam. For those who challenge this narrative, what is at stake is the legitimation of their denomination.

Often it is the minority Shi'a adherents who must file grievances because they are forced to share space with Sunni followers. Despite the ancient traditional differences, such a policy delegitimizes certain groups and reflects a consensual view of the tradition, which fails to recognize divisions, differences, and adversarial aspects of the various sects. By casting Muslims as a unitary whole, not only are adherents left feeling offended and feeling their tradition disrespected, but the policies can also make the groups antagonistic toward one another. As a result, individuals have been forced to sue to have their own worship space, free from Muslims of different denominations, a problem that has been litigated for decades.[12]

One of the most recent challenges to such policies involves the *Holt v. Hobbs* plaintiff, Muhammad, who is part of a pending lawsuit alleging violations of the First and Fourteenth Amendments to the US Constitution, RLUIPA, and Section 1983. It is quite a remarkable statement that this person, who already won a case at the Supreme Court, continues litigating other claims, including this one alleging the defendants failed to accommodate his sincere religious practices and failed to ensure his group is granted separate space for worship like the various Christian denominations. A similar victory on this issue would settle another area of prison law, which has disgruntled Muslims for decades.

Muhammad's latest legal struggle details his quest to worship freely, especially free from individuals he would not consider to be a fellow Muslim.[13] The 2019 complaint filed by Muhammad and his two co-plaintiffs indicates that, like Muslims on the outside, the denominations in prison may be deeply divided. Sometimes Muslims are engaged in culture war behind bars with themselves. Here Muslims are forced to wage struggle on two fronts: one against the administration for not recognizing their denomination, and another against other Islamic followers, to vie for control of some of the narrative in order to be recognized. As Muhammad's complaint argues, the Arkansas prison policy of combining all Muslim groups into a single meeting is insufficient and unseemly, compared to the prison's accommodation of Christians. Although this facility needed at minimum three different meeting spaces—for Sunnis, the NOI, and the Five Percenters, the prison combined their congregational meeting into a unitary mass. This was not a salutary move because, according to Muhammad, the "deliberate and willful failure to recognize the religious differences between Islam, NOI, and NGE has caused significant tension and discord among the inmate populations that adhere to Islam, NOI, and NGE across ADOC's facilities."[14] In this case, Muhammad took a radical stand by refusing to congregate with others whom he believed practiced a different religion, as the complaint details: "Two of the Plaintiffs—Mr. Martin and Mr. Stewart—have been forced to choose to attend the weekly combined religious services because they felt compelled to do so to maintain their designations as Muslim and to preserve their rights to other religious accommodations, such as participating in the Ramadan meal program. Mr. Holt, on the other hand, has chosen not to attend the combined religious services in accordance with his sincerely held religious beliefs; and, as a result, in 2017 he was forced to sacrifice other religious accommodations."[15]

Muhammad's complaint arose in a context where no other faith groups, including a variety of Christian groups, were forced to choose between

attending religious services led by other faiths or forego religious obligations. Christians were also not forced to sacrifice their status as Christians
by failing to attend religious services. In addition, the prison prevented
Muslims from wearing *kufis*, subjecting them to discipline if they wore the
headgear without permission of the prison. The complaint itself touts
Muhammad's previous court victory, describing it as a "landmark precedent elevating religious protections for all prisoners of all faiths nationwide."[16] Furthermore, the complaint cites a Fifth Circuit decision, which
applied *Holt* to hold the Texas Department of Criminal Justice had failed
to justify its restriction on a Muslim wearing a *kufi*.[17] Thus, Muhammad's
Supreme Court victory already began to pay dividends and, remarkably
enough, even to Muhammad himself.[18] One study showed that after *Holt*
prisoner-plaintiffs received an increase of 29 percent of pro-prisoner votes
in RLUIPA cases, demonstrating the expansive effect this case has on
judicial decision-making.[19]

Muhammad's suit followed several others that have raised issues in this
area. A recent case concerned a Michigan prison's failure to provide equal
access to the Eid feast for Sunni Muslims and the NOI.[20] In that case, corrections officials twice prevented the plaintiff Maye from participating in
Eid al-Fitr, and one told Maye he could attend only if he changed his religion from NOI to Al-Islam. The court held for the plaintiffs and ordered
the prison to allow all Muslims to participate in Eid. This challenge was
not the first against the prison's policy, and even after a previous court victory that allowed Muslims to access Eid celebrations, the prison still would
not let some attend the feast.[21] In essence, the case was a victory that
cleared a path for Muslims to attend Eid, but the prison officials said he
must change religions and told Maye he was not really a Muslim. Hence,
even with an underlying victory, Muslims must fight against institutional
inclinations to preclude some from enjoying the same rights that others
do. But the prison's ignoring of this very decision came back to haunt the
institution because the *Maye* court used this decision to determine prison
officials could not be shielded under qualified immunity because their
conduct violated clearly established statutory or constitutional rights a
reasonable person would have known.

Among other cases was *Salahuddin v. Goord,* where the Second Circuit
saw merit in a complaint by a Sunni Muslim that the prison's policy of

forcing Sunni and Shi'a followers to hold joint Ramadan worship services was a violation of the Free Exercise Clause.[22] In that case, the court vacated the district court's summary judgment and found Salahuddin stated sufficient facts to demonstrate a burden on his free exercise of religion. With that, the burden shifted to the prison officials to prove the regulation was grounded in legitimate penological concerns. Although prison officials cited the regulation was implemented in the name of prison security, finances, space, and staffing limitations, the court asserted they offered no evidence on the record to show the policy was based on legitimate penological grounds. Instead, the court saw facts that amounted to the violation of Salahuddin's RLUIPA and First Amendment free-exercise rights, granting him the right for the lower court to take a genuine look at his claims. The case was a textbook example of how policies that ignore religious differences could essentially extinguish another's religious rights.

Two years later, the same prison official would face litigation by a Shi'a Muslim.[23] This individual sued for Shi'ite Muslims' right to have independent worship space to conduct their services separate from Sunni Muslims and to have services conducted by a Shi'ite leader. In addition to Free Exercise claims, the petitioner made others based on the First Amendment's Establishment Clause. He claimed the prison regulations established Sunni Islam as the official Islamic religion of the prison system and the prison was advancing one interpretation of Islam over another. Sympathetic to these arguments, the court reversed the summary judgment and found there were indeed disputed issues of whether the regulations were related to penological interests. When it came to his Free Exercise claims, the court relied on *Salahuddin* to establish the legal standard for this case, which mirrored the former as another instance of a genuine claim by a Muslim being rejected in federal court. Perhaps more astonishing is that the court refused to recognize the claim of qualified immunity on behalf of prison officials. Again, citing *Salahuddin,* the court assessed that qualified immunity was not appropriate at the summary judgment stage where "genuine issues of material fact exist." In essence, the court was saying that not only were the regulations wrong, but officials knew they were wrong too, or at least should have been aware of the *Salahuddin* case itself. This suit on behalf of Shi'ite prisoners is indebted to the prior suit by a Sunni Muslim. In this way, the denominations have been building on each other's struggles to dismantle the one-size-fits-all, consensual understanding of Islam.

This and other cases demonstrate the ability to worship freely is still a goal for some in prison, and the quest for constitutional rights remains an ongoing struggle. This general struggle embodies a variety of issues that implicate the free exercise of religion, of which the most prominent are discussed next.

GROOMING, DRESS, DIET, AND HOLIDAYS

For Muslims in prison, grooming and dress habits of the religion are an important part of faith, and much litigation regarding grooming and dress underscores that all are not treated equally under the law. It is little wonder, then, that Muslims have been involved in ongoing litigation to determine the boundaries of the ability to practice the tenets of tradition. Muslims have sued for the right to wear particular clothing, headwear, medallions, and shoes, and many cases center around Muslim rights to grooming and hygiene. Already discussed is Holt's nationwide victory for those wishing to wear a beard, but there was quite a history leading up to the decision. Previous to this case, there was nothing that resembled a uniform rule about beards: there were different rules for state and federal facilities, and circuit splits in federal courts provided for disparate treatment. Until the Court's ruling, there was still litigation on this point arising in various jurisdictions, while in others, facial hair was not even an issue. One need only imagine the situation from a Muslim perspective, where in one place in the country, Muslims are allowed to grow a beard fully, while in others there are length limitations. Yet, in others like Arkansas, it was prohibited altogether. The same holds true for a range of practices and articles of faith, which showcases the law's lack of uniformity because what is legal may depend solely on where one lives and have very little to do with legal principles. When the law's impact on life is governed by a stroke of jurisdictional luck or by popular vote of citizens, concepts like fairness and equality may seem distant.

The ability to wear certain articles of dress is one of the prominent areas of litigation. Muslims have been prohibited from wearing turbans, *tarboosh,* and *kufi* caps.[24] A more recent case has been more favorable to Muslims. In *Ajala v. West,* a Wisconsin federal district court held the prison had not shown that banning a Muslim from wearing a *kufi* outside his cell or group worship was the least restrictive means of furthering a compelling government interest.[25] In other actions, Muslims sued for the right to wear traditional robes, Islamic clothing, and prayer beads.[26] In the case of prayer beads, regulations prohibited the display of the beads altogether, but in some systems, there have been prohibitions on the color of bead, which officials assert conveys gang symbolism. Beyond, Muslim plaintiffs declared that due to adherence to the Sunnah of the Prophet Muhammad, they are required to wear a turban as a religious headdress.[27]

Due to practices of Islam typically involving holiday observances and dietary restrictions, including fasting and abstinence from pork, these have become regularly litigated issues. A 1968 case gives a grave sense of how difficult eating may have been for Muslims in the early days of litigation. Pork, according to witnesses, was used to prepare items such as hamburgers, meatloaf, chili con carne, and gravies served with non-pork meats. Although the prison denied allegations, there was testimony from cooks and foodservice individuals about how food was cooked, including one individual who admitted: "That beside pork in its more obvious forms, it is present in macaroni and cheese, hot dogs, cold-cuts, and various cooked luncheon meats. The chief steward stated that pork is used to season about half of the green vegetables, as well as beans, onions, stewed tomatoes, and other side dishes."[28]

In this institution, about two-thirds of the meals served contained pork, and no substitutes were offered. Such a dire situation illustrates how a Muslim might be practically starved out of existence for complying with the religious duty to refrain from pork. In *Finney v. Hutto,* a similar situation was found by a federal court, namely that vegetables were routinely prepared using pork grease.[29] In this case, the court did not go so far as to substantiate Muslim mistrust of food handlers by ordering a separate kitchen for Muslims. However, it enjoined the prison from serving pork to Muslims and exposing them to food that has been contaminated by contact with pork or pork grease, which laid the foundation for Muslims being free from handling pork under threat of punishment.

Other cases illustrate the difficulties Muslims face in prison to be observant of religious customs. Cases have gone from prisons refusing to recognize Ramadan as a legitimate holiday to some prisons today, which fully accommodate the holiday and Muslims who break the fast at night. In early cases such as *Walker v. Blackwell*, Muslims in federal prison made out several claims, including being denied a halal-compliant meal after sunset during the month of Ramadan.[30] The court sided with the prison reasoning "considerations of security and administrative expense outweigh whatever constitutional deprivation petitioners may claim."[31] While the opinion makes clear the costs would have been nominal and the risks minimal, this case shows that Muslims early on began advocating for dietary and holiday rights and that courts sometimes relied on the flimsiest of rationales to deny them. Sometimes Muslims relied on previous prison policies that granted Jewish accommodations, and the Jewish establishment of kosher food, in fact, has benefitted Muslims in prison. On the one hand, Muslims have consistently been able to point to the accommodations of Jewish adherents as a means of invoking equal protection under the law. On the other, Muslims benefitted practically because many times kosher meals were a Muslim's best opportunity to stay compliant with Islamic dietary laws and not starve, and because prisons have been willing to serve Muslims kosher meals. The establishment of kosher foods for Jews in prison has helped to feed the Muslim litigation engine and feed Muslims literally.

Indeed, among complaints from Muslims about prison conditions, foodservice and accessing halal meals have been chief. Hundreds of court decisions have upheld the denial of halal meats[32] and other compliant foodstuffs.[33] Other cases revolved around food service employment, and some have sued to avoid handling pork meat, including packing and moving pork products.[34] Sometimes, Muslims are even denied donated halal meals.[35] According to the plaintiffs at one such institution, while Muslims were denied donated food, Jewish followers were served kosher meals three times a day, seven days a week, by the prison. In another case, Muslims lost a class action bid against New York prisons to compel the prison to serve halal meals three to five times a week.[36] At the time of the suit, Muslims were fed halal meat once a week, whereas Jewish prisoners were given kosher meat four times a week. Even though courts rationalized their decisions, the result was Muslims often had to work harder to figure ways to be compliant with dietary laws than their religious counterparts.

Some of the cases are remarkable with respect to the nature of accommodating Muslims' dietary needs. One recent appellate court ruling held, among several claims that succumbed to summary judgment, that two survived—a Muslim's request for a halal diet and halal meat to celebrate a holiday feast.[37] In that case, the prisoner-plaintiff claimed he must eat a halal diet that includes halal meats. At the time, he ate no meat and was sustaining himself on the vegetarian meal option offered by the prison. Under RLUIPA, he claimed that the prison's policy of not providing halal meals or meat amounted to a substantial burden on his free exercise of religion, which the court seemed to agree: "It is a reasonable inference that (the Department of Correction's) failure to provide a halal diet either prevents Mr. Abdulhaseeb's religious exercise, or, at the least, places substantial pressure on Mr. Abdulhaseeb not to engage in his religious exercise by presenting him with a Hobson's choice—either he eats a non-halal diet in violation of his sincerely held beliefs, or he does not eat."[38] Under this rationale, the case was sent back down to consider whether the prison could meet its burden of showing a compelling interest and showing they used the least restrictive means to implement the regulation.

The other claim the court allowed to move forward was the prison's failure to provide halal meat on Eid-ul-Adha ("Feast of the Sacrifice"). This Islamic holiday is ranked among the holiest of the religion, which celebrates Abraham's willingness to sacrifice his son, Isaac, as an act of obedience to God. As a holiday, it is comparable to the feast celebrating the end of Ramadan, but the prison would not supply any special food items for this occasion. However, in its ruling, the court rejected the lower court's finding there was no RLUIPA violation because Muslims could buy meals from an "approved vendor." Yet, there was no vendor listed on the record, and as one commentator notes, "as a result, the court concluded that there may have been periods when there was no approved halal vendor for (the prison); thus, there may have been a time where Abdulhaseeb's religious exercise was substantially burdened."[39]

The case stood for the notion that an individual's lack of a halal-specific diet and access to halal were grounds for finding a substantial burden on his religious practice. In its ruling, the court notes that more than one court has held the lack of a halal diet to be a substantial burden on a Muslim's exercise, and others found a genuine issue of fact as to whether the lack of a halal diet may create a substantial burden. Many prisons escaped such a determination by providing vegetarian or other types of meal options, and courts tended to uphold such options as sufficient to prevent a finding of substantial burden. However, this individual made a case that the options were not sufficient, and that his religion requires him to have some halal food and meat. As such cases demonstrate, Muslims' push to expand the boundaries of free exercise behind bars make it highly likely food and holiday rules will remain areas of contention.

Although Muslims continue to struggle for dietary rights, some prisons are more accommodating than others. In California, for example, The Religious Meat Alternate Program was implemented in all adult corrections facilities, which provides for two vegetarian meals (breakfast and lunch) and dinner with halal meat. In addition, Muslims, like other faith groups, may be permitted up to two events each year where the prison provides foods with recognized religious significance in place of the regularly planned meal. The policy includes kosher and vegetarian options as well. When considering the nature of some of the lawsuits mentioned, this policy, while not perfect, could be a step forward in recognizing the sensitive nature of dietary needs and the need to accommodate an individual's religious beliefs. To be sure, with such simple programs in place, there would likely be less litigation in this area.

ACCESSING SPIRITUAL LEADERS, BOOKS, AND PARAPHERNALIA

The quest to have access to spiritual advisors, reading materials, and other religious items remains an area of litigation. From the earliest periods, Muslims struggled to access legitimate spiritual leaders from the outside. As a result, they often have had to step up to the role of leadership behind bars, which had unfortunate consequences for the development of Islam in prison. In some systems, allowing incarcerated individuals to lead services is disallowed because the prison does not want an individual to be seen as a leader or seen as having a higher rank than others. The lack of access to Muslim leaders from the outside is paralleled by a lack of access to religious books. As shown, Muslims have had to litigate to get prisons to recognize even the Quran as a legitimate holy book. Beyond that, there have been expungements to rid libraries of books that were considered too extremist or inflammatory, while the direct censorship of specific titles is an ongoing practice. According to the Equal Justice Initiative, "there is arguably no government institution that censors reading material more broadly and arbitrarily than American jails and prisons."[40] In addition to that type of censorship, Muslims had to deal with prisons censoring letters from religious leaders and organizations. In the way Muslims are forbidden from accessing these people and books, they are often disenfranchised from possessing articles of worship. Focus on these issues shows the ongoing struggle for Muslims to practice religion in prison, and the myriad ways prison officials use prison rules and regulations to frustrate access to genuine leaders and articles of faith.

The problem of being cut off from religious leaders is one that Muslims have had to contend with at both state and federal levels. Of course, there was no question of Muslims getting access to outside religious leaders in the early days because they were not even recognized as a religion. Over time this status changed, and prisons have been more porous when permitting Muslim leaders. However, after the attacks of 9/11, the pendulum shifted drastically in the other direction. In the wake of that event, several policies were implemented, including policies by the Federal Bureau of Prisons (BOP) that restricted outside imams from entering federal prisons. The measures were rooted in alarmist rationales that perceived leaders from the outside to be extremist influences that would radicalize Muslims behind bars. The shortage of outside help was compounded internally because the Bureau effected a de facto hiring freeze on imams to service the federal Muslim population. At one point, the Bureau had fallen well below what the Chaplaincy Services Branch defined as a "critical shortage" of chaplaincy when it was operating at a ratio of one Muslim chaplain for every nine hundred Muslims in prison.[41] The resulting shortages often put the burden on incarcerated Muslims to lead religious services. Often neophyte and inexperienced leaders took up the task, and there were few positive consequences from this development. One need only imagine a scenario of Muslims who have never even prayed in a mosque leading other Muslims in worship. At best, the lack of authentic influence watered-down traditions; at worst, the shortages gave space for some to spout messages rooted in gang rivalry or extremist ideology rather than traditional messages. There is a similar gap in state prisons, as one Pew survey on chaplains identified Muslims as the most underserved religious group in prisons. Meanwhile, in 2020 it was reported that 199 of 236 federal prison chaplains, or 84 percent, were Protestant Christian, even though Protestants make up only 34 percent of the total incarcerated population.[42] In this modern scenario, equality is discarded, leaving most of the Islamic religious programming and education in the hands of individuals who frequently lack basic understanding about Islamic doctrine and liturgy, while Christians have an overabundance of resources.

Cases previously discussed underscore the Muslim quest to make Qurans and other literature available in prisons. Sometimes it is claimed that even when Qurans are permitted, they are destroyed by prison staff.[43] It is a struggle that has been long and strenuous, beginning with materials from Elijah Muhammad, which were seen by prison administrations as racist and hostile, to the Quran, all the way to other authors whom prison authorities have censored.

In the post-9/11 era, these practices returned in full swing, with censorship of Muslim reading materials and the purging of prison libraries of certain books. At the federal level, the BOP implemented the Standardized Chapel Library Project, which sought to inventory all current holdings and determine their permissibility under the BOP's security policies. In addition to whatever other discriminatory treatment it wreaked against Muslims, this project offered a compelling example of how suppressive tactics can backfire and antagonize Muslims rather than reduce hostility. The Bureau's removal of texts was reported to have greatly frustrated individuals, some of whom had been reading a particular book for decades but were now told it was off-limits. From a Muslim's perspective, this policy was paternalistic and penally unsound. It may have also overlooked how such literature may help counter extremism and thus produce a normalizing effect by acting as a repellant, for the great majority of non-imprisoned Muslims are averse to extremist literature. This harmful strategy also potentially hindered effective monitoring of individuals suspected of extremist tendencies, as one panelist at a 2011 congressional hearing noted: "if an individual in a correctional institution possesses these types of radical material, it's actually, in a way, an investigative benefit because that person is then self-identifying as someone that bears further inspection and someone that can be monitored by the correctional staff."[44]

Litigation surrounding these issues paints a picture of two different standards—one enforced upon Muslims and one to which Christians are held. For example, while the Quran and other Islamic texts and authors have been banned, it is rarely, if ever, the case that the Bible has been banned. Although the Old Testament is replete with stories of debauchery, war, and violence, it is a wonder this text would not suffer the same fate. Same for the Christian Bible, which contains equally subversive messages. Despite passages in the Revelation of John that depict graphic violence and cataclysmic suffering, prison officials never seem to recognize this double standard. By comparison, Elijah Muhammad's community newspaper that advocates for Black empowerment and justice is relatively tame compared to some of the narratives of the Christian Bible. Yet, it is Muslim works of literature that are subject to prohibition. Such writings are banned while the biblical sources from which they build are widely available and hardly even raise an eyebrow among prison officials.

Incarcerated individuals face multiple hurdles in the quest to obtain liturgical items necessary to practice Islam, but there have been advances. Muslims sued for the right to possess prayer oils, incense, leather socks, halal toothpaste, a compass, and prayer rugs, in addition to other religious paraphernalia. Like other rights, the struggles to obtain items pertaining to worship exist in a world of double standards. Here, it is worth again noting California, which allows individuals to wear or carry religious items, including headbands, wristbands, beaded chokers, religious medallions and chains, religious headgear, and prayer beads, among other items. In a world of restriction, this policy appears to be a progressive step in affirming the importance of religion for people in prison. Not only is it a way to dislodge the wedge that separates followers from the faith, but it is also likely a move that saves the state money by avoiding a range of litigation, not to mention promoting goodwill between keepers and the kept.

ESTABLISHMENT CLAUSE CLAIMS

Claims by incarcerated Muslims include those based on the Establishment Clause of the First Amendment. Although less frequent than Free Exercise claims, Muslims have used this constitutional protection that prohibits the government from encouraging people to be religious or promoting one religion over another. The central inquiry in these cases is whether a prison action or rule endorses or supports one religion over another. Here, "religion" can mean a different religious group completely or denominations within a religious group. Although district courts are split on the test to determine such cases, the litigant's central task is to show a prison or official acted in a way that endorsed, supported, or affiliated themselves in some way with religion. Depending on the jurisdiction, the prison action will pass constitutional muster either if it is designed for a purpose that is nonreligious, does not advance or set back a religion, and does not encourage excessive government entanglement with religion, or it will pass the action if it is not found to force an individual to support or participate in a religion.

Muslims litigate establishment claims based on an array of circumstances. Cases include one that alleged the expenditure by the state to support and teach the Protestant religion represented a union of church and state in violation of the Establishment Clause.[45] In one case, *Brown v. Livingston,* a federal court held incarcerated Muslims in Texas prisons were being treated differentially by prison staff in violation of the Establishment Clause.[46] That court examined a prison policy that prohibited religious adherents of a particular faith from gathering in groups of more than four for religious services unless a prison staff member or outside volunteer provided direct supervision. As such, the policy naturally favored larger denominations and those denominations able to be housed together. Muslims were disadvantaged and were able to participate in religious activities for only one hour per week. In contrast, Catholic and Protestant adherents had access to six hours or more of religious activities per week. The court also noted Jewish followers were housed to bring them closer to Jewish religious volunteers. The prison assigned incarcerated Native Americans to housing units that would make religious services more available to them. Yet, the prison made no effort to house Muslims to give them a similar advantage to participating in more religious activities.

More recently, in 2020, Muslims in Virginia's Riverside Regional Jail successfully showed Establishment Clause and Equal Protection violations based on the jail's "God Pod" facility.[47] The ruling was handed down by a Virginia federal court, which held the jail's Christians-only area of the facility, known as the God Pod, had established an official preference for Christianity. According to the court, that part of the facility had the effect of creating a religiously segregated area of the jail. The jail paid Good News Jail & Prison Ministries nearly $84,000 in 2018 to provide chaplain services to individuals of all faiths incarcerated at the jail. According to court documents, this organization's vision is "to reach every inmate in the world with the Good News of Jesus Christ that they might become growing disciples." While the jail was paying for such services, Muslims at the jail had difficulty procuring Qurans and other Islamic materials. In addition, Muslims submitted multiple grievances stating Christians had greater opportunities for bible study classes and other religious services, while Muslims could only congregate for Friday Jumu'ah. More critically, while the God Pod allowed individuals to live in the separate area if they agreed to study Biblical principles, there was neither facility for Muslims who wished to do the same nor did they get access to microwaves and other privileges that came with being in "minimum custody."

As the only religious programs pod in the jail, which was paid for and supported by the jail, the Establishment Clause violations were clear—paying for Christian chaplaincy while forcing Muslims to rely on volunteers established a preference. Meanwhile, as the only sort of program, which is essentially for Christians only, the treatment is differentiated by religion, including one group getting perks and benefits over others, including being in a less regulated environment. Such a benefit was impossible for Muslims unless they were willing to convert. These actions made Christianity preferred at the jail, while Muslims were left to cobble together whatever programming was feasible, which is essentially the same reason that their Equal Protection claims succeeded as well.

While the typical Establishment claim involves a prison administration accommodating or preferring one religious group over a different religious group, sometimes violations occur within different denominations within a group. The *Maye* case mentioned earlier is an example of such a violation, where the Michigan Department of Corrections denied members of the NOI the opportunity to participate in Eid celebrations at the close of Ramadan.[48] Despite the plaintiff being a devout adherent for over two decades who had missed only two biweekly services in the previous two years and considered a leader and spokesperson for the NOI at his respective facility, he was denied participation solely because he was a member of the NOI. As you may recall, prison officials stated that to participate in Eid, the plaintiff "must change [his] religion from the NOI to Al-Islam," whose members were allowed to participate. The petitioner did not change and was ultimately not allowed to participate. Uncertain as to whether the *Turner* standard or the strict scrutiny standard of review applied, the appellate court found the Establishment Clause was violated under either standard.

This case was particularly egregious on other counts as well. For one, Michigan's corrections facilities had already been embroiled in other lawsuits for not accommodating Muslim holidays yet allowing Jewish adherents the ability to participate in Passover. From that litigation, the Michigan facilities revised their policies to allow NOI members to participate in Eid, rules they did not even follow, as seen in *Maye*. Here, the prison's decision not to follow its own protocol shows yet again that even when the law is changed, it can be an uphill battle for Muslims to enjoy the benefits afforded. Accordingly, as the district court magistrate found, the failures of the prison to follow its own rules "underscore the disparity in treatment, amplify the wholesale nature of the deprivation, and readily support a finding of purposeful discrimination."

EQUALITY UNDER LAW

> Despite decades of litigation and grievances regarding its failure to accommodate basic Islamic religious practices— including Friday prayer services, growing beards, and wearing kufis—ADOC continues to fail to provide Muslim inmates with the basic and necessary accommodations to practice their faith.[49]

As the God Pod case demonstrates, "equal protection of the laws" is another viable avenue of litigation. Despite the government being prohibited from denying people equal protection of its governing laws, it is still common. This protection is rooted in the Fifth Amendment to the US Constitution and requires the federal government to treat an individual in the same way it treats others in similar conditions and circumstances; the Fourteenth Amendment requires individual states to entreat their citizens the same. The essence of equal protection is to make a state official impartial and not to make distinctions based on differences that are irrelevant to a legitimate government objective.

From the earliest days of litigation, a significant part of Muslim grievance was rooted in the fact that Muslims in prison were treated differently than their Christian counterparts. The grievances continue, as seen in a 2016 case, where the plaintiff sued because Christian prisoners were being treated more favorably than Muslims.[50] Another lawsuit shows the range of favoritism by which Christians were allowed "(i) the use of better venues for religious services, (ii) the availability of a greater selection of religious books in the SDC library, and (iii) official observances of Christmas and Thanksgiving, without similar observances of Ramadan."[51] The court, however, distinguished Christmas as a "nationally recognized holiday, not a religious feast," and found no merit in the argument that similarly situated Muslims were not being treated equally because no Islamic holiday was subsidized in the same way. In its tortured logic, the court looked at Christmas and its secular influences rather than acknowledging the holiday's plainly religious core. In contrast to this decision, the *Abdullah* plaintiffs mentioned earlier successfully argued Muslims were denied equal protection of the law based on their treatment by prison officials, which complained that "faiths such as Judaism, Hindu, Sikh, Buddhism, Catholicism, and 'others'" were being accommodated, but not Muslims.

Muslims have made equality arguments based on other grounds. For example, one individual brought an equal protection claim due to a Texas prison's grooming policy forbidding keeping a beard.[52] He argued that the grooming policy explicitly differentiates between male and female inmates. As the court described, the prisoner-petitioner "says that female inmates are permitted to 'express their femininity' by growing long hair, as an 'inherent characteristic' of a female's natural or cosmetic trait, but male inmates are prohibited from expressing their masculinity by growing their facial hair." In the same case, the petitioner claimed it was also a violation of equal protection. The prison created an exception to the grooming policy for medical reasons but not for religious reasons. He acknowledged that the exception was not a security-based decision but claimed his religious needs were just as important, arguments that would be echoed in *Holt* soon after.

As litigation illustrates, the ability to lead a religious life behind bars is a difficult proposition for Muslims, even when the law favors their side. The cases demonstrate unique struggles and obstacles to access the most basic of religious provisions. From the Muslim view, what is "law" for others is not the "law" to which they are subject. Often, they are forced to prove themselves, eschew religious items and practices, or group for worship in ways other groups are not required. Taken this way, prisons themselves have much to do with the legacy that was created by Muslim prison litigation—because they have consciously deprived Muslims of the rights and benefits they freely distribute to others. Collectively, prison policies worked to disenfranchise Muslims from one of the most cherished ideals of the American polity, the freedom of religion, which here is abandoned in favor of direct religious repression.

5 Holding Prisons Accountable

> When prisoners emerge from the shadows to press a
> constitutional claim, they invoke no alien set of principles
> drawn from a distant culture. Rather, they speak the
> language of the charter upon which all of us rely to hold
> official power accountable.
>
> —*O'Lone v. Estate of Shabazz* (1987)

It was an hour and a half ride south to S.C.I. Huntingdon, the maximum-security prison that would start a journey for one young man, which continues to the present. On May 25, 1983, the Court of Common Pleas of Philadelphia sentenced this young man to death. One need only imagine the transport bus that took convicted individuals to the prison, which made for a loud, choppy ride that rattled the bones of some unfortunate ones who were headed to their new home, shaking the bodies of already shaken souls. Although the ride was relatively short, it must have seemed like an eternity for those headed to their final destination. These individuals breathed tense air, mired with the fog of fear and depression. The passengers swallowed lumps of uncertainty under the best poker face one could manage. If the ride itself was bumpy, it was like a wild roller-coaster ride inside the mind of passengers. Passengers' thoughts raced at light speed, and emotions were unbound. There may be hateful thoughts about the judge, jury, prosecutor, or even about one's own lawyer. However, these feelings may give way to the sorrows of leaving behind one's family, friends, and loved ones, sentiments that traumatic thoughts about personal loss may displace—of one's job, home, and plans in life, not to mention the physical separation.

As difficult as these issues may be in the minds of the passengers, they are secondary to the anticipation of entering prison. The gravity of being incarcerated is all-consuming, and it is this existential trauma—the terror of time—that grounds all others. Hence, regardless of how one postured for the ride, be it with head held in hands, laid back, or deadpan, everyone eventually thought of their fate that awaited.

For one passenger, this was no ordinary cab, but more like a messenger of death. Before this ride, Mumia Abu-Jamal was sentenced for the 1981 murder of Philadelphia police officer Daniel Faulkner. When he checked in and received his prison clothes, Abu-Jamal was a relatively unknown personage. Although his case had some notoriety when it occurred, he did not know he would go on to become a cause célèbre in America. Abu-Jamal was a staunch member of the Black Panther Party and involved in John Africa's M.O.V.E. movement. As years went by, Abu-Jamal's case would garner support, some of which was based on the unfairness of the trial proceedings and the evidence used against him. Some was based on the recordings he made from prison, which depicted him as a calm, rational thinker, who has won over many sympathetic fans. For others, he simply holds the status of a living saint.

During his nearly three decades on death row, Abu-Jamal fiercely critiqued the police, courts, and prison systems. His books *Live from Death Row, Jailhouse Lawyers,* and *Death Blossoms* offer harrowing glimpses into the world of prison, and collectively announce an indictment of a system where justice is often checked at the gates. As an author, educator, and litigator, Mumia Abu-Jamal achieved national and global recognition, and has been described as the most famous Muslim in American prison and the most famous incarcerated individual in the world.[1] Rivaled perhaps only by his Muslim colleague, H. Rap Brown, aka Jamil Al-Amin, Abu-Jamal became a cultural and international phenomenon. His voice and image are widely recognized at home and abroad.

Abu-Jamal's status in hip-hop culture is legendary. He is revered in Muslim circles and beyond. Numerous songs sample from his lectures and recordings, and many are dedicated to him, including "Free Mumia" by KRS One and "Mumia 9/11" by the Unbound Allstars. Other odes were composed by Tupac Shakur, Immortal Technique, and Snoop Dogg. Some of these tracks feature Muslims explaining Jamal's situation as trapped by a godless society, as Public Enemy's Chuck D put it:

> After all, I feel the bruisin of the Constitution
> When my back's against the wall, manifesting in their destiny
> Shit, they just testin me, Mumia's spirit blessin me
> No alibi, I know Allah is not their ally
> I believe I can fly, but their type of freedom is a lie
> So fuck the government, C.I.A. and F.B.I.[2]

Songs like this reveal the respect and appreciation of Abu-Jamal that compel rappers to honor him. Some of it is due to his social criticism and explanation of hip-hop as a challenge to the social order. In his opinion, hip-hop is a sign of struggle, a particular danger that warns of some in society who are in critical danger of demise. He explains:

> To think about the origins of hip hop in this culture and also about home-land security is to see that there are at the very least two worlds in America. One of the well-to-do and the struggling. For if ever there was the absence of homeland security it is seen in the gritty roots of hip hop. For the music arises from a generation that feels with some justice that they have been betrayed by those who came before them. That they are at best tolerated in schools, feared on the streets, and almost inevitably destined for the hell holes of prison. They grew up hungry, hated and unloved . . . and this is the psychic fuel that seems to generate the anger that seems endemic in much of the music and poetry.[3]

As this and other recordings of Abu-Jamal postulate, there are considerable gaps in prison accountability. Underscoring these problems, his works sparked the minds of a generation who see him as a poster child for injustice in America. Perhaps some of this support ultimately played into his removal from death row, which the Superior Court of Pennsylvania affirmed in 2013. For many, his legend was already cemented long before these recent events, but, for others, this change of tide has given hope and inspiration that he may see the outside of prison once again.

His efforts, however, have not been merely rhetorical flourish. He has gone to courts to fight to enforce his rights. For example, he litigated free speech claims and sued to get Hepatitis C treatment behind bars. In prison, his health deteriorated. Dealing with an illness, which was diagnosed in 2012, court documents describe 70 percent of his body was covered with a severe rash. He was suffering from hyperglycemia to the point of losing consciousness and having to be admitted to the prison's medical center. His willingness and determination to take such actions represent the quest to advance rights behind bars and hold prisons accountable as public institutions. He stands as a shining example of a multifaceted approach to dealing with grievances in prison. Although his primary means were through teaching and writing, he made headlines by filing complaints through the courts as well. His efforts show that he was an individual who understood that prisoners' rights and criminal justice reform were different sides of the same coin. Abu-Jamal's advocacy shows how Muslims, more than other religious groups, have shown an affinity for using courts and other adjudicatory bodies to achieve justice.

In addition to his contributions to civil litigation, Abu-Jamal has been fighting his own criminal conviction since he was sentenced in 1982. The complexity of this case is astounding and spans decades, yet it represents a whole other aspect of litigation in which he is involved. At the very end of 2018, Abu-Jamal supporters were elated to hear that a Philadelphia court granted him the opportunity to appeal his case to the Pennsylvania Supreme Court. After decades in prison, this opportunity represents the first chance of any such hope he may be freed. Were such a momentous occasion to occur, it would be a huge victory and milestone in the saga of Muslim prisoner litigation. His release would inspire further hope and would likely encourage further litigation by Muslims.

"NO ONE IS ABOVE THE LAW"

The struggles described in this book originated in the "hands-off" era, when prison wards were deemed "slaves of the state" and their treatment by state officials was insulated from judicial review. This point is obvious when it came to First Amendment claims. For the first century and a half of the country's existence, the constitution's religion clauses applied only to claims against the federal government. Because states were not bound to abide by the amendments in the Bill of Rights, the states owed the federal government no obligation when it came to religious freedoms. It was a momentous shift for those incarcerated in state prisons as the Supreme Court began to make the Bill of Rights applicable to the states piecemeal through the doctrine of incorporation. Before the Court began applying the amendments to the states, federal courts rarely interfered in state punishment practices, but now people in prison had a constitutional hook to intervene. *Cooper* would open an entirely new era of law that had a profound effect on correctional institutions. As one scholar noted: "It is clear that the ability of prisoners to file civil rights actions, although burdening the federal courts with a steady stream of cases, has provided the basis for improving the conditions at correctional institutions and preventing the kinds of flagrant abuses that commonly existed for most of American history."[4]

Muslims were a critical component of the prisoners' rights movement, which took root amid these legal developments. Those incarcerated in state prisons began to sue in growing numbers. Over time, the scale of lawsuits would spawn a political backlash to curb the number of lawsuits by people in prison. The most important piece of legislation to accomplish this end was the Prison Litigation Reform Act (PLRA), which shifted the needle back to something just short of the "hands-off" era. As one legal researcher found, the number of lawsuits reduced drastically in the years following the enactment of this legislation.[5] Even in such a monumental attempt to scale back litigation from prison, Muslims continue to be avid litigators and contribute meaningfully to expanding freedoms and rights behind bars. Their struggle to push boundaries of the status quo is ongoing despite legislation intentionally designed to make suing prison officials harder for those incarcerated than the general population. The natural effect of such legislation is that genuine violations will go without redress.

As the cases and court opinions indicate, the challenges ran far and wide, covering a vast range of subjects: from individuals like Mumia Abu-Jamal, who sued for the right to have access to necessary drugs and medical procedures, to Martin Sostre, who waged war against the prison's wanton use of solitary confinement. These suits worked to improve prison conditions and worked to benefit all who suffered under lock and key, thus shaping prison culture in critical ways.

At the same time, it is a mistake to think religion is completely divorced from some of these claims. Sometimes the two cannot be separated. For example, an Eighth Amendment claim of cruel and unusual punishment is typically mutually exclusive of religious-based claims. Nevertheless, it would hardly be surprising to understand that sometimes the punishment claim arises in the first place because the guard who physically mistreats an individual may do so because of the individual's religion. In these instances, religion is inextricable from some of these seemingly secular struggles because the constitutional claims arise out of religious prejudice.

There are also cases where other physical conduct by prison officials impinges on religious rights. Muslims often must litigate to maintain their physical integrity concerning touching and viewing that violates religious codes. Instances include when female officers can see males in the nude during shower time or strip searches. In one case, an individual brought an RLUIPA action in Massachusetts state court to challenge the prison's policy of allowing female guards to pat down males in the genital and buttocks area.[6] In this case, the court credited expert testimony about Islam and noted, "it is demeaning and humiliating for Muslim males to be touched by female corrections officers, particularly in this manner."[7] Despite the defendants attempt to argue that disallowing women to do this type of pat-down would result in gender discrimination against the female employees, the court shut this argument down, citing other cases that upheld similar injunctions. The court noted at the prison in question, there were only 26 female officers out of 268, which would make it a rare occasion where a male would not be available for a pat-down. The court effectively exposed the defendants were not using the least restrictive means for conducting the security search, netting a win for the right of individuals in this state prison system to be free from such searches absent emergency situations.

These challenges are sometimes the only means of justice and guaranteeing that nobody sits above the law. One of the pillars of this reputation has manifested in the phenomenon of jailhouse lawyering. As it has been described, individuals often face harsh punishment for violating rules that prohibit them from helping co-captives with legal assistance. In his book, *Jailhouse Lawyers: Prisoners Defending Prisoners v. the U.S.A.*, Mumia Abu-Jamal describes the plight of those in prison who helped others with legal aid: "Before Johnson v. Avery, jailhouse lawyers were routinely thrown into the hole for their writ-writing activities. In Johnson's wake however, states across the country lost a series of cases brought by jailhouse lawyers who, as a direct consequence of their violation of prison regulations, had lost good time, or a cut in one's term and other amenities."[8] He notes that despite the Court's ruling opening the doors to allow jailhouse lawyers the legal right to assist others, prison administrators continued to find ways to punish them, particularly those engaged in actions against the prison administration. Despite the *Johnson* decision in 1969 that opened up protections for assisting with habeas corpus writs and later for civil rights actions, Abu-Jamal cites a report spanning American prisons from 1945 to 1990 showing no segment of the modern US prison population has been punished more than jailhouse lawyers—not Blacks, gays, gangs, or other similar groupings.[9] Such stark reporting indicates how the basic hurdle of trying to get legal assistance has been a major uphill battle for those incarcerated.

Muslim litigants in prison proved they are willing to sacrifice themselves and subject themselves to further punishment to fight for justice. Muslim jailhouse lawyers are known for helping people from non-Muslim backgrounds with legal assistance and for being among the more legally minded individuals in prison. Muslims were also active at mediating between individuals incarcerated and between them and outside forces. Jailhouse lawyering is a symbol of oppression, desperation at the hands of a prison system that operated with near impunity.

Muslims in prison made their mark in prison law by contesting their treatment and conditions of confinement. Among a range of extralegal treatment, Muslims had to endure hardships, unlike others. Previous ethnographic research by the present author describes guards ridiculing Muslims by calling them "Muhammad" or "Al-Qaeda," referring to traditional clothing as "nightgowns," and repeatedly confiscating worship items, including incense, oils, beads, and foodstuffs.[10] In addition, prison guards have been known to host "gladiator" fights by putting rivals in a common area and taking bets on fights. Guards have also placed helmets on individuals to conceal beatings and gave some "flashlight therapy" with their lights, as well as moved individuals around so that family members cannot access an individual, preventing them from seeing bruises and cuts from beatings.

There are also the "legal" avenues the guards can take to make an individual's life difficult. For example, defending oneself against a guard's aggressions could be simply deemed as assault, which could result in disciplinary action by the prison. Disciplinary action can include loss of privileges, loss of good time credits, as well as leaving behind a negative mark on one's record, which could be detrimental to obtaining parole. Finally, of course, of all tools at the administration's disposal, the ability to transfer an individual from the general population into a solitary space is the most terrifying and brutal. Although such confinement may result from disciplinary action, in many systems, this need not be the case because individuals may be put there for simply "administrative" purposes, which may translate into whatever need the administration may have. Indeed, this is where the term "ad-seg" derives—shorthand for "administrative segregation." To illustrate, in some prison systems, simply reporting a sexual assault could become a one-way ticket to whatever form of solitary confinement is instituted at that facility. In theory, the individual is not being punished but is there because the administration deems it necessary for the protection of that individual. The executive decision effectively admits that the prison is incapable of protecting the complaining individual otherwise short of instituting this type of response, which functions as a forceful deterrent to reporting wrongdoing in the first place.

The landmark case, *Sostre v. Rockefeller,* headed by Martin Sostre, recognized a civil rights action against the governor and warden for sending Sostre to punitive isolation. Sostre argued he was kept in solitary for over a year without due process of law. He alleged he was punished because of his legal and Muslim activities during his incarceration. The court agreed with Sostre and held he was punished because his political views were found offensive by officials. The court ordered the governor and wardens to submit proposed rules and regulations governing future disciplinary charges where possible punishments included punitive segregation and loss of good time credits.[11] For Sostre, it was a major win that reverberated in prisons throughout the country and proclaimed that people in prison were not simply some commodity that could be shifted to extreme punishment at the prison's whim. While at the time it may have seemed like a great victory, in time, the victory would amount to very little. The use of solitary has become so commonplace that it is not strange to hear of individuals who have spent years in such housing facilities, including those on death row who can spend decades living this way. In some prison systems, simply being validated as a gang member can be a ticket to solitary housing. These developments made Sostre's great victory more of a bleep on the prisoners' rights radar.

Recent Muslim litigation echoes charges in the past, including harassment and retaliation for the very act of engaging in litigation efforts. In *Allah v. Al-Hafeez*, Allah's complaint included twenty-six defendants, mostly prison officials, which alleged the officials harassed Allah in retaliation for filing the lawsuit. The claims, however, were ultimately rendered moot when the prison transferred him.[12] Complaining is a risky business for other reasons as well. In *Salahuddin v. Goord*, the Muslim plaintiff claimed that his right to be free from cruel and unusual punishment under the Eighth Amendment was violated when prison officials delayed treatment for a Hepatitis C infection. In this case, it was months until a prescribed course of treatment would begin, which included a liver biopsy.[13] The treatment was delayed for months, in part because of his transfer to another prison. Such cases give a taste of the hardships endured by those incarcerated at the hands of the wardens and how the ability to transfer a ward only magnifies the power gap. Simultaneously, the process extinguishes all the exhaustion of remedies and other legal legwork that went into following the proper channels to get to court in the first place.

As described previously, sometimes the litigation involves enforcing the rights of Muslims against Muslims of other denominations. Whether it be competition for meeting space or scarce resources, sometimes Muslim denominations are forced to vie for credibility. This crisis in narrative control often occurs in spaces where the administration takes on a monolithic view of Islam and lumps all the adherents into a consensual framework. The point is vivid in one case that involved a Shi'ite individual who claimed the coordinator, a member of what the court calls a "rival sect," violated his constitutional rights.[14] In essence, the Sunni Muslims commandeered over the practice of Islam within the facility, facilitated by the coordinator who was more than willing to curb the religious rights of Muslims of different denominations. For his role as a willing assistant to the intentional oppression, he was a named defendant. Among other curtailments, the Shi'ite Muslims were intentionally removed from the prison's Muslim roster, which prevented them from participating in certain religious functions. At the same time, the prison determined that Muslims of different faiths did not require separate space for their meetings. Under this scheme, Shi'ites were not deemed significant enough to warrant their own congregation space, and they could not participate in several other religious functions.

As these cases and histories indicate, the scope of litigation by Muslims is not simply about fighting for religion. The oppression is multilayered, the struggle is more expansive, and the impact reaches beyond Muslims in prison. Moreover, the arc of Muslim litigation is bent on holding institutions accountable for the wrongs committed. This dialectical approach to litigation resulted in greater freedoms for those incarcerated and, at the same time, has shined a light on extralegal and illicit practices by prison officials. As an institution like prison is hidden away from the prying eyes of society, it is like a fiefdom of its own, ruled by the warden. Thus, the litigation efforts of Muslims should be recognized as living documentation of the struggles that those in prison face simply to survive.

THE POST-9/11 ERA

The attacks of September 11, 2001, mark the most important moment for Muslims in American history. The attacks ushered in a bleak period for American Muslims, who were caught in between the American thirst for vengeance and a fear of all things Islamic. Soon after the attacks, the country engaged in a War on Terror, which focused American military power on specific Muslim regions of the world. To make a case for this war, as Todd Green notes, "U.S. political elites constructed and perpetuated an Islamophobic narrative that featured the larger-than-life Muslim enemy as the most significant threat to U.S. values and freedoms."[15]

The physical War on Terror was accompanied by a culture war that made Muslims the target of cultural oppression and social stigma. After the attacks, Muslims in the United States experienced unprecedented levels of discrimination and violent treatment. There were marked increases in hate crimes, workplace discrimination, school bullying, and mosque vandalizations.[16] Treatment of incarcerated people was no exception. It may be argued that Muslim prisoners suffered greater oppression because much of the treatment went unseen and unheard, secluded behind concrete walls and barbed wire fences. While hate crimes against Muslims spiked in this period, those in prison suffered their own hardships wrought by a new era of fear and hatred. However, behind bars, the situation was different since prisons were nestled within a long pedigree of bigotry and Islamophobia, giving rise to a new wave of animus that saw prison officials resort to recycling time-tested practices that disenfranchised Muslims alone. As in previous times, Muslims were signaled out for discriminatory treatment that included special restrictions, censorship of religious books and paraphernalia, and abuse by prison staff.

Some of the iron fists that dominated Muslims inside were the result of fierce fearmongering by politicians on the outside. Hence, this new era was not simply a return to xenophobic attitudes based on ignorance and racism like those experienced by Muslims in prison in the 1960s but instead was a part of a vehement and countrywide cultural backlash. Prison sat within a larger cultural milieu where Muslims were attacked; mosques were burned down, anti-sharia bills were enacted, not to mention the killing of individuals who were mistaken for being Muslim. It was a conscious venting of fear and hatred that came from all quarters: from politicians beating drums who warned of prisoner radicalization to scholarly talk of prison "jihadization," all the way to commentators who talked about prisons as fertile soil for Al-Qaeda style recruitment and violent prison jihad.[17] Moreover, in some instances, Homeland Security dollars were at stake for prisons that could demonstrate problems with prisoner radicalization. In such a social and political climate, it was nearly impossible to decipher fact from fiction regarding the Islamic influence on prisons.

The harsh cultural backlash opened the doors to Muslims being vilified by prison officials and politicians alike. For example, there were no fewer than three congressional hearings dedicated to issues at the junction of prisons, Muslims, and radicalization in the decade that followed.[18] Among the chief fearmongers was Congressman Peter King, who was notorious for depicting prisons as breeding grounds for extremist violence. His efforts single-handedly propagated the notion that Muslims in American prisons were influenced by Muslim terrorist groups abroad. To this date, however, none of these machinations ever materialized. Since then, he dropped the issue and walked away quietly, but it is remarkable and worth noting how he used his government position to promote a particularly hateful attitude about Islam, which itself proved to be constructed on a false narrative. His anti-Islamic attitude helped to make life miserable for Muslims in prison, vilified the religion, and made conversion to Islam synonymous with radicalization.

The irony in these events is that all the while these narratives were portraying Muslims in prison as a public enemy, many behind bars were living law-abiding lives, engaging in rehabilitation and continuing a legacy of litigating for their rights. The alarmist claims about violent prison jihad were not simply false—they overshadowed the true jihad that was taking place in courts, a nonviolent, civil struggle that was far more in line with the rule of law than the doomsday campaigns would have us believe.

One of the true and tested ways prison officials disenfranchised Muslims was by labeling some groups as a gang rather than a religion. These attitudes harkened to past efforts to delegitimize Muslims, as one legal commentator noted in 1962 when prison officials moved to classify Muslims as "a threat to order, but also to declare that they are a sham religion, not entitled to any assistance in the efforts to practice their faith."[19] Nearly half a century later, the same tactic was launched to rebrand some Muslim groups under the "gang" or "security threat group" moniker, which was simply a new iteration of an old run in the Islamophobia playbook. This approach alleviated the prison from having to give religious rights to some groups and greenlighted the institution's harsher punishments against the same. By categorically excluding individuals, prison officials set the stage for litigation that continues to the present by individuals in both federal and state prisons.

Already discussed was how prison officials clamped down on allowing Muslim leaders to enter prisons. The Bureau of Prisons (BOP) claimed it lacked a legitimate Islamic organization to recommend chaplains, which was the underlying rationale for not hiring. However, to this day, these organizations, including the Islamic Society of North America, have never been formally charged with terrorism or other crimes. A 2005 Senate investigation eventually cleared them of any wrongdoing.[20] The restrictions rendered all Muslim chaplains as potential terrorists and subjected imprisoned Muslims to additional preventive actions and overt penalization, despite no such policy being applied to any other demographic group.[21] These actions supported the narrative that Muslims posed a unique threat and paved the way for differential treatment, which was a direct cultural response to the attacks of September 11th.

These actions were unfortunate because not only did they set an example for state prisons to follow, they also overlooked how such policies may catalyze radicalization—how they could work to encourage extremism in the name of preventing it. Already, we have seen how officials radicalized individuals like Cooper and Sostre by subjecting them to prolonged periods of solitary confinement—now, their restrictions on Muslim leaders threatened the same. A result of this gap in leadership is that much of the Islamic religious programming and education fell on the shoulders of other individuals. Prison personnel frequently lacked a basic understanding of Islamic beliefs and practices and typically had very few Muslims on staff. The restrictions on external imams left a gap in leadership; as one official at the BOP noted, "a substantial portion of Islamic services [were] being led by inmates."[22] While there is nothing doctrinally that would oppose such developments, sometimes the situation led to negative outcomes. Some evidence suggested the vacuum in leadership was sometimes filled with undesirable inmates. One Muslim inmate affirmed such a situation inside a California prison where he describes, "maverick" imams took over the pulpit and were fearless in their condemnation of government policy, sometimes presenting a "fundamentally anti-american or militant picture of Islam."[23]

In the wake of 9/11, prison officials returned to the familiar policy of banning certain Muslim texts, which forced Muslims back into court to sue prison officials. In the same way that Muslims in prison were forced to litigate to receive basic texts, including the publication *Muhammad Speaks*, they found themselves once again in the same position. Back then, the writings were considered racially inflammatory and based on hatred; certain texts were now considered off-limits for fear that they could radicalize Muslims in prison.

Another drastic measure by the BOP in this era was implementing the communication management units (CMUs). The CMUs were designed as special facilities within a self-contained federal prison that severely restricts, manages, and monitors an incarcerated person's external communications, including telephone, mail, and visitation. These units were implemented as a part of the War on Terror to limit communication for individuals in federal prison due to their offense of conviction, offense conduct, or other verified information.[24] The first unit was installed in 2006 at the Federal Correctional Complex in Terre Haute, Indiana. Four years later, a second opened in Marion, Illinois. Communications by individuals in the CMU have their verbal communications monitored by counterterrorism agents remotely.

At the outset, it became apparent Muslims would bear the brunt of these facilities. Reporting on the first year of the Indiana facility showed that of the 213 individuals in the prison's CMU, all but two of them were Muslims. In the Illinois facility, the CMUs were predominantly occupied by Muslims as well. In Indiana, the CMU restricted Muslim group prayer to once per week, according to a 2010 lawsuit filed by Enaam Arnaout and John Walker Lindh, the latter widely known as the "American Taliban" after being captured in Afghanistan fighting for Taliban forces. His claim was filed under RFRA where he argued the BOP staff interfered with what the district court found to be a central tenet of his faith—"the obligation to engage in five daily prayers, or Salat." Noting there was scant evidence of disruptive behavior by Muslims during their group religious observances, all of which were under constant surveillance, the court entered a permanent injunction in favor of Lindh against the restrictions on worship. In addition to finding the regulation resulted in a "substantial burden on religious exercise" that failed to adopt the least restrictive method of supervising the gatherings, there was no compelling government interest that excused the BOP's non-compliance with RFRA. Beyond this victory for religious freedom, the court granted a total of nearly $170,000 in fees and costs to be paid to Lindh's attorney, which punctuated the illicit policy.

Other lawsuits on behalf of Muslims filed by the ACLU and the Center for Constitutional Rights challenged the policies and conditions of both known CMUs. In 2011, a lawyer for the Center described "a tenfold overrepresentation of Muslims prisoners at the CMUs," with about seventy percent of the inhabitants of the CMUs being Muslim.[25]

These figures offer a startling look at the disproportionate application of CMUs to house Muslims in prison. The criteria for being referred ostensibly could include a wide array of criminals, from drug kingpins to leaders of street and prison gangs to those who attack doctors who perform abortions. Most dramatically, one is left to wonder why these units are not overflowing with individuals with an inclination toward white supremacy and domestic terrorism. After all, national security intelligence has shown that white nationalists and militias are the country's greatest security threat. FBI data recognized the Aryan Brotherhood as the most murderous group behind bars, accounting for 18 percent of prison murders despite comprising fewer than 1 percent of the prison population.[26] Meanwhile, white supremacist organizations are the most capable of detonating IED bombs behind prison walls.[27] With so many individuals who fit the criteria for being referred to these units, why are most spaces occupied by Muslims? The answer to this question gives a glimpse into what oppression looks like from the Muslim perspective. It shows Muslims are signaled out for differential treatment, which makes the rule of law more myth than meaningful in prison.

RECENT ISSUES

The latest litigation efforts by Muslims include both novel claims and those that characterized Muslim life in prison historically. As in the past, there have been defeats, but the victories have been significant. Already discussed was the *Holt* victory that resulted in the state being made to allow the wearing of, at minimum, a half-inch beard. However, there have been other victories through the efforts of Muslims and advocates outside of prison.

In one victory, Muslims challenged group prayer limits at a federal prison in Kentucky. In this lawsuit, Muslim Advocates and federal detainee William Doyle challenged a BOP policy that restricted group prayer that was enforced only against Muslims. At first, the lawsuit seemed destined for failure when Doyle sued the McCreary Federal Penitentiary in Kentucky in 2018. In that filing, he claimed violations under RFRA and the Fifth Amendment right to equal protection due to the prison's policy that limited his ability to pray in groups by requiring him to get advance permission each time and by limiting prayer to groups of at most three prisoners. In contrast, the prison allowed Christian adherents and other faiths to pray in groups without requiring staff permission. Furthermore, the prison authorized other nonreligious group activities that involve more than three people.

The case eventually reached federal court. Almost reflexively, the district court granted summary judgment for the defendants on the RFRA claim and dismissed the equal protection claim, but the decisions were appealed. In the appeal, Doyle argued the BOP "has no system-wide policy limiting the number of prisoners who can pray together. Instead, McCreary adopted its own prison-specific institutional supplement restricting the availability of group prayer by prisoners."[28] More critically, the filing argued the district court erred by simply accepting the defendants' assertion that the prison had a compelling interest in the policy without sufficient evidence and it abused its discretion by granting summary judgment before discovery commenced. On the equal protection claim, the appeal argued Doyle indeed stated a valid equal protection claim, namely "that non-Muslim prisoners—and only non-Muslim prisoners— are permitted to 'pray more than three [persons at a time] on the yards, in the dining hall, and at the table in the housing unit' without being disrupted or threatened with discipline for violating the policy." Meanwhile, "prison officials decline to enforce the policy against Christian prisoners who pray openly at dining tables in full view of prison staff . . . [and i]n contrast to the Christian prisoners who are permitted to pray openly in groups of four in the dining hall . . ." which Doyle argued is a clear pattern of treatment that itself demonstrated intentional discrimination.[29]

The result of the litigation is noteworthy. In response to the appeal, the BOP changed its group prayer guidance for all federal prisons, and the McCreary Penitentiary withdrew its policy restricting group prayer. With a string of defeats based on religious claims, it is likely the BOP saw the writing on the wall and recognized the appeal was likely going to be successful and expose further unfair tactics by the Kentucky prison. The victory, however, extended beyond the Kentucky prison, as the BOP developed new guidance for federal prisons, outlined in the agency's Religious Beliefs and Practices Manual, which was sent to all the nearly 150 federal prisons. Among the provisions of the new guidance was the removal of previous recommendations that restricted group prayer to no more than three prisoners, a clear statement that requests for group prayer should be treated the same way other group activity requests are treated, and staffers should accommodate all group prayer requests, only denying when security or order of the facility would be jeopardized.

Diet and food services is another area that has seen a spate of legal action in recent years. Among the more infamous cases are from Alaska and Michigan, which look to be extensions of long-standing battles between incarcerated Muslims and prison administration. The cases detail how Muslims sued to have prisons accommodate religious practices such as permitting meal schedule changes to celebrate Ramadan, requiring kitchens to serve some halal meats, removing pork products from other foods, or simply allowing individuals to purchase or receive religiously compliant foodstuffs. Despite extensive litigation and time spent in court, Muslims still struggle to be compliant with their religious dietary duties.

In Alaska, the situation was egregious. In 2018 the Council on American-Islamic Relations (CAIR) sued the Alaska Department of Corrections on behalf of Muslims housed in the Anchorage Correctional Complex.[30] The suit alleged prison officials violated Muslims' rights under the First, Eighth, and Fourteenth Amendments of the US Constitution, RLUIPA, and Section 1983 by denying them proper meals and necessary calories during Ramadan. According to the prison standards, wards are to be given three meals a day, two of which are hot meals that typically range between twenty-six hundred to twenty-eight hundred calories. In contrast, "cold meals" were given to Muslim individuals during Ramadan with a caloric range of five hundred to eleven hundred calories. Like allegations made in other lawsuits, Muslims saw lessor food on their plate that sometimes contained pork products, which forced them to go with even less food. Claiming that the policies amounted to a "starvation diet" for Muslims, the suit asserted, among other violations, Muslims were subject to cruel and unusual punishment. Among several grievances, the plaintiffs alleged they stocked food in their cells due to the policies, which they saved to eat later in the evening. However, their food was confiscated, and they were further prohibited from participating in Ramadan because they saved food in their cells. For their insolence, the plaintiffs were told they would be removed from the Ramadan list as an added disciplinary measure. According to the complaint, "that day neither Plaintiff . . . were given any bagged meals to eat; and accordingly, they ate nothing that day."[31]

In a stunning turn of events, the Alaska Department of Corrections set-tled the lawsuit in September 2019. As a part of the arrangement, the Department agreed to a $102,500 settlement to cover damages, attorney fees, and costs. Perhaps more critically, it also agreed to certain policy changes that included providing observant Muslims with two hot, pork-free meals containing a combined minimum of three thousand calories, weekly Friday congregation, and the freedom to participate in daily con-gregational prayers and study groups.

In Michigan, Muslims found themselves in a similar situation. However, in this instance, Muslims were given a starker choice for Ramadan: either break their fast with the general population or go beyond their religious obli-gations and starve. Led by NOI members, Muslims filed suit in federal court. One of the plaintiffs was dismayed that they had to struggle so hard for the ability to fast appropriately: "[w]e have young people trying to change, improve their lives, and religion is one of the tools to make change . . . We're stopping fists and saying 'for [thirty] days, let's be spiritual. For [thirty] days, let's keep peace.'"[32] The plaintiffs, in this case, were each awarded punitive damages between $650 to $1,300, which were in addition to compensatory damage awards. While the awards may not have been as much as the plain-tiffs sought, the victory was tremendous for two reasons; as one of the plain-tiffs noted, "one, the jury believed us. Second, the jury actually awarded puni-tive damages." In this regard, he is correct, for in all the cases covered in this book, it is a rarity for a court to award any substantive punitive damages. If anything, courts are accustomed to giving nominal damage awards of one dollar, which underscored the windfall of the Alaska settlement.

Other issues that forced Muslims in prison to take their causes to the courts come from women's prisons and jails. In the last few years, the legality of women wearing hijabs has been brought to the fore of legal issues. Already we have seen Muslim males in prison struggled to wear kufi or fez caps, and Muslim women find themselves in the same predica-ment for wearing headscarves. The use of headscarves raises unnerving questions because on the surface it is automatically subject to the same security concerns that were leveled at males. Nevertheless, how much is based on security concerns, and how much is the result of cultural disdain for the practice? The question is valid because opposition to the hijab is an ongoing aspect of the culture war globally.

Although the issue is not new, there have been various iterations of prison policies that inspired litigation in this area. Among the earliest cases was in 2005, when the ACLU represented a Muslim woman in federal court who took her son to visit his father at Columbia Correctional Institution. At the gatehouse, the guard on duty told her she would have to remove her headscarf to check for weapons. She was ultimately forced to remove her headpiece in front of male guards and others, which was practically sacrilegious because she always kept her head covered in public. "I felt naked," she described. "I felt I disgraced my family and my religion."[33] While it is clear prisons have legitimate reasons to scour visitors, it is also true visitors need not check their religious freedoms at the gate. This lawsuit was ultimately dismissed because the prison changed its policy, and now allows headgear as long as it does not conceal the wearer's identity.

Recent lawsuits center on a Muslim's freedom to wear a hijab while being booked and photographed for jail. For example, one woman sued the Louisville Metro Corrections, a jail where booking officers made her remove her hijab in front of dozens of male officers and individuals for her photo to be taken. Like the previous case, the jail changed its policy and now allows for "male and female detainees to retain religious headwear while incarcerated, and specifically during booking photography."[34] In another case, a Minnesota Muslim woman alleged she was forced to strip in jail and remove her hijab for a booking photo. This case not only saw the jail change its booking policy to accommodate wards with religious headwear when taking booking photos, but the jail settled the case for $120,000. More recently, the Council on American-Islamic Relations filed a lawsuit against the Michigan Department of Corrections for forcibly removing a woman's hijab for a booking photo shoot. This lawsuit, however, is not just an isolated incident. This lawsuit represents the latest efforts from other CAIR chapters around the nation, which have filed similar suits to protect the rights of Muslim women who are in the custody of local and state police departments or being housed in jails and prisons.[35]

As these cases show, Muslims continue to experience degrading and humiliating treatment at the hands of state officials. In some situations, the treatment is more invidious because in the case of the hijab, the actions are not just ones that disenfranchise religious adherents. Instead, these are acts that get straight to the core of Muslim modesty and strike in ways that leave women feeling vulnerable, threatened, and as one woman described, the treatment was "one of the most humiliating and harmful experiences" of her life.[36] Hence, these actions are a unique form of oppression because they involve cultural differences, mainly because the hijab is often worn as a buffer against the gaze of males. In these instances, however, the women are forced to uncover themselves directly in front of male officers, or in some instances, incarcerated males, which makes the state action particularly heinous and reflects the depth of cultural dominance.

Recent legal activity around hunger strikes on behalf of Muslims in prison offer other aspects of state dominance. Although the practice of fasting in protest of one's imprisonment or because of one's treatment in prison is nothing new in American history, including the American-run prison at Guantanamo Bay, Cuba, it is a recently growing phenomenon. Like their Guantanamo counterparts, Americans have consciously chosen to refrain from eating as a mode of protest. One of the largest protests occurred in 2013 and was widely known as the California prisoner hunger strike, which involved over twenty-nine thousand individuals held in California prisons and included Muslim participants. The strike was in protest of the state's use of solitary confinement practices. The *Los Angeles Times* reported the strike was timed to coincide with the beginning of Ramadan, and according to individuals reached by the *Times*, the decision was intended to provide "a measure of protection for Muslim inmates participating in the protest, who were less likely to be cited for violating the rules."[37] Weeks into the strike, the California prison system secured a federal court order to begin force-feeding strikers and was granted the ability to ignore "do not resuscitate" forms strikers signed. While the strike achieved mixed results, it undoubtedly put the issue of solitary confinement practices back in the public eye and political sphere.

In addition to coordinated striking, Muslims also engage in individual strikes. One of the recent cases comes from the federal "supermax" prison in Florence, Colorado. "Supermax" is home to Umar Farouk Abdulmutallab, also known as the "underwear bomber," serving multiple life sentences for trying to detonate an airliner in 2009. He sued the Justice Department, claiming, among other grievances, the prison force-fed him when he went on hunger strike. His seventy-three-page complaint is a document that offers a glimpse into his life in the highest security prison in the country.

Among other issues, the complaint describes Muslims are harassed during prayer by white supremacists while the guards do nothing about it. In addition, Abdulmutallab claimed that he was repeatedly force-fed in a manner that is described as unnecessarily painful, abusive, dangerous, and degrading. On one occasion: "The force-feeding tube was placed down his windpipe instead of his esophagus, causing the nutritional supplement liquid to enter his lungs and resulting in [his] feeling like he was being drowned in a manner akin to waterboarding . . . . Additionally, the BOP force-fed him with substances that are "haram," which he is religiously forbidden to consume."[38]

New issues continue to arise, which impel Muslims to seek legal redress, and more critically, demonstrate the unique oppression and mistreatment Muslims suffer at the hands of prison policies and staff. However, in all situations, this brief survey illustrates the power of the state in full force—the ability to strip prisoners naked in front of the opposite sex, to force tubes down peoples' throat for feeding, or on the contrary, to starve individuals from the bare caloric necessities—the cases throw into deep relief the subordinated position of Muslims in prison while simultaneously underscoring the power of the state over the bodies and minds of people imprisoned. More than anything, the cases demonstrate that often courts are the only recourse available to those in prison and that litigation is likely to continue as a viable means to pursue justice behind bars.

6 Muslim Litigiosity

On a cold February evening in Atmore, Alabama, death row at Holman Correctional Facility was in a somber state. It was the first execution in 2019, a ten-month reprieve since the last time a man was put to death in the confines. Even though mortality pervaded the air, lawyers for the man on death row made last-ditch legal filings to postpone the execution. Despite these eleventh-hour efforts to prevent the execution, all hope was dashed when the US Supreme Court lifted the pause in the execution and allowed Alabama to proceed with the killing.

The little glimmer of optimism gave way to the familiar scene of a "dead man walking." After all, this was Alabama, a state with a distinct proclivity for killing. Alabama has the highest per capita killing rate of any state in the country, and in some years, its courts impose more death sentences than Texas, which has a population five times as large. Moreover, this is a state that did not hesitate to execute an eighty-three-year-old the year before, making it home to the oldest person executed in the modern era.

In hindsight, the state's thirst for killing was probably not likely to be stopped by such last-second lawyerly attempts. Instead, the case represents another instance of the state's spectacular killing history. However, this execution was different. It was not the typical Catholic priest with the dead man walking, but an imam, and the condemned, a Muslim, was Dominique Ray. It was also different because the imam was barred from entering the execution chamber, the inner sanctum where the lethal injection was administered. As prison policy had it, only employees of the prison could enter that part of the chamber and the only religious figure who was an employee was a Christian chaplain. For Ray, the ultimate choice was befuddling—either choose the chaplain of a different faith or face death in the chamber alone.

When Ray realized the prison would not allow his adviser to accompany him into the execution chamber, he petitioned federal court for a stay of execution. Ray claimed the policy violated RLUIPA and the Establishment Clause of the First Amendment to the US Constitution. The court denied his request and upheld the prison's decision to refuse his adviser into the chamber. Ray appealed the decision to the Eleventh Circuit Court of Appeals, which granted a stay on February 6, 2019, to resolve Ray's religious claims, adding, "the Clerk of Court is directed to EXPEDITE this appeal so that we may promptly resolve these claims."[1]

The next day, however, the US Supreme Court made short shrift of the Eleventh Circuit's decision by granting a last-minute application to allow the state to move forward with Ray's execution. The Court did not speak to Ray's religious claims, only that he had not met the relevant filing deadline for relief. Nevertheless, a 5–4 majority of the Court voted to let his execution move forward—such that the state could kill Ray that very evening. By 10:12 p.m., he was pronounced dead.

A four-member dissent, led by Justice Elena Kagan, was livid at the turn of events. Perhaps most critically was that Ray acted within five days of learning the prison refused to let his adviser into the death chamber. Justice Kagan chastised the majority for deciding the issue with little briefing and no argument, "just so the State can meet its preferred execution date." Quoting Court precedent, the dissent also underscored the legal issue surrounding Ray's Establishment Clause claim and argued one religious denomination could not be officially preferred over another: "But the State's policy does just that. Under that policy, a Christian prisoner may have a minister of his own faith accompany him into the execution chamber to say his last rites. But if an inmate practices a different religion—whether Islam, Judaism, or any other—he may not die with a minister of his own faith by his side."[2]

Justice Kagan noted the state failed to show how the prison's policy is narrowly tailored to serve a compelling state interest. She questioned pointedly whether allowing Ray's adviser would result in a security risk and noted the State offered no evidence to show its prohibition on outside advisers was necessary to achieve the prison's interest in security. Asking why Ray's imam could not receive the training for execution protocol that Christian chaplains received, she answers her own question: "The State has no answer. Why wouldn't it be sufficient for the imam to pledge, under penalty of contempt, that he will not interfere with the State's ability to perform the execution? The State doesn't say."[3]

In dramatic fashion, this case showcased a conservative group of justices floundering the opportunity to denounce religious discrimination and uphold religious rights. Rather than issue a bold statement on the First Amendment's guarantees, the Court bowed to the state's killing schedule. Instead of allowing the litigation pending in federal appeals court to play out, the justices cut it short and allowed a murky timing issue to dictate justice. At worst, it outright ignored Justice Kagan's startling contention: "Ray has put forward a powerful claim that his religious rights will be violated at the moment the State puts him to death." While it may be more accurate to say his religious rights were violated before execution, the point is clear—his religious claims should have been adjudicated first because they may have resulted in an outcome that bears procedurally on the execution itself. The Court's decision, then, despite its innocuous grounding in procedure, allowed Alabama to proceed with a killing whose optics looked more like religious persecution than protection of religious liberty.

Ray's legal fate mirrored that of most Muslim litigants in prison—they tend to lose in court—yet unlike most litigants who return to their cell empty-handed, Ray was heading to the execution chamber to face death alone. The case was unlike most because it grabbed widespread attention and sparked public outcry across the country. Some of the voices included religious leaders of all faiths who condemned Alabama's policy as heartless and cruel. Thus, even though he lost his bid in court, the case reverberated nationwide. The magnitude of the issue was evident in a Supreme Court ruling handed down just two months after Ray's execution, which showed a Court suddenly willing to address a similar question about Texas's execution protocol. In that case, *Murphy v. Collier,* the Court halted the execution of a Buddhist who was not allowed to have a spiritual advisor of his faith be present in the killing chamber. The prison policy allowed only Christian and Muslim chaplains in the chamber, which was held to be religious discrimination.[4] In a concurring opinion, Justice Kavanagh outlined two potential solutions for prisons seeking to avoid constitutional violations in the future: "(1) allow all inmates to have a religious adviser of their religion in the execution room; or (2) allow inmates to have a religious adviser, including any state-employed chaplain, only in the viewing room, not the execution room."[5] In response to the court order, Texas elected not to allow anyone in the killing chamber. The Court, in turn, stopped the execution again and determined Murphy could not be killed until his late appeal was considered or unless the prison allowed his Buddhist spiritual advisor into the death chamber or a Buddhist advisor of its choice.

Soon after, in another case, it became clear that option two would not be feasible for prisons moving forward, and, symbolically enough, it was an Alabama policy that was once again under the spotlight before the Court. Through the execution of Ray, the state of Alabama set in motion several cases bearing on the issue. After the execution, the Department of Corrections changed its policy of allowing only Christian chaplains in the killing chamber, and followed Texas's system of not allowing anyone in the room. The Court struck the policy and mandated that individuals who are to be executed must have a religious leader present in the execution chamber. The opinion was a boost for religion because rather than deny a religious leader to all individuals condemned to die; the Court guaranteed the right to all. By guaranteeing such, the Court ensured state killings would not be as depraved as those committed by some of the very individuals now condemned. The decision made Kagan's critique in *Ray* somewhat prophetic because this case ultimately proved her point. Under the law of this case, Ray's religious rights were indeed being violated as he was being executed.

As these developments illustrate, *Ray* shook up prison law and produced a net win for individuals awaiting execution throughout the country. Ray's case ignited a backlash that led to reform of what can only be described as a deprivation policy and created a bright-line rule for executions. Now, all prisons in the country were on notice that if a state is going to be in the business of putting people to death, it must figure a way of allowing the condemned person's spiritual advisor in the killing chamber. Thus, even though Ray himself was unable to benefit from his advocacy, in the end it would lay the foundation for greater religious freedoms for individuals of all faiths on death row. Finally, Muslim prisoner litigation offers a glimpse of an idea that may seem counterintuitive to many—namely, the efforts of Muslims effectively expand the rule of law. In an era where even political leaders are worried about Muslims wanting to install Sharia law in the country, Muslim court action embodies the ideals inherent in the rule of law, strengthening and expanding rights, so that more rights and more people are protected, but also so that prisons themselves are not above the law.

A CRITICAL CONTRIBUTION TO PRISON LAW JURISPRUDENCE

By now, hopefully this work convinces the reader of Islam's profound influence on prison law. Muslims have collectively, perhaps like no other faith group, looked to courts as a means of pursuing justice. Through individual and organized efforts across different denominations, the cases pursued by Muslim litigants contributed to prison culture in important ways, including helping to establish laws that would benefit all people in prison. These achievements contribute to a living, breathing legacy of Muslim prison litigation, which shows no sign of slowing, even in the face of onerous legislation like the PLRA and AEDPA (Antiterrorism and Effective Death Penalty Act), which diminishes the likelihood of making a successful claim in federal court. Against such odds stacked against them, including retaliation by guards, Muslims continue to shape prison law and policy.

The contributions of Muslim litigants also reflect sustained critique of a justice system that is sometimes anything but just. Under incarceration, people who have already lost their physical liberty are often deprived of other rights, or worse, deprived of physical integrity and basic safety. The experiences may be compounded by racist or anti-Islamic attitudes of guards, which make life particularly difficult for Muslims. The litigation thus not only represents a profound contribution to prison law but offers up a powerful indictment against the government and the treatment of Muslims in prison.

Muslim prison litigation is the by-product of a struggle between oppressor and oppressed. It is a reality that fits neatly within the religious concept of "jihad," and "prison jihad," to be more exact. When prison officials force Muslims in prison to take their grievances to court, it results in a zero-sum game between the institution and the believer who believes he is following the will of his God. It is no exaggeration to suggest the litigation is a species of jihad that is grounded in general principles of Islamic doctrine. Muslims are on the righteous side of the law, trying to ensure justice is served for those who suffer injustice at the hands of the criminal system. For Muslims, the adversary is clear and the objective is known, making this struggle no different from others that Muslims experienced in the past.

Prison jihad is a real thing, but it is far from the hype that makes headlines. This battle is decades-old yet hardly appears on society's radar. Perhaps it is overlooked because the machinery of Muslim prison litigation works at a slow, lumbering pace and deals with issues that have little bearing on life on the outside. It is far from the type of jihad discussed in the news, such as spectacular acts of terror and shock that can happen instantly and produce life-changing impacts on society. Moreover, this phenomenon portrays something American audiences have not been exposed to much— a heroic tale that features Muslims upholding the law and positively impacting society. This phenomenon is as spectacular as the violent acts that get all the airplay and attention, yet it remains a rather obscure reality for most Americans. Unfortunately, these very audiences would benefit most by understanding how Muslims directly support some of the most cherished ideals in society, particularly because they are often the same audiences that are inundated by negative reporting on Muslims and Islam.

As it stands, Muslims are no strangers to having their contributions to civilization overlooked or deleted from the annals of history; the legal efforts of imprisoned Muslims are not excused from this. However, the facts remain, in just half a century, Muslims in various denominations have collectively steered the course of prison law. Muslim prisoner litigation and the Muslim influence on penal institutions are subjects that have yet to be treated meaningfully by research and scholarship. The early cases brought by the NOI "began the process through which the Muslims' litigation would develop a legal legacy of enhanced, albeit limited, constitutional protections for all prisoners."[6] Although these achievements are monumental, they are more astonishing when considering how few Muslims there are in the United States. According to the latest polling, Muslims make up 1 percent of the American population. In prison, Muslims are a much greater percentage of the population. As Muslims are disproportionately represented in prison, they are disproportionately involved in litigation. Though numerically small, Muslims have left an indelible mark on American prisons and continue the struggle to this day.

However, this work does not mean to say Muslims believe the courts are the only way to seek justice, or that there is full confidence in the court system. After all, Elijah Muhammad himself saw the limitations of relying on the very system that persecuted Muslims writing, "the white man's court is ruled by the will of the white man. We can never hope to have equal justice in the courts of the land belonging to a people who are our enemies."[7] This skepticism indicates Muslims did not have blind faith in the courts and legal processes. However, given his own experiences behind bars, coupled with the successes that his followers were able to obtain, litigation was understood as one dimension of the struggle.

The same holds for the influence of religion—it is not the case that religion motivates all, and religion is not a necessary condition. As we have seen, religion pervades multiple aspects of the litigation, but, for some, it can play a minor or no role at all. This point was evident from one individual who described his case: "I can not say that Islam or Religion has sparked my desire to fight . . . I despise the thought that someone believes that they can make me their victim."[8] Such sentiments show that religious influence, while undeniably a motivating force in litigation, is certainly not the only one.

REIMAGINING THE ROLE OF RELIGION

> You asked what motivates me to litigate: Justice and the
> taking of power from oppressors who seek to destroy Islam
> by watering it down. Islam enjoins the right and forbids the
> wrong, so . . . as righteous Muslims we have a duty to resist
> and disobey. So our form of resistance at the present time is
> court action.
> —Abdul Maalik Muhammad[9]

> What inspired me is my faith. How even though I'm Muslim
> & others are not. Islam (Quran & Sunni) still tells Muslims to
> stand up for the right even if they are not Muslims. So I
> always felt, whatever I win on behalf of Islam, the non
> Muslims can even benefit.
> —Individual in Florida State Prison[10]

When we look at what religion "does" behind bars, one thing is certain—it is not a sedative. For Muslims it is a force that has mobilized individuals and inspired them to take up the arduous work of suing in court. For some, religion provides a theological frame to a seek justice through spiritual activism. By engaging in litigation, individuals align ideology, action, and the rule of law. This untold aspect of the lawsuits forces us to reimagine how religion influenced litigation efforts. Moreover, they demonstrate individuals who are putting religious prescription to work in the real world. One individual described that "Islam played the only role in filing my [religious] claim . . . Islam commands all Muslims to stand against oppression to fight in the cause of the religion (not a physical fight), not to mention my rights secured by the federal constitution to do so as well."[11]

There are three important ways religion exerted influence on litigation.[12] One obvious way is when the litigation involved claims about religious rights, and religion itself is the very motivation for suing. At a base understanding, an individual might interpret his action as advocating on behalf of or in the cause of Islam. Religious influence is also displayed in the organizational efforts by Muslims in prison and on the outside. When litigation spawned in the 1960s, NOI members encouraged and supported such litigation. Not all cases were the result of spontaneous action, but, instead, from the organizational strategies of groups and individuals to streamline litigation. Finally, there are those for which religious ideology inspires the willingness to take a stand for justice. The messages of Islam are central motivators, and litigants draw on Islamic traditions of action. This aspect of religion's influence is an important supplement to critical work on prison litigation, which to date has overlooked the religious dimensions of litigation efforts.

For those cases that directly involved religious freedom claims, religion is the motivating force. After all, the outcomes of this type of case directly impact how one gets to practice religion. In the foundational period of litigation, Muslims struggled to establish Islam as a legitimate religion and had to inch their way to gaining greater rights, including actions brought to obtain the Quran, other religious literature, and access to faith leaders. By default then, the cases implicated deeply held practices and beliefs, which infused the struggles with spiritual significance.

Beyond explicitly religious claims are those efforts by religious organizations and individuals. The NOI offered a clear example of how to orchestrate challenges to prison officials in court. Both Elijah Muhammad and Malcolm X shared a tradition of "religiously motivated prison activism" that saw Muhammad preaching to men like Malcolm in prison, and Malcolm encouraging incarcerated men to file civil rights claims in courts. In addition to the NOI's anti-prison bent were the individuals on the inside who supported litigation efforts materially and encouraged others to pursue legal actions. Martin Sostre and Thomas X Cooper offer prime examples of individuals who stayed preoccupied in litigation or in assisting others with the same. Sostre was staunch in his belief and was willing to risk further punishment to assist others with their legal cases. These efforts were so noticeable they gained the attention of courts, one of which seemed suspicious at the pattern of the lawsuits, writing "these are not cases where uneducated, inexperienced, and helpless plaintiffs are involved ... taken together with the number of complaints directed to this court by these plaintiffs and others of the same sect, indicates that these applicants are part of a movement."[13]

Perhaps the most telling influence of religion on litigation efforts is how messages of faith motivate individuals to take up litigation. This proposition is nothing new since such activism is evident among Muslims from Elijah Muhammad's NOI to present Muslim involvement in the Black

Lives Matter movement. In prison, individuals like Sostre engaged in activism as a direct result of ideology. From his perspective, because pens, papers, and notebooks could create court petitions, they were like "dynamite," but more critically, "most essential weapons to fighting Shaitan." These sentiments from decades ago have not diminished, as described by one individual incarcerated in Tennessee, who has "helped many inmates with civil and criminal litigation over the years":

> I believe that I have been commanded to fight to establish Allah's Religion if it is being oppressed from its establishment. In the prison environment, the pen is the mightiest weapon given to an inmate. As a martial artist in Wing Chun and Ti Quan Do martial arts, I have mastered the art of writing as a means of self-defense technique against the prison administration. I only fight (write) when I am forced to.[14]

These words echo those of a prison convert, Brother Clyde X, who in the 1960s, details his preaching efforts and how justice was the centerpiece of his understanding: "the main thing I would tell them was how the Muslims wanted freedom, justice, and equality and unity of the Blackman . . . I told all the other brothers that I wasn't going to fight physically anymore because that was the wrong."[15] More importantly, he saw the law as the best way to continue his struggle:

> The only way I could win was to fight him with his own weapon which was law enforced by the state and Federal Government. I began studying State and Federal law. As I studied I wrote petitions seeking religious privileges in order to hear a Muslim Minister speak the word of Islam. I filed petition after petition, but in each court it would lose. So I began writing. I even wrote for other prisoners—getting them out of prison and back home again . . . As I was preparing myself for freedom, justice, and equality, the authorities were preparing to stop me in every way they could.

Such individuals are the epitome of the Muslim prison litigator—individuals who have experienced oppression but refused to fight physically. Instead, they chose to learn the law, learn to write, and learn to litigate to fight against injustice for themselves and others.

Muslim litigants continue to draw inspiration from the edicts of Islam, and religious ideology continues to be an important, if overlooked, area of influence. As the petitioner in *Holt* describes about his efforts in court,

"This form of action is one of the means of resisting oppression that the hadith refers to when it states that you can fight oppression by using your tongue." As such, his work as a litigator fits squarely within his understanding of Islam:

> Lawsuits surrounding Islamic issues are also a form of dawah or calling because it educates the non-Muslims about what true Islam is. . . . I believe that when I stand before Allah (swta) on the Day of Qiyam, when I receive my Book of Deeds inshallah in my right hand, that my actions here will be the things that allow me to run across the Sirat bridge into Paradise. As Imam Jamil Al-Amin said: I seek truth over a lie, I seek justice over injustice, and I fear Allah (swta) more than I fear the state.

Muhammad's quote of Al-Amin is noteworthy since Al-Amin, formerly known as H. Rap Brown, has been a longtime civil rights leader, known for his firebrand preaching and writings like *Die Nigger Die!* But more importantly, he has also litigated from prison, including one case where he claimed prison officials violated his constitutional right to access the courts and free speech.[16]

ADVANCING THE RULE OF LAW

> But for many if not most defendants, the period from arrest to
> verdict (or plea) is only a preamble to an extended period
> under state control, whether on probation or in custody. It is
> during the administration of punishment the state's criminal
> justice power is at its zenith, and at this point the laws
> constraining the exercise of that power become most crucial.[17]

This section examines the "rule of law" as a cherished principle of governance and considers how Muslim prison litigation advances core aspects of the concept. As an initial consideration, the phrase is imbued with the vestige of power. The "law" "rules" everyone and there is no one above the law or outside it. While this may be the centerpiece of the idea, in prison, however, this concept loses its luster and looks quite different for those who often fall on the outside of the law's protection. Rather than prove their fealty to the rule of law, correctional facilities often prove disloyal to the ideal. Their wards experience the protections of law at their weakest and are left to fend for themselves in a world where they are practically powerless. They are under incarceration as a punishment and to help them lead a law-abiding life, yet they sometimes exist in a world of lawlessness, where the rule of law tends to look more fantasy than anything factual. Muslims in prison have undertaken all sorts of sacrifices to try to ensure prisons and officials are not above the law or beyond its reach. In doing so, they have been guardians of this bedrock principle of American civilization and have advanced its presence behind bars.

There are competing and contested interpretations of what this idea entails.[18] As a general matter, the concept is central to the legitimacy of a government, its laws, and its institutions. It is "regarded as either a principle of law or as a principle of governance" that is concerned with consistency and "defining either a minimum standard which something has to meet in order to be law or as an aspiration standard identifying what it means to be good law."[19] Perhaps the simplest and foremost underpinning of the rule of law is that it is diametrically opposed to the "rule of men."[20] It is the dual notion that all are subject to the law and that all are protected by the law, summed up in the notion of "getting one's day in court." For decades, the "hands off" doctrine deprived prisons of the rule of law, and, even today, in some systems, the concept sits as but a gutted ideal. Perhaps of all places, prisons represent the fringe of institutions where the rule of law is suspended the most. In this environment, where people are at their most vulnerable and the state is at its height of power, Muslim prison litigation arises with suits that decry the rule as missing in action.

Among the constitutive elements of the rule of Law, three central tenets are critical for recognizing their abandonment in prison.[21] First is allegiance to constitutionalism, which comprises the procedural and substantive limitations on government authority and arbitrary action. Second, the rule is characterized by rule-based decision-making, which is intimately related to constraining arbitrariness. Third is adherence to neutrality principles as a base for decision-making, instead of ad hoc discretion. In the prison, arbitrary and oppressive action by the government sometimes violates all notions of the term. So, even if the rule is intended as a constraint against government powers, it has its failures, which is perhaps why it has been said that the rule of law is unattainable.[22]

As we have seen throughout this book, there is a rich, long history of Muslims in prison trying to ensure that the law operates there. The struggle for equal protection of the law is for real, as is mistreatment by guards, staff, and administrative policies. In the quest for substantial equality, imprisoned people have encountered great difficulty accessing courts, spanning from the "hands off" era to penalties for jailhouse lawyering to the present, where legislation like the PLRA exemplifies the codification of this mentality. Implementing higher barriers to access courts is the antithesis of what the rule embodies.

These realities make prison a place that suffers a scarcity of the rule of law and benefits from Muslims' allegiance to law and the legal system. As the court cases demonstrate, Muslims have constantly received extra-legal treatment and punishment by guards and administrative policies that burden Muslims unconstitutionally. Muslim attempts to advance prisoners' rights through lawsuits must be seen for what they are: a fortification of the rule of law. It has been noted one of the simplest ways the NOI could justify its turn to law and the courts to protect and advance Muslims' rights was the organization's consistent support for law and order.[23] Researchers found support for this idea among many of the research subjects who perceived Islam as a way of preventing them from carrying out illegal activities in the future after leaving prison.[24] Despite the fact that statements about the ineffectiveness of courts and Elijah Muhammad's periodic attempts to distance the organization from entanglement with law enforcement and prison litigation, on the back of almost every *Muhammad Speaks* are the statements, "We want justice. Equal Justice under the Law. We want justice applied equally to all regardless of creed, class or color."[25] Beyond were unequivocal statements by Muhammad himself that accentuated the point: "We recognize and respect American citizens as independent people, and we respect their laws which govern the nation."

Previous chapters demonstrate Muslim litigants in prison were directly involved in expanding the law's application there when correctional facilities first started coming under the scope of federal courts. From that point,

Muslims began a long-standing history of turning to the courts to combat hostility, oppression, and unlawful treatment. By struggling in this way, sincere Muslims paved the way for Islam to become a recognized religion and for the law's protection of various Muslim denominations for the foreseeable future. They worked to expand this aspect of the rule of law. Not only have they secured rights that other incarcerated individuals enjoy, religious and secular alike, but they were also involved in some of the first cases that took the notion of civil rights in prison seriously.

Speaking on the prisoners' rights movement generally, in 1980, James B. Jacobs hypothesized several impacts that litigation behind bars had on prison administration. These developments must be understood as effectively ensuring the rule of law expanded in the correctional setting. Chief among these were the *bureaucratization of the prison and a new generation of administrators.*[26] He notes prior to litigation efforts, prison administrators operated by intuition: "[t]here were no written rules and regulations, and daily operating procedures were passed down from one generation to the next ... Early lawsuits revealed the inability of prison officials to justify or even to explain their procedures."[27] However, courts began demanding rational decision-making procedures and written policies, which resulted in an overhaul of prison systems that put in place rules and regulations that put some restraint on officials and normative expectations of those incarcerated. Moreover, Jacobs notes the movement *"expanded the procedural protections available to prisoners."*[28] Individuals were not entitled to even the most rudimentary procedural protections when faced with losing good time credits or receiving extra punishment. These gaps led to the development of legislative and administrative procedures, including grievance procedures for formal dispute resolution, arbitration, and "minimum standards" to certify compliance by prison officials. Finally, the movement *heightened public awareness of prison conditions.* As media and other coverage brought the brutality of prison to the world outside, it helped mobilize support for change. This development spurred legislative, regulatory, and supervisory bodies that adopted rules and facilitated correctional improvements.

Described earlier were the various lawsuits necessary to implement Islam as a bona fide religion in prison. Prisons did not recognize Islam and Muslims were not given the status of a religion outright. Unlike

Christian denominations, followers of Islam were forced to prove themselves before they were accorded First Amendment rights. These early lawsuits thus extended the law's protection to cover an entirely new class of subject: The Muslim. Although the litigation would extend the law's protection to a growing class of incarcerated, this hardly meant all Muslims enjoyed these protections because some groups still face uphill battles to be recognized by prison officials as a genuine religious group.

Another, perhaps not so obvious, way Muslim prison litigation supports the rule of law is by providing precedent for future litigation efforts and creating a greater body of law. Cases involving Muslim litigants show how they struggled to obtain rights, including freedom of speech and association to freedom from cruel and unusual punishment. More specifically, the rules set in many of the religious claims are generally applicable to individuals of other faiths, which means prisoner-petitioners can rely on those cases as a legal basis to pursue other legal claims that have nothing to do with Islam. Effectively, the efforts of Muslims have created ground rules and precedent for individuals of other faiths to enjoy ongoing expansions of religious liberty and to build upon in tomorrow's legal battles and, in cases like *Ray*, to spark fervor to change the law.

The push to expand the law's coverage and extend its reach to protect more people is the result of Muslims pushing for equality under the law. For this outsider population to push back against a system that outpowers them in every conceivable way, it is remarkable to understand how the efforts attempt to equalize the playing field. The overall thrust is due to the pursuit of equality under the law. The fact people inside prison have their rights curtailed in ways that are foreign to people on the outside shows the law at its most unequal; efforts to obtain more rights for incarcerated people is a means of equalizing a lopsided situation between the inside and out. In *Holt*, we witnessed how Muhammad relied on practices and court opinions in other jurisdictions to push for one-half-inch beards as a minimum for all behind bars. This litigation equalized the situation within prisons because, prior to that decision, some Muslims behind bars could not grow a beard at all.

LITIGATION PRAXIS

> As a Muslim, I believe in self-defense. I also believe in the
> right to freedom of religious choice. Religious oppression is
> the worst form of oppression. Islamic beliefs dictate the view
> that oppression is worse than killing. Therefore, as a Muslim,
> I am given the permission and the responsibility to fight
> against all oppression from being able to practice my First
> Amendment rights to the freedom of religious exercise. These
> views are dictated by the Qur'an in several verses therein.[29]

When Muslims engage in litigation due to the belief that they are following what their religion prescribes, it offers a snapshot of praxis at its pur-
est. Such individuals operate consciously by dovetailing religious ideology
with activism in the real world. For an onlooker, it would be a mistake to
think that being Muslim is just coincidental to litigation; for some litigants, there is a connection, a causal relationship—it is not simply that a
Muslim is involved in litigation, but, rather, he is involved in litigation
because he is Muslim. When one's belief takes him all the way to the court-
house steps, under a firm conviction that his religion sanctions the suit,
such use of the courts and the law demonstrates the essence of praxis.
Such an attitude was iterated by another individual who, in a civil complaint, recited a hadith where a companion of Prophet Muhammad asks
him to advise him. The Messenger told the companion to not become
angry. The dialogue continues with the Messenger giving the same
response two more times. The individual explains how this saying informs
his present actions: "When staff play with the sahur meal by not putting
food items in the bag or when you break fast the food trey is light, this
causes one to become angry. How can I get the benefits and blessings of
my fast if I'm mad all day because staff is playing with my food. So, the
only way to fight these issues in my opinion was to file a lawsuit and
inshallah someone (a lawyer) take my case."[30]

While most may be familiar with liturgical acts, such as lighting
incense, ringing bells, or partaking in sacrament, few people would imagine the work of litigation as something spiritual. However, it is proper to
talk about "Muslim litigiosity" to describe how Muslims express faith

through litigation. This praxis further demonstrates why litigation may be seen as a form of religious expression, which forces us to expand our consideration of what constitutes a spiritual or sacred act, and recognize that sometimes what might be perceived as mundane acts may be imbued with religiosity. And just as some might fast or perform other rituals as expressions of faith, litigants in prison undergo severe austerities to get their day in court, and sometimes must literally fast as well under mistreatment by staff. Muslim prison litigation blurs the conceptual line between sacred and profane, because by engaging in the exhaustive work of litigation, Muslims put faith into the legal system—the very system that landed them in prison in the first place. While this paradox may seem perplexing, when mapped against Islamic attitudes about justice and equality, the practice of suing in court appears as a natural sequitur of accepting Islam.

7 Conclusions and Final Thoughts

When Thomas Bratcher asked Malcolm X to testify as an expert witness in the case of *SaMarion v. McGinnis,* he articulated the relationship between incarcerated Muslims and those outside through the metaphor of war. "The fighting man cannot win a war without the moral support of the homefront." Black prisoners saw the courts as a breach in the walls, which allowed them to express their claims before the world outside.

—Garrett Felber, *Those Who Know Don't Say*

The data and theoretical points detailed in this work suggest several distinct takeaways. Perhaps, above all, they stress the importance of Muslims to the development of prison law, policy, and culture. Examination of Muslim prisoner litigation provides an untold chapter to both prison law in America and the study of American Islam. Together, they tell a history of the outsider, the most downtrodden in society, and the battles they waged against religious repression wielded in the belly of the beast. These lawsuits, for some, are more than mundane filings that seek to achieve some worldly goal; they are about seeking justice, which is the essence of religious conduct.

Muslims certainly launch these lawsuits from a disadvantaged position. They exist within a lopsided institution that benefits from judicial deference and legal loopholes that give the state nearly absolute power over Muslims. In turn, Muslims in prison sit among the most marginalized groups in the country, powerless as an intersectionality of despised identities. Their lawsuits offer a piercing example of how the law operates when it applies to the lowest of the low, and how they propound a powerful indictment of American prisons for perpetrating religious oppression, violence, extralegal punishment, and other misconduct against those whom they are supposed to watch and protect. While such state actions made life behind bars anything but lawful, the Muslim response, by and large, has been to deal with these problems civilly using the legal system.

Muslim litigiosity embodies a unique response to state oppression and is a modern manifestation of religious devotion in the prison context. Whereas Americans may see Muslims as inherently violent or prone to violence as a form of problem-solving, this story paints a different picture. After all, many of these issues pertain to an individual's most deeply held beliefs and convictions. Yet, the state-sponsored violence and the denial of religious and other rights has not provoked violence. Instead, the Muslim modus operandi used formal channels to complain, first through the prison grievance procedures and then through courts. Compared to the ongoing, concentrated stream of litigation that has come to define this legacy of Muslim lawsuits, extremist violence is but a footnote in the story. Rather than resorting to violence, Muslims proved quite adamant at settling grievances through the court system. This history of Muslim prisoner litigation undermines the alarmist notion the prisons are fertile fields for extremist violence and instead underscores the Muslim reputation for being clean, disciplined, and regimented, and for being successful at keeping out of prison once released.

AN OUTSIDER'S VIEW: LESSONS IN STATE DOMINANCE

> This [Outsider Jurisprudence] methodology . . . offers a
> unique description of law. The description is realist but not
> necessarily nihilist. It accepts the standard teaching of street
> wisdom: law is essentially political.[1]

OutCrit jurisprudence is a fruitful venture in the quest to understand Muslim prisoner litigation. In classical form, the application of critical jurisprudence reveals "the indeterminacy of law as well as the way power asymmetries have marginalized and subordinated countless groups."[2] More than anything, the power of narrative brings the realities of prison alive to "breach" the walls to the outside world; it validates the litigation as a strategy against state subordination and stands ripe as one of the hallmarks that supports OutCrit analysis. After all, it is narrative that is brought to bear on the conduct of state actors, Muslims telling their stories to the courts, and both figuratively and literally, praying for relief. As history has shown, some of the litigation occurred within marked periods of American culture wars where Islamophobia played a prominent role as a villain-foil for Americans for decades.

The OutCrit perspective emphasizes the great importance of recognizing just how isolated prisons and their wards are from the public eye. Not only are individuals in prison located sometimes a thousand or more miles from their hometowns, but prisons are generally built on remote lands, which are cheaper and therefore more cost-effective for new construction. Moreover, since the mid-1970s, the Court has held the media and the public may be denied access to prisons, which only further isolates prison policies and practices from public accountability.[3] As there are already legal obstacles to prevent those in prison from giving an unfettered, authentic account of what happens on the inside, their narratives become the only practical lifeline to greater knowledge for those on the outside.

As we have seen in the early 1960s, there was much suspicion and animosity directed at Muslims imprisoned. These attitudes translated into reporting by prison authorities that cast Muslims as belligerent, violent troublemakers. They were some of the earliest and strongest voices of Islamophobia, who controlled the narrative about Muslims, which conveniently omitted details about their own role in antagonizing and ostracizing Muslims in prison. These were the first accounts of Muslims in prison, and they painted a bleak picture about their character. With these descriptions, a blueprint was laid for the tactics and weapons that would be used in culture wars to come.

Based on these developments, a strong case is made that the American prison is a ground-zero of modern American Islamophobia. Correctional officials were an authoritative voice that was instrumental for framing Muslims as a threat to good order. Their characterizations would reach outside of prison and influence the perceptions of law enforcement on the outside. The early treatment of Muslims in prison is emblematic of the American fear of Islam. While these stereotypes would wane over the years, they returned with a vengeance after the attacks of 9/11. Indeed, there were at least three congressional hearings on Muslim radicalization in prison despite little evidence of extremist violence or foreign influence on American prisons. Hence, the litigation itself may be viewed as a response to the waging of a culture war in the correctional setting. For many of the early cases, Muslims sought equal protection under the law. To be granted the status of religion was the first legal step necessary, and Muslims have fought to enforce their rights ever since. This perspective unveils how prisons dominate the kept and how litigation is a way to resist.

The outsider perspective prioritizes the experience of subordination to offer a phenomenology of religion and the law. Religion itself ignites individual and institutional acts of victimization that arise out of hatred and fear. In practice, the state dominates in multiple and apparent ways. As a near-total institution, prisons govern practically every aspect of a person's life. It is a place where fundamental constitutional and civil rights are outright suspended or severely curtailed, and there is no such thing as a right to privacy, an illegal search, or, as the court noted in 1984, no reasonable expectation of privacy in one's prison cell.[4] However, prison officials are notorious for breaking whatever laws are in place and engaging in the most heinous conduct, including participating in massive cover-ups and shuffling incarcerated individuals to conceal wrongdoing and obstruct justice.

As in bygone years, people in prison experience minimal rights and privileges, yet institutional actors often abrogate even those scant rights. Moreover, state officials not only disavow this thin film of law that protects people imprisoned, but they also proved capable of inflicting all sorts of other evils, much of which will never be adjudicated in a court of law. Such a sobering reflection of the awful power prison wields over individuals illustrates a lived reality that harshly falls on the most downtrodden outsider groups in the country. Their treatment indicates that people in prison, specifically Muslims, were the target of a cultural war that state agents provoked; the government picked this war to wage. Prison litigation is a cultural response to this struggle.

Such a powerless being in the hands of a seemingly omnipotent prison system casts a doubtful shadow on the rule of law. This point rings particularly true in light of the long and hard battle it has been to mandate prisons to provide legal assistance and other resources so individuals can represent themselves in court. It is not simply that there have been deficiencies, but many instances of outright hampering of the ability to have one's day in court. After all, it took several lawsuits to prevent prisons from punishing individuals who provided legal assistance to their incarcerated peers. Assisting others with legal aid was dangerous business, and doing so landed many a Muslim in solitary confinement. Thus, the rule of law suffers a double blow since such prohibitions effectively mount a barrier between people in prison and the promise of getting one's day in court.

The situation is graver, however, when layered with religious repression against Muslims in particular. If those in prison are the most loathed and outcast in society, Muslims occupy this role among those imprisoned. Understanding these attitudes within the correctional context offers a shiny example of Khaled Beydoun's notion of "structural Islamophobia," the "fear and suspicion of Muslims on the part of government institutions and actors. This fear and suspicion are manifested and enforced through the enactment and advancement of laws, policy, and programming built upon the presumption that Muslim identity is associated with a national security threat."[5] For some, the prison experience has often involved additional pain and suffering simply for trying to be a good Muslim. The mistreatment of Muslims was noted early in the writings of Eldridge Cleaver, who in the 1960s described that prison officials would "periodically bundle up the leaders of each Mosque and transfer them to another prison, or place them in solitary confinement so that they could not communicate with the other members of the mosque."[6]

The litigation decries prisons as the oppressive institution extraordinaire when it comes to the treatment of Muslims. The tactic of simply denying a person in prison the status of Muslim has disenfranchised people for decades. Prison officials have dubbed Muslims as anything but religious. Taken to its logical extreme, the posture can be used as a means of disqualifying Muslims from First Amendment and other religious rights, whether by ignorance or intent. As the court opinions expose, some of the court judges in the early cases hardly seemed to know that such a thing called "Islam" or a "Koran" existed, let alone understand the global popularity of each. The efforts in the present have an uncanny resemblance to what prisons have been doing for decades: denying individuals the status of Muslim and denying some groups the status of a religious group at all.

In fact, several prisons still list Five Percenters as a gang, even though all evidence suggests that, above all, they are a religious group. This point is true even if members themselves may not acquiesce to the notion they fit the definition of religion.

At its most basic, Muslim prisoner litigation is an effort to take a stand against the beast. It is a snapshot of those most in the underclass with nowhere else to look but the courts. Muslims used courts to sue so that prison conditions and treatment improved, not to try to avoid punishment, as Moore notes, Muslim litigation was about changing prison conditions, "*not* to sue for release . . . By asking for judicial intervention, in the management of prisons, the inmates sought not only a means to resist the unchecked authority of prison administrators, but more importantly to transform existing conditions."[7]

One of the ways "unchecked" state dominance continues to inflict repression is with the unfettered ability to transfer wards involuntarily. The ability of prison officials to move a person to a different prison facility is based on a pair of cases in the 1970s when the Supreme Court declared that absent some state law or other created rights, individuals in prison have no protected liberty interest in the right to stay at one's current prison or a right to notice and hearing when involuntarily transferred to another prison.[8] There is practically no way to contest one's transfer from one facility to another, demonstrating the tremendous power behind this practice.

When the raw ability to transfer fuses with the judicial doctrine of mootness, it creates an irresistible force that can effectively gut the rule of law. A finding of mootness has the power to extinguish an RLUIPA or Section 1983 claim, which demonstrates its awesome potential. When a correctional system can move people around at will, it sometimes can be a strategy to absolve prison staff from constitutional and statutory violations. This point was noted by the plaintiff in *Holt*. Fearful of this tactic being used against him as his case was progressing at the highest level, he made a request and wanted the court to understand this problem: "As part of that injunction, it stated that in my petition—because this is something that's become a real issue with me there at the penitentiary, at Cummins Unit, that—that the defendants be banned or barred from transferring me to another institution in retaliation for this litigation. It's a common tactic ADC uses to disrupt litigation. You understand what I'm saying?"[9]

Accordingly, the number of Muslims bringing and winning cases in court would seemingly be greater were it not for a prison's ability to move people around and, subsequently, benefit from a doctrine that can magically make the case go away. Being transferred from a facility that was the locus of a plaintiff's allegations necessarily moots claims for declaratory and injunctive relief against officials of that prison. As a result, case after case shows courts ignoring what officials have done at a prison merely because the prisoner-petitioner has been shifted to another facility or because they stopped the violative conduct. According to earlier research, the head of the Prisoner Litigation Bureau of the Attorney General's office, about 15 to 20 percent of cases are disposed of by settlement or by mootness.[10] The overall impact represents a significant gap in justice.

The outsider perspective is valuable for conveying the multitiered struggle for Muslims in prison. They struggled to have their day in court and had to contend with a repressive institution that has historically fostered varieties of Islamophobia. Understanding the law from this perspective validates Muslim litigiosity as an ally of the rule of law.

ROLE REVERSAL: THE CRIMINAL AS ENFORCER

> Immunity from judicial scrutiny led to a tradition of lawlessness in the corrections phase of the criminal process. The elaborate constitutional protections afforded the accused before and during trial stopped at sentencing. What happened to the convicted after that was not a matter of judicial or, indeed public concern.[11]

> The Muslim prisoners' cases have a profound impact upon the entire correctional system because they helped to change the existing relationships between "keeper" and "kept" and they provided the legal vehicles for all incarcerated persons to attempt to vindicate their constitutional rights.[12]

The role of litigation sometimes is to ensure existing laws are followed. The "hands-off" era marked a time of unfettered state conduct when it came to treatment of people in prison. Even when this posture changed and civil rights in prison were slowly established, it hardly guaranteed the laws would be followed, or, more critically, that the rules of the prison would be followed either. Litigation by Muslims points out this truth, as do court opinions. Like prison policies, officials may sometimes ignore policies, but they do not result in viable legal claims. For example, when an individual follows formal procedures to get an identification card with one's spiritual name printed on it, officials may refuse to call an individual by that name and face no consequence, which seemingly undermines the purpose of such a policy in the first place.[13] Of course, much of prison governance is local, and there is a vast range of decision-making by prison administration and staff. In theory, decision-making is supposed to be guided by rules, policies, and regulations. The litigation shows that this is often not how it goes. *Abdullah v. Wisconsin Department of Corrections* offers a snapshot of such a case, which states the problem from the prisoner-plaintiff's point of view: "Defendant Frank and his employees stated herein have failed to act in accordance with their own rules, policies and procedures as set forth in the Wisconsin Administrative Code. . . . In doing the aforesaid, the defend-ants sought to circumvent their own rules and policies governing religious practices/property . . . and intentionally and repeatedly turned a blind eye to the violation of plaintiffs' civil/constitutional rights, by failing to prop-erly investigate complaints submitted . . . thereby not providing plaintiffs with an adequate remedy that will give voice to legitimate grievances."[14]

In this facility, the staff circumvented the law through its acts and omis-sions and, worse, failed to provide a means to remedy legitimate griev-ances. In other words, Muslims were not afforded their day in court; rather than affirm the rule of law, the prison's actions subverted it. In these moments of role reversal, Muslims are cast as enforcers of the law—the criminal following the law while prison officials are mired in illegality and rule-breaking. This reality indicates the Muslim struggle in prison is not just about defining what is constitutional in the correctional context, but also about guaranteeing the current law is implemented. This point extends to the judiciary as well, as one individual explains, "One factor that needs to be brought to the light that affects so many people . . . The refusal of many judicial justices who refuse to follow, adhere [to], and implement the laws as they are sworn to do."[15]

The courts are not the only space where Muslims tried to make their legal case. Indeed, Muslims went beyond and sought international intervention. For example, in 1970, individuals on death row filed charges to the Committee to Petition the United Nations against genocide, citing a range of human rights violations with emphatic punctuation, including the State of New Jersey and officials denied people "the very laws that they (officials) say are equally applied to all Inmates . . . who are also unfortunate to fall victim to the 'Big Business' of the criminal court system of these United States."[16]

While these charges ultimately amounted to very little legally, they provide another example of Muslims attempting to enforce the rule of law. This time, rather than trying to get courts to get state and federal prisons to follow the law, they lobbied an international body to protest that the United States was not fulfilling its international obligations. It is an extreme example of Muslims trying to get their day in court to get their own country to follow the law. It is of no consequence that, in the same way that litigation efforts usually ended up with Muslims losing, the UN could do very little for the plight of Muslims. The important point to note is they were willing to press for justice—even if it meant trying to go over their own country's head and place their grievances in the hands of a foreign governing body.

While Muslims clearly illustrate upholding of the law in a black-letter sense, in a more sublime sense, Muslims in prison are enforcers of a different stripe—they are also enforcers of Muslim traditions. When a Muslim imposes an Islamic regime on his lifestyle, the self-enforcement perpetuates religion itself. Whether it be keeping Jumu'ah, Ramadan, the dress and diet, or learning to kneel, traditions of Islam are performed and practiced behind bars and are reinscribed daily. Prisons are hubs of Islamic activity that ensure the repetition of ritual and prayer that keep the tradition alive. The self-patrolling of Muslims, both individually and collectively, enforces a code that produces specific outcomes relevant to purposes of punishment. In the case of Muslims in prison, the impact of religion has contributed to the goal of rehabilitation. Studies indicate religion is often a contributing factor for helping people stay out of prisons.[17] The outcomes are even more robust for Muslims, with submission to Islam being more congruent with rehabilitation than other religious traditions.

This self-monitoring is even more effective than Foucault's perfected panopticon because not only do Muslims become their own warden in prison, but they live a stricter lifestyle than that prescribed by the penal regime, and they are aware of it. Unlike those in Foucault's prison, who are unaware they are doing the prison's work by self-monitoring, for Muslims, it is praxis—they are fully conscious of their self-regulation as a part of the responsibility that comes with submission to God. The power of submission effectively displaces the prison's attempt at reform because the enforcement of Islamic regulation over their own lives proves a stricter regime than what the prison prescribes and proscribes. The impact of adopting Islam in prison correlates with a decreased probability of returning to prison once released and points to the notion that religion may be better at the game of reforming than correctional facilities themselves.

The situation births a paradox whereby the consummate outsider, the "criminal," becomes the law's enforcer. To the naked eye, the situation looks as counterintuitive as anything imaginable, but when understood within the context of religious faith, much of the enigma dissipates. When seeking justice is understood as integral to one's ideology, and litigation is a means of its achievement, it should be little wonder Muslims created a rich and long-standing tradition that is still largely an unsung achievement in law. As such, their willingness to voice their grievances acted as a mirror to reflect the ongoings of prison and document some of the very worst in oppression by the state. It is a history that teaches us not just about Muslims seeking justice in the name of religion, but also about the government at its worst. The lawsuits are like journals that document the terrorism, criminality, and lawbreaking administered upon those who are in the care of the government that is supposed to be "correcting" them. Muslims flip the script and instead showcase what it is to uphold the law. They live a regulated spiritual life and pursue litigation in a way that does just that and, in the process, effectively support foundational principles of American law.

Still, it must be reiterated that just because Muslims gain a particular victory, it does not always amount to a victory for the rule of law. Even when courts favor Muslims in litigation and issue favorable rulings, it does not mean the law will be upheld. This is notable throughout several cases—where prisoner petitioners gain a small victory, only to have prison officials fail to comply. These omissions demonstrate how powerless people in prison are against their keepers and indicates the zenith of oppression. Such conduct was seen in *Holt*, where at the district court level, the plaintiff was granted an injunction to wear a half-inch beard until the court could hold an evidentiary hearing on the issue. In that hearing, he describes the trouble he faced after obtaining the injunction, which hints at the extralegal struggle individuals involved in litigation must face:

> I would also point out to you that even though there has been a restraining order in place, that I've still been subjected to harassment on the part of ADC staff at various times. In fact, being locked up in ad seg under investigation on the grounds that Major Robertson stated that I had been in the law library and had typed an order up on the law library computer. When I told him that the order was valid, he tried to state that I had forged Judge Miller's signature. Even though I was let out of the segregation several hours later, after it was determined that the order was in fact valid. Going down the hallway—I even had to go and ask Warden Warner for assistance because I would carry the order in my pocket because certain shifts weren't notified that the order was in effect and that I was allowed to wear the beard, so officers and people in positions of authority would try to harass me and threaten to lock me up for having the beard and would say they didn't care what the order said, they didn't care that—if it came from a federal judge or not, this was the Department of Correction, this wasn't the feds . . . I couldn't even go to breakfast in the morning times because I was being harassed by staff in the hallways.

Muhammad's case lends credence to the notion that the rule of law is a political fantasy, for even when the law is clearly handed down, prison staff can snatch rights away through their malicious conduct. Thus, while Muslims are champions in seeking to uphold the law in the prison context, prison officials sometimes care little about what the law says. Aside from the unsightly appearance of prison officials being lawbreakers, it also has the unsavory effect of deterring individuals from engaging in litigation and makes it such that only the most durable will be able to withstand such egregious treatment for trying to do things by the book.

Sometimes simply filing a grievance can be the basis for negative treatment by prison officials. Muslims have described the tendency of officials to retaliate against them for reporting misconduct. Retaliatory actions include searching one's prison cell without cause, which effectively means officials can tear through one's cell and turn it upside down. In addition, confiscations are common, as are threats against individuals. In one case, an individual claimed he had items taken from his cell after a search in retaliation for filing a grievance and the officers filed false charges against him.[18] The court sided with the Muslim petitioner, who was able to show enough wrongdoing on behalf of prison staff to proceed with this case.

These cases demonstrate the blatant rule-breaking and abuse of authority on behalf of prison officials. The conduct is especially egregious because it represents illegal conduct being waged on individuals trying to play by the rules. Through their conduct, prison officials are effectively stalling the ability of individuals who seek to complain through the proper legal channels. Their actions take away an individual's primary tool for righting wrongs in prison. It is conduct that amounts to another blow against the rule of law, helping to create a lawless environment character-ized by a dual dearth of justice: officers who break the law and captives who are discouraged from using it. Under such a system of supervision, justice begins to look like a faraway concept, and the rule of law is con-spicuous by its absence.

As devotees of the rule of law, Muslim litigants are cast in a role-reversal of sorts, whereby the person in prison, the convicted criminal, plays the role of law-enforcer, and the institution and its employees, the law-breakers. Muslims perform the institutional function of being watchers of the watcher, and are willing to go to great legal lengths to ensure prison officials and staff are not above the law. Although such a check on govern-ment power may be expected to come from one of the other two branches of government or, more ideally, from the executive branch itself, incarcer-ated Muslims are the ones struggling as reformatory agents. In effect, they are a constraining force on the government, which may strike some as counterintuitive—people in prison strengthening the very underpinnings of American law.

LESSONS IN RELIGIOUS STUDIES

By now it is clear that legal analysis alone is insufficient for approaching Muslim prisoner litigation. The influence of religion looms too large to be ignored and enters the discussion at multiple entry points. By carefully understanding the religious influences at each level of analysis, the reward is a better understanding of the phenomenon and a better understanding of religion. Considering religious issues involved in the legal battles provides better depth and clarity about why individuals in prison litigate, and as a bonus, we learn more about religion itself. The study of religion is enriched with greater insights about religiosity, and specifically, as expressed in the prison context.

Muslim litigation as a phenomenon behind bars feeds into religious studies debates about the nature of religion. Early religious studies theorist, Mircea Eliade, advanced a model of religion that served as the launchpad for understanding the essence of religion. In his worldview, religion revolved around the center—the "axis mundi"—that split the worlds into sacred and profane. For Eliade, "every Microcosm, every inhabited region, has a Centre; that is to say, a place that is sacred above all."[19] This vision was critiqued for being ahistorical, apolitical, and consensual.[20] Later theorists challenged Eliade's model and proceeded to show how his approach was flawed; whereas he thought he was making a history of religions, there was little by way of historical analysis, and as one religious scholar describes, "historians work with events and individuals, but individuals, real historical actors, are curiously absent in much of Eliade's work. We might say today that his paradigm lacks 'agency' and is an ahistorical paradigm."[21]

The study of Muslim prisoner litigation shows the exact opposite. Under Eliade's model, because there are no historical actors, there is no politics. However, this reasoning is flawed, for as this work has shown, the litigants and their religious motivations at times are steeped in historical or political motivations. Even the "political prisoner" concept has been exemplified in the NOI and embraced from at least the 1960s.[22] For Muslims in prison, law and politics are often a centerpiece of Muslim life. The notion that religious conversion may be a driving force of prisoner litigation demonstrates how sometimes the religious and political are inextricable. The same holds for the strict division into sacred and profane, where, in prison, both are present at once. A prison is a place of profanity, literally and figuratively, and in these hellish conditions, people live spiritual lives and engage in God's work to advance justice.

Further illustrating this political bent are groups like the NOI and Moorish Science Temple, groups often described as "nationalist" or

"separatist," which underscores the political orientation of the organization—they are followers of Islam with political aspirations. One need only
recall individuals, such as Muhammad Ali, Martin Sostre, and Mumia
Abu-Jamal, who are often viewed as political figures first and Muslims
second. In addition to the political advocacy of such individuals, since the
earliest formations Muslim groups have always expressed faith through
political practices, including Moorish Science followers, who carry nationality cards so members can proclaim their nationality as Moors.
"Nationality," according to the organization, means "belonging to a nation
or state. Nationality determines the political status of the individual, especially with reference to allegiance, while domicile determines his civil status." Similarly, the Nation of Islam has always proclaimed separatist ideals
and taken a long-standing, unabashed stance against the government's
use of prisons for political dissidents. In his *Message to the Blackman in
America,* Elijah Muhammad outlined a core set of beliefs about what the
NOI wants. Steeped in political overtures, the list includes demands for
"equal justice under the law"; "an immediate end to the police brutality
and mob attacks"; "the government of the U.S. to exempt our people from
ALL taxation as long as we are deprived of equal justice under the laws of
the land"; and perhaps most relevantly, "freedom for all Believers of Islam
now held in federal prisons. We want freedom for all black men and
women now under death sentence in innumerable prisons in the North as
well as the South."

In a similar fashion, the litigation makes it difficult to claim Muslims in
prison can be described as consensual in any meaningful way. As Eliade
stated, internal divisions of religion were reconcilable, and his model was
described as unitary: "there were no necessary conflicts, no contestations
of meaning, and religious traditions were essentially traditions of great
unity."[23] Muslims in prison tend to divide themselves along denominational lines that betray such formation. In the competing and contested
interpretations of Islam, there is often a lack of cohesion, including that
groups often splinter into subgroups due to theological and practical disagreement. This reality was reiterated in a recent letter sent by an individual
on Missouri's death row, who inquired about this book's approach to the
subject matter. In doing so, he obliterates the notion of nonconsensual and
shows that sometimes groups see themselves as deeply divided from other

groups and may disavow other denominations completely: "in your research, did you include such un-Islamic groups such as the Nation of Islam, MSTA, Five percenters, Ahmadiyyah, Shia, and the likes? Or did you just write generally—and lump everyone together?"[24] As the questions suggest, American Muslims, like those in the Middle East, can be at greater odds than simply nonconsensual—they can be in straight up opposition.

Recent litigation bears the point as another recent claim was brought in the name of Muslims wanting separate prayer space from other Muslim groups. As the complaint notes, "requiring Muslims to attend religious services led by adherents of the Nation of Islam or Five-percent Nation is akin to requiring Christians to attend religious services led by a Jewish rabbi, or Jews to attend religious services led by a Christian priest."[25] This analogy makes it clear that the characterization of religion as "consensual" is flawed, because the different denominations are often involved in an intra-faith conflict, some of which even spills over into court. In this case, the analogy is particularly revealing because it suggests that adherents attend services of an entirely different faith, despite all groups involved considering themselves as Muslim.

Muslims in prison likewise deal a blow to the idea that religion is ahistorical. Litigants believe in various foundational dates for the faith that are equally important for adherents as the historical events of the Prophet Muhammad and other biblical prophets. In the NOI, for example, the importance of Saviors' Day cannot be overstated. This is the tradition's most important gathering of the year, attracting the largest audiences of any event. For adherents, religion is not some timeless wonder trapped in the ancient world as Eliade would have it, but, rather, religion revolves around ever-evolving dates of holy birthdates, events, appearances, and disappearances that animate adherents and create newfound histories and origin stories.

Finally, the study of religious conversion is a critical piece that effectively ties religion and law together. When considering the impetus and determination that sustained these efforts over decades, it is without doubt that converts took their newfound beliefs as a springboard to dive into the world of law and politics. Muslim groups understood the appropriation of courts as a central piece of their political struggle. The fact many Muslims have ended up in court filing lawsuits is not by accident, because it is a part of a more elaborate scheme to appropriate the legal system for the advancement of civil rights. Muslim prisoner litigation is a critical legal development that advances religious study.

DECONSTRUCTING MUSLIM STEREOTYPES

The litigious nature of Muslims in prison stands opposed to narratives attempting to demonize Islam and Muslims or portray adherents as violent and a threat to institutional and national security. However, this work contends such portrayals miss the analytical mark because they misapprehend what Islam looks like to a convert. As all newcomers to Islam learn, the meaning of "Islam" is related to the same root that produces the word "salam," the Arabic word for "peace." The connection between submission and peace makes violence somewhat antithetical to one on a path of peace. Specifically, Muslim converts may be less susceptible to extremist orientations because they are in a reformation process that charts movement away from violent and chaotic lives. In the case of former gang members, this is certainly the trend. For those dedicating their lives to the faith, messaging that involves violent extremism may contradict the very core of what makes Islam attractive in the first place.

The long history of Muslims appropriating courts to deal with grievances shows that viewing Muslims as a unique force of extremism is misplaced. Instead, it shows quite the opposite—Muslims are quite content to conform to the legal system and the normal channels of complaint, which members of society are expected to employ. While Muslims have looked to the law, they traditionally have been depicted as anything but lawful. "Although the Black Muslims before 1975 preached hostile rhetoric, vilifying white America, they actually precipitated little violence."[26] Additionally, they became known as an orderly, clean-cut group who were model citizens behind bars. They were wont to partake in the deviant aspects of prison subculture, and in some riots, Muslims were known to have helped protect prison officials. As James B. Jacobs described, soon after the War on Drugs began, "Muslims became a quiescent and stabilizing force in many prisons, which began to be rocked by new cohorts of violent and disorganized ghetto youth."[27] Even though Muslims have been a positive influence on the prison environment with their disciplined regimes, aversion to drugs and alcohol, and restrictions in hygienic, sexual, and dietary habits, perhaps the most positive influence of Islam in prison is the positive impact on rehabilitation. Among other benefits to prison culture, research shows that of all religious individuals, Muslims are the least likely to recidivate, making Islamic religious programming a boon to the institution and the administration of criminal justice.

These realities of life similarly counteract dominant narratives that followed the attacks of September 11, 2001. In the years that followed, American alarmism set itself on prisons as an area ripe for violent jihadist extremism, which was just the recycling of oppression that characterized Muslim life in prison since at least the 1950s. Only now, officials were free to import Islamophobia into the prison context wholesale by superimposing fears of violent extremism on followers who were largely peaceful and content to use courts to express discontent. In addition to politicians drumming up congressional hearings on Muslims in prison based on the flimsiest evidence, federal prisons were quick to crack down on Muslim populations. Despite violence perpetrated by Muslims being the exception to the rule in the previous decade, and the government's congressional research service suggesting there was no jihadist or foreign network recruiting going on in prisons, Muslims continued to bear the brunt of harsh policies and regulations that were seemingly, but not unfamiliarly, directed at them alone.

Such were the attitudes of some in academia whose conclusions tended to portray Islam as a security issue like no other. For example, in one report produced by the Strategic Studies Institute of the US Army War College, an author notes, rather ominously, that "other breeding grounds for Islamist activists and terror groups are prisons . . ."[28] Without substantiating this claim with proof or any evidence, the piece goes on to vilify the work of Muslims in prison, stating, "we must also consider the possibility of foreign-sponsored infiltration of U.S. prisons to develop homeland terror cells . . . Today, Islamist movements are more likely to grow and emerge out of our own state or federal prisons." But why are they more likely? Are there any concrete instances of such a thing happening? More importantly, why has there not been any corroboration by researchers of this foreign-infiltration thesis? The answers to these questions show just how alarmist and extreme such views are when laid against the practical realities of American prisons.

Mainstream commentary propels similar notions about Muslims and prisons that make violent radicalization and terrorism inextricable from Islam. Whether prisons are described as "fertile soil" for jihad or breeding grounds for terror, some authors have labored to make the argument that Muslims are a unique threat to others in prison, to the good order of the prison administration, and even to the security of the country. As time has shown, however, the ominous tidings have yet to manifest. Although these messages are becoming dated at a rapid rate, it hardly means they have not damaged Muslims inside and outside of prison. As we have seen, the language and attitudes found in C. Eric Lincoln's study of the NOI became the fuel to oppress members of that very group as well as Muslims from other denominations, the likes of which still inform prison administration attitudes toward Muslims. Unfortunately, such attitudes toward Muslims have been the basis for signaling out Muslims for harsher treatment and increased surveillance. These misinformed practices create the oppressive conditions that trigger the very litigation discussed throughout this book. Thus, the bad political press, the shoddy scholarship, and the bad writings contribute to a climate of fear of Muslims in prison, despite that, empirically, time has called their bluff.

Far-right commentary moves beyond the physical threats and depicts the work of Muslims in court as something far more sinister. Some have employed the term "litigation jihad" or "lawfare" to describe the use of litigation as a weapon to overthrow or instill the American legal system with sharia law.[29] While these terms may have some validity, in these instances, they are disparaging terms intended to delegitimize litigation. This version of jihad suggests that litigation is a means for frivolous or harassment suits, despite that in prison, the claims often involve deeply held religious beliefs and practices. In the most extreme cases, a lawsuit can mean the difference between life and death. Muslims have indeed struggled against their treatment in the classical sense of jihad; however, the turn to litigation has been largely defensive—to protect people in prison—rather than as an offensive strategy to undermine the legal system.

Rather than fulfill these doomsday prophecies, incarcerated Muslims continue fighting for rights in prison. Collectively, they continue nudging prisons closer to the Constitution and place their faith in the process of using courts to settle grievances. Rather than attempt to influence their environment through physical action, Muslims undermine this alarmist call and instead bring their actions to court. This unsung tradition is remarkable in the annals of prison history and shows Muslims being upright and lawful in dissent.

TOWARD GREATER JUSTICE

Muslim prisoner litigation is a phenomenon that definitively advances the rule of law. Such a finding naturally leads to the consideration of how such litigation efforts may be further supported. If the rule of law is to be meaningful, it must apply to all, including those behind bars. In practical terms, this point means establishing and enforcing the rights of people in prison and holding prisons accountable to the law and their own rules. Because incarcerated Muslims proved effective at expanding the rule of law through litigation, there should be increased support to continue this important work. There are practical measures that can help ensure that all legitimate claims get their day in court.

It is somewhat astonishing that despite the positive associations between Islam and rehabilitation, prisons remain intent on placing high bars for Muslims to practice religion freely. As court opinions detail, Muslim litigants have been in a perpetual struggle for the right to practice religion as freely as those of other religious traditions. This situation is unfortunate because one would hope prison administrators would understand the benefits of religious freedom and recognize religious programming and other opportunities are convergent with penal goals. Moreover, rather than clamp down on the practice of religion, prisons would do better to understand individuals who take up Islam behind bars contribute to a more orderly institution and are less likely to recidivate. It makes little sense that so many penal institutions persecuted Muslims for so many years on these counts alone.

Of course, one of the greatest remedies to fight recidivism is education, which can function as an important means of supporting Muslim prisoner litigation. Unfortunately, people in most jails and prisons were legislatively banned from receiving Pell Grant funding for education in the mid-1990s. When this ban occurred, postsecondary opportunities behind bars were effectively wiped away, and only a handful of programs were left behind, which relied on private funding and volunteers. Education is a critical tool for supporting the work of the jailhouse lawyer as well. Such lawyers are an important pathway to getting one's day in court, but these individuals are often untrained and lack basic skills of practice and knowledge of procedure. Unfortunately, their help, as deficient as it might be by professional lawyer standards, could be the very best aid one can obtain behind bars. There is much that could be done to increase the quality of education and the training of individuals who render this type of aid in prison. Now that Pell grants have been restored to people in prison, it is important to assist those who qualify for Pell Grant funding and assisting programs and other directives to set up services in prison. The reinstatement of Pell Grant funding is a tremendous opportunity to help rehabilitate individuals, but it also contributes to the institution's intellectual culture and orderliness. The boon of Pell Grant funding directly supports prison litigation because individuals can major in subjects such as pre-law, legal studies, and vocational paths such as paralegal training and legal certificate training. These degrees and vocational skills would directly support litigation efforts and contribute to employment prospects for reentry.

Another avenue to enhance the scope and quality of legal representation is for more law schools and lawyers to provide legal services for those incarcerated. At this intersection is a glaring interest convergence, where greater skills training is emphasized in law when the United States happens to be the world leader in incarceration. Perhaps more than any other demographic group, people in prison lack legal aid. The union of law students, lawyers, and law schools can produce a multiple-win situation—incarcerated people get badly needed legal assistance, students get legal experience, law schools fulfill accreditation requirements and missionary goals, and lawyers fulfill ethical duties to provide pro bono services. Hence, for law schools, particularly those seeking to create more experiential learning opportunities for students or those whose mission is embedded in social justice paradigms, such a program that connects students to people in prison aligns with and would fortify litigation efforts. The practical result of such skills training is students can assist among the most indigent and least educated segments in American society. In addition to law school faculty, such work could be overseen in internship/externship by other legal professionals, including those sponsored by corporate firms aiming to fulfill pro bono goals. This tremendous legal gap experienced by those behind bars is one that law schools, law students, and lawyers can help to shrink.

Using law school students and resources to assist those incarcerated is also in accord with lawyer ethics and the notion that a lawyer is a steward of justice. Unfortunately, legislation like the PLRA makes prison-based litigation a losing bet for lawyers: the odds are stacked against prisoner-petitioners, and there is little financial incentive for lawyers to take on cases. For students, however, the cost-benefit balancing is different: their job is to learn practice readiness. The work and ideas fit together well because by assisting incarcerated individuals, who are deeply entrenched in litigation efforts, they are also helping to advance justice. The American Bar Association, which accredits law schools and sets education requirements, overwhelmingly supports law students and schools working together to provide greater opportunities for students and the bar to serve those in prison. For example, in a recently passed resolution, the Association urged "bar associations, law schools and other stakeholders to develop and increase educational initiatives, clinics, and other experiential courses through which law students provide legal assistance to pretrial detainees, immigration detainees, and incarcerated individuals reentering society."[30]

This work cannot rest without reiteration of what mootness and transfer represent in the world of prison litigation. With this doctrine, prison officials can effectively avoid having to answer to litigation because, by their use of transfers, they can effectively render a claim moot and kill class action lawsuits before they can take root.[31] Even though the prison can turn around and continue to engage in the very same practices that led to the lawsuit, the individual who experienced them can be involuntarily transferred to a different facility and never see justice for the mistreatment. The ability to transfer is thus an awesome power that allows prison staff to engage in unlawful conduct with impunity. To appreciate this power fully from the incarcerated perspective is difficult, particularly because prior to getting a case to court, the prisoner-petitioner has already jumped through an array of administrative hoops and PLRA hurdles. Prison can make all these legal efforts null and void by simply transferring the individual, thereby causing legitimate claims to vanish and never be adjudicated in a court of law, regardless of how miserable prison staff made an individual's life.

When fused with the ability to transfer unchecked, this doctrine subverts the entire notion of getting one's day in court. Because getting one's day in court is a core principle of the rule of law, the mootness doctrine must be scaled back from the court's repertoire in the correctional context. Equally so, transfer policies must require greater accountability than at present. At minimum, prisons should be prohibited from transferring one who has a live and pending case in court. This seems to be a simple solution that could alleviate a lot of suffering and a total undermining of the notion that no one is above the law. It would also remove a huge deterrent to individuals filing claims in the first place, because they would at least be guaranteed that their case will be heard. At the very least, a prison should be forced to show cause to obtain court approval before transferring such an individual. Otherwise, unrestricted transferring simply dooms individuals in the future to suffer unlawful harm, which is never addressed.

In addition to these issues, when incarcerated individuals must transfer involuntarily, there can be tremendous disruptive impacts on a person's life. It is not easy for one transferred to continue receiving mail, medication, counseling, therapy, or other needs. These may all become compromised when one is forced to get up and move at the whim of a prison's administration that knows all too well how this doctrine functions in court. This is a cumbersome edict, especially when one has litigation pending because court documents must follow the transfer, which creates the distinct possibility of delayed responses or losing mail, ultimately weakening one's case.

More ominous than these considerations is the genuine rupture in the life and rehabilitation potential for the transferee. A transfer often means the end of relatives, friends, or other existing support systems to visit and stay in physical communication. Family members and friends who were once able to see their children may be disenfranchised from this basic opportunity, which indirectly forces these people to pay for the draconian measures of the administration—decisions that may be premised on the prison's wrongdoing in the first place. Moreover, the transferee will have to establish himself in a new prison environment and start in a new place all over again. Whatever friendships were forged, jobs held, and goodwill established with staff is all made to vanish. Such a rupture in routine, including educational and religious programming, is erased. Furthermore, one is made to become the new kid on the cellblock, a change that represents a tremendous strain on an individual's psyche—the very individual who suffered at the hands of prison officials to the point of filing a claim. The situation lends the impression that a transfer is a de facto punishment for filing a lawsuit.

Of course, even with the resolution of these looming obstacles, it is still a huge uphill battle for individuals in prison to seek justice due to the strictures put in place by the PLRA. As this act was intentionally designed to stem court filings by people in prison, it increased fees, decreased attorneys' fees, limited the number of filings, and limited damages. Within the first two years of its enactment, there was a steep decline in both filing and filing rates, and after sixteen years, the number of filings would shrink by 60 percent.[32] This piece of legislation stands as another formidable hurdle that effectively ensures some genuine grievances will never be heard in a court of law. This sentiment was expressed by one individual incarcerated in Missouri, who had a claim for denial of religious rights, which was dismissed on summary judgment. He writes, "I could have probably won on appeal but because of the Prison Litigation Reform Act, I couldn't afford it."[33] This legislation affords less protection to the people who need it most and, as a result, diminishes both justice and the rule of law.

While this work is a litany of the mistreatment of people in prison, reform of this practice should rank high in criminal justice priorities. In the present era of Black Lives Matter, which has forced greater attention on law enforcement and police practices on the street, the moment is opportune to consider the police of prison. In comparison to what happens in prison, what happens on the street is merely the tip of the proverbial iceberg. Like police on the outside, those inside are shielded by qualified immunity, which allows them to engage in all sorts of wrongdoing without ever facing judgment.

Although the mootness doctrine proclaims a bleak outlook for prisoner litigation, it says a lot more. Studies have long shown most prison-based civil rights suits are dismissed in the early stages of litigation.[34] The moot-ness doctrine, more specifically, admits another means by which claims by people in prison have been muted. More gravely, it means we are not get-ting the whole story when it comes to the oppression of Muslims in prison. Indeed, while the opinions studied in this book are important cases in prison-law jurisprudence, many of the claims in appellate rulings are con-spicuously absent because they have succumbed to the mootness doctrine by a prison transfer. The outsider perspective invites us to recognize that this doctrine has silenced a world of claims about prison officials, prison policies, and the abuse of those incarcerated. If mootness endures, the notion of justice will continue to ring hollow for those who experience injustice behind bars, only to be bested by the injustice of having no recourse in court.

Notes

INTRODUCTION

Epigraph: James B. Jacobs, "Stratification and Conflict among Prison Inmates," *Journal of Criminal Law and Criminology* 66, no. 4 (1976): 476.

1. Spencer Ackerman, "Peter King Pioneered the Persecution of American Muslims," *Daily Beast*, November 12, 2019, https://www.thedailybeast.com/peter-king-pioneered-the-persecution-of-american-muslims.

2. Donna E. Arzi, "The Role of Compulsion in Islamic Conversion: Jihad, Dhimma, and Ridda," *Buffalo Human Rights Law Review* 8 (2002): 15–44.

3. Christopher Smith, "Black Muslims and the Development of Prisoners' Rights," *Journal of Black Studies* 24, no. 2 (1993): 139.

4. United States Commission on Civil Rights, *Enforcing Religious Freedom in Prison*, ed. Quentin Willems (U.S. Commission on Civil Rights, 2008), 70.

5. Archive of Muhammad Speaks, *Muhammad Speaks*, no. 30, April 14, 1967, 6.

6. "The Most Remarkable Revelatory Letter Ever Written by Malcolm X," Moments in Time, accessed August 6, 2022, https://momentsintime.com/the-most-remarkable-revelatory-letter-ever-written-by-malcolm-x/#.YR0awy1h0TZ.

7. Quran 49:13.

8. Quran 30:22.

9. Sunan al-Tirmidhi, *Book of Tafsir of the Quran*, vol. 5, Hadith 2955.

10. Musnad Aḥmad, *Book of Tafsir of the Quran,* vol. 5, Hadith 2297.

11. Vincent Copeland, *The Crime of Martin Sostre* (McGraw-Hill, 1970), 127.

12. Kenneth B. Clark, "Malcolm X talks with Kenneth B. Clark," in *The Negro Protest: James Baldwin, Malcolm X and Martin Luther King Talk with Kenneth B. Clark* (Beacon Press, 1963), 22.

13. Khaled A. Beydoun, "Islam Incarcerated: Religious Accommodation of Muslim Prisoners before Holt v. Hobbs," *University of Cincinnati Law Review* 84, no. 1 (2018): 105.

1. AT THE INTERSECTION OF RELIGION AND PUNISHMENT

1. Cantwell v. Connecticut, 310 U.S. 296 (1940) (Free Exercise); Everson v. Board of Education, 330 U.S. 1 (1947) (Establishment Clause).

2. Muslim Advocates, "Fulfilling the Promise of Free Exercise for All: Muslim Prisoner Accommodation in State Prisons," July 2019, https://muslimadvocates .org/wp-content/uploads/2019/07/FULFILLING-THE-PROMISE-OF-FREE-EXERCISE-FOR-ALL-Muslim-Prisoner-Accommodation-In-State-Prisons-for-distribution-7_23.pdf.

3. These individuals were contacted and solicited for their thoughts on litigation. Forty individuals were initially contacted, with approximately one quarter responding and offering responses and further commentary.

4. Clair A. Cripe, Proceedings of the 106th Annual Congress of Corrections, Denver, August 22–26, 1976 (American Corrections Association, 1977), 25.

5. Felecia Dix-Richardson and Billy R. Close, "Intersections of Race, Religion, and Inmate Culture: The Historical Development of Islam in American Corrections," *Journal of Offender Rehabilitation* 35 (2002): 97.

6. Kathleen Moore, "The Case for Muslim Constitutional Interpretive Activity," *American Journal of Islamic Social Sciences* 7 (1990): 69.

7. Cooper v. Pate, 378 U.S. 546 (1964) (holding that the lower court erroneously dismissed prisoner-petitioner's claim, which stated a viable cause of action).

8. Garrett Felber, *Those Who Know Don't Say: The Nation of Islam, the Black Freedom Movement, and the Carceral State* (University of North Carolina Press, 2019).

9. *Enforcing Religious Freedom in Prison,* ed. Quentin Willems (Nova Science Publishers, 2010), 20.

10. Ibid, 70.

11. Ibid, 12.

12. Dan Berger, *Captive Nation: Black Prison Organizing in the Civil Rights Era* (University of North Carolina Press, 2014), 264.

13. Siraj Islam Mufti, "Islam in American Prisons," Umma Forum, December 14, 2006, http://www.ummah.com/forum/showthread.php?106570-Islam-in-American-Prisons.

14. Karl Marx, "Introduction: A Contribution to the Critique of Hegel's Philosophy of Right," *Deutsch-Französische Jahrbücher* (1844).

15. Felicia Miyakawa, *Five Percenter Rap: God Hop's Music, Message, and Black Muslim's Mission* (Indiana University Press, 2005), 31.

16. Edward E. Curtis, IV, *Islam in Black America: Identity, Liberation, and Difference in African-American Islamic Thought* (State University of New York Press, 2002), 6.

17. Herbert Berg, *Elijah Muhamad and Islam* (New York University Press, 2009), 106.

18. Harry R. Dammer, "Piety in Prison: An Ethnography of Religion in the Correctional Environment" (PhD diss., Rutgers University, 1992), 23.

19. For further reading, see Khaled Beydoun, *American Islamophobia Understanding the Roots and Rise of Fear* (University of California Press, 2018); Todd Green, *The Fear of Islam: An Introduction to Islamophobia in the West*, 2nd ed. (Fortress Press, 2019).

20. Dan Berger and Toussaint Losier, *Rethinking the American Prison Movement* (Routledge, 2017), 53.

21. Jim Thomas and Barbara H. Zaitzow, "Conning or Conversion? The Role of Religion in Prison Coping," *Prison Journal* 86, no. 2 (2006): 242.

22. William James, *The Varieties of Religious Experience* (University Books, Inc., 1963), 196.

23. Rudolf Otto, *The Idea of the Holy: An Inquiry in the Non-rational Factor in the Idea of the Divine and its Relation to the Rational*, trans. John W. Harvey (Oxford University Press, 1917), 12.

24. Ibid, 18.

25. Karl F. Morrison, *Understanding Conversion* (University Press of Virginia, 1992), xvi.

26. Todd R. Clear et al., "The Value of Religion in Prison," *Journal of Contemporary Sociology* 16, no. 1 (2000): 53–74.

27. Malcolm X, *The Autobiography of Malcolm X* (Grove Press, 1965), 190.

28. Berger and Losier, *Rethinking the American Prison Movement*, 60.

29. Sahar Aziz, "'Whosoever Sees an Evil:' Muslim Americans' Human Rights Advocacy," *Oxford Encyclopedia of Religion* (2020), 10.

30. Margaret Moore Jackson, "Confronting 'Unwelcomeness' from the Outside: Using Case Theory to Tell the Stories of Sexually-Harassed Women," *Cardozo Journal of Law & Gender,* 14 (2007): 79.

31. Richard Delgado, "The Inward Turn in Outsider Jurisprudence," *William & Mary Law Review,* 34 (1993): 744.

32. Ediberto Roman, "Afterword: LatCrit VI, Outsider Jurisprudence and Looing Beyond Imagined Borders," *Florida Law Review* 55, no. 1 (2003): 583 (describing LatCrit as "an experiment of outsider scholarship.")

33. William J. Aceves, "Critical Jurisprudence and International Legal Scholarship: A Study of Equitable Distribution," *Columbia Journal of Transnational Law* 39, no. 2 (2001): 299–394.

34. Olympia Duhart, "Soldier Suicides and OutCrit Jurisprudence: An Anti-Subordination Analysis," *Creighton Law Review* 44 (2011): 893.

35. Francisco Valdes, "Outsider Jurisprudence, Critical Pedagogy, and Social Activism: Marking the Stirrings of Critical Legal Education," *Asian American Law Journal,* 10, no. 65 (2003): 66–67.

36. Felber, *Those Who Know Don't Say,* 5.

37. Garrett Felber, "'Shades of Mississippi': The Nation of Islam's Prison Organizing, the Carceral State, and the Black Freedom Struggle," *Journal of American History,* 105, no. 1 (2018): 73.

38. Jackson "Confronting 'Unwelcomeness' from the Outside," 79.

39. Shulamit Almog, "As I Read, I Weep: In Praise of Judicial Narrative," *Oklahoma City University Law Review,* 26, no. 2 (2007): 488.

40. James Davison Hunter et al., *Is There a Culture War?: A Dialogue on Values and American Public Life* (Brookings Institution Press, 2006).

41. Timothy Marr, *The Cultural Roots of American Islamicism* (Cambridge University Press, 2006).

42. Herbert Berg, *Elijah Muhamad and Islam* (New York University Press, 2009), 12.

43. Ibid, 13.

44. Carlo A. Pedrioli, "Constructing the Other: U.S. Muslims, Anti-Sharia Law, and the Constitutional Consequences of Volatile Intercultural Rhetoric," *Southern California Interdisciplinary Law Journal,* 22 (2012): 66–67.

45. Richard Delgado, "Storytelling for Oppositionists and Others: A Plea for Narrative," *Michigan Law Review* 87, no. 8 (1989): 2412.

2. ISLAM IN AMERICAN PRISONS

1. A. J. Willingham, "By 2040, Islam Could Be the Second Biggest Religion in the US," CNN, January 10, 2018, https://www.cnn.com/2018/01/10/politics/muslim-population-growth-second-religious-group-trnd/index.html#:~:text = The%20Muslim%20population%20is%20growing,to%20a%20Pew%20Research%20study.

2. Claude Andrew Clegg, III, *An Original Man: The Life and Times of Elijah Muhammad* (University of North Carolina Press, 1997), 107.

3. Clegg, III, *An Original Man,* 107.

4. Clegg, III, *An Original Man*, 98.

5. Malachi D. Crawford, *Black Muslims and the Law: From Civil Liberties from Elijah Muhammad to Muhammad Ali* (Lexington Books, 2015), 144.

6. Manning Marable, *Malcolm X: A Life of Reinvention* (Penguin Books, 2011), 94.

7. Malcolm X and Alex Haley, *The Autobiography of Malcolm X* (Random House Publishing Group, 2015), 176.

8. Ibid, 173.

9. Dannin, Robert, "Island in a Sea of Ignorance: Dimensions of the Prison Mosque," in *Making Muslim Space in North America and Europe*, ed. Barbara Daly Metcalf (University of California Press, 1996), 139–140.

10. Warfare History Network, "Vietnam War: Muhammad Ali's Draft Controversy," *National Interest*, January 12, 2021, https://web.archive.org/web/20210117132706/https://nationalinterest.org/blog/reboot/vietnam-war-muhammad-alis-draft-controversy-176177.

11. Clay v. United States, 397 F.2d 901 (5th Cir. 1968).

12. Zoe Colley, "'All America Is a Prison:' The Nation of Islam and the Politicization of African American Prisoners 1955–65," *Journal of American Studies.*, 48, no. 2 (2014): 401.

13. C. Eric Lincoln, *The Black Muslims in America* (Beacon Press, 1973), 84.

14. Archive of Muhammad Speaks, *Muhammad Speaks*, no. 26, March 17, 1967, 6.

15. Hamid Reza Kusha, *Islam in American Prisons: Black Muslims' Challenge to American Penology* (Taylor & Francis, 2009), 146.

16. Archive of Muhammad Speaks, *Muhammad Speaks*, 11, no. 28, March 24, 1972.

17. "Muslims in American Prisons Face Battles to Practice Religion: Courts Offer Insight for Peaceful Facilities," *Corrections Professional* (2005): 10.

18. Jane I. Smith, *Islam in America* (Columbia University Press 1999), 165.

19. Michael Waller, *Terrorist Recruitment and Infiltration in the United States: Prisons and Military as an Operational Base*, Testimony before the Subcommittee On Terrorism, Technology and Homeland Security of the S. Committee on the Judiciary, 108th Cong., 2003.

20. Office of the Inspector General, Department of Justice, "A Review of the Federal Bureau of Prisons' Selection of Muslim Religious Services Providers," *Department of Justice* (2004), http://www.justice.gov/oig/special/0404/final.pdf.

21. Asma Gull Hasan, *American Muslims: The New Generation* (Bloomsbury Academic, 2000), 75.

22. Sulayman S. Nyang, *Islam in the United States of America* (ABC International Group, 1999).

23. US Congress, Senate, *Committee on Intelligence of the United States Senate*, 108th Cong. (2005) (Robert S. Mueller, III, Director, Federal Bureau of Investigation).

24. Hasan, *American Muslims*, 76.

25. James Baldwin, *The Fire Next Time* (Taschen, 1963), 51.

26. James B. Jacobs, *Stateville: The Penitentiary in Mass Society* (University of Chicago Press, 2015), 63.

27. Nathan McCall, *Makes Me Wanna Holler: A Young Black Man in America* (Random House, 1994), 209.

28. Tupac Amaru Shakur, "I Ain't Mad at Cha," track 13 on *All Eyez on Me*, Death Row Records, 1996, compact disc.

29. *Islam in America*, Christian Science Publications, 1991–1992, Videocassette documentary.

30. Berger, *Captive Nation*, 57.

31. C. Eric Lincoln, *The Black Muslims in America* (Beacon Press, 1973), 120.

32. Muslim Advocates, "Fulfilling the Promise of Free Exercise for All."

33. Dannin, "Island in a Sea of Ignorance," 139–140.

34. Robert Dannin, *Black Pilgrimage to Islam* (Oxford University Press, 2002), 176.

35. Jacobs, *Stateville*, 60.

36. Berger, *Captive Nation*, 264.

37. Rodney Stark, "Why Religious Movements Succeed or Fail: A Revised General Model," *Journal of Contemporary Religion*, 11 (1996): 133.

38. Dannin, *Black Pilgrimage to Islam*, 176.

39. Archive of Muhammad Speaks, *Muhammad Speaks*, 6, no. 16, January 6, 1967.

40. Archive of Muhammad Speaks, *Muhammad Speaks* 5, no. 23, February 25, 1966.

41. Todd R. Clear et al., "The Value of Religion in Prison," *Journal of Contemporary Sociology* 16, no. 1. (2000): 53–74.

42. Hearns v. Terhune, No. 02–56302, 2005 U.S. App. Lexis 13034 (9th Cir. 2005) (wherein a Muslim man alleged adequately that prison officials knew of a threat to him from other Muslims in prison).

43. Other cases were precursors to the *Cooper* decision, which laid the groundwork for that decision—for example, Pierce v. La Vallee, 293 F.2d 233 (2nd Cir. 1961); In Re Furguson, 55 Cal.2d 663 (Cal. 1961); Sewell v. Pegelow, 291 F.2d 196 (4th Cir. 1961); Fulwood v. Clemmer, 206 F.Supp. 370 (D.C.D.C. 1962).

44. Toussaint Losier. ". . . For Strictly Religious Reason[s]: Cooper v. Pate and the Origins of the Prisoners' Rights Movement," *Souls* 15, no. 1–2 (2013): 28.

45. Cooper v. Pate, 382 F.2d 518 (7th Cir. 1967).

46. SpearIt, "Muslim Radicalization in Prison: Responding with Sound Penal Policy or the Sound of Alarm?," *Gonzaga Law Review* 49 (2014): 37.

47. From individual in Florida State Prison, letter to author.

48. From individual in New York State Prison, letter to author.

49. From individual in Georgia State Prison, letter to author.

50. Howard v. Foster, 208 F Supp.3d 1152 (D.Nev. 2016).

51. Ibid.

52. Archive of Muhammad Speaks, *Muhammad Speaks,* 1, no. 3, January 1962.

53. John X, "Muhammad Subject of Wide Press Coverage," *Muhammad Speaks* (1960): 10.

54. Ibid. The word *"adl"* is the prominent term that is translated as "justice," which in the Islamic context may be to straighten, sit straight, to amend or modify, to run away, depart or deflect from the wrong to the right path, to be equal or equivalent, to be equal or to equalize, to balance or counterbalance or to be in a state of equilibrium; see Majid Khadduri, *The Islamic Conception of Justice* (Johns Hopkins University Press, 1984); Tufail Ahmad Qureshi, "Justice In Islam," *Islamic Studies* 21, no. 2 (1982): 37 (analyzing Quranic justice as containing four components: Equality, Moderation, Trust, Solidarity).

55. Quran 4:36.

56. Quran 2:83; 4:36; 6:151; and 17:23.

57. Quran 4:135.

58. Quran 4:75–76.

59. Quran 16:90.

60. Khalid Bin Ismail, "Islam and the Concept of Justice," *Centre for Islamic Thought and Understanding,* https://ir.uitm.edu.my/id/eprint/32047/1/32047 .pdf.

61. The word *fitra* describes the state of purity in which humans are born, which is innate submission to God.

62. Surat al-Rum 30:22.

63. Ahmad Hasan, "Social Justice in Islam," *Islamic Studies* 10, no. 3 (1971): 209; Ahmad Zaki Yamani, "Social Justice in Islam," *Islamic Studies* 41, no. 1 (2002): 5 (outlining the Western concept of "justice" and its alignment with Islamic ideals that are advanced by the words *Adl, Qist,* and *Taswiyah*); Sumanto Al Qurtuby, "The Islamic Roots of Liberation, Justice, and Peace: An Anthropocentric Analysis of the Concept of Tawhid," *Islamic Studies* 52, no. 3–4 (2013): 297.

64. Ismail, "Islam and the Concept of Justice."

65. Amal Qutb, Nazir Khan, and Mahdi Qasqas., "Islam and Social Justice," in *Spirituality and Social Justice,* eds. Norma Jean Profitt and Cyndy Baskin (Canadian Scholars' Press, 2019), 131.

66. Imam Omar Suleiman, "How Can We Make It Right? What the World's Religions Have to Say about Justice," interview by Carol Juruvilla, *Vox* (2021), https://www.vox.com/the-highlight/22419487/religion-justice-fairness.

67. Farouk Peru, "A Muslim on the Idea of Protest," Muslim Institute, accessed August 22, 2022, https://musliminstitute.org/freethinking/culture/muslim-idea-protest.

68. From individual in Missouri State Prison, letter to author.

69. Sahar Aziz, "'Whosoever Sees an Evil:' Muslim Americans' Human Rights Advocacy," *Oxford Encyclopedia on Religion* (2020), 3.

70. Imam Nawawi, *A Translation and Commentary of Riyad Al-Salihin*, vol. 1, Hadith 1–601, trans. and ed. Moulana Afzal Ismail (Muslims at Work Publications, 2015), 259.

71. Aziz, "Whosoever Sees an Evil," 4.

72. Crawford, *Black Muslims and the Law*, 67.

73. Archive of Muhammad Speaks, *Mr. Muhammad Speaks* 1, May 1960; *Muhammad Speaks*, no. 1, December 1961, 2. (The first few editions were called "Mr. Muhammad Speaks," but then it was revised to Muhammad Speaks.)

74. Archive of Muhammad Speaks, *Muhammad Speaks* 10, no. 22 February 12, 1971.

75. Archive of Muhammad Speaks, *Muhammad Speaks* 1, no. 3, January 1962.

76. Archive of Muhammad Speaks, *Muhammad Speaks* 7, no. 5, October 20, 1967.

77. Malcom X and Alex Haley, *The Autobiography of Malcolm X (As Told to Alex Haley)* (Ballantine Books, 1992): 188.

78. Ibid., 214.

3. THE STRUGGLE TO BE RECOGNIZED BY PRISONS

Epigraph: James B. Jacobs, *Stateville: The Penitentiary in Mass Society* (University of Chicago Press, 2015), 59.

1. Losier, " . . . For Strictly Religious Reason[s]," 19.

2. "Report 12 Bar Robberies and Murder Solved," *Chicago Daily Tribune* August 29, 1952, 16.

3. "2 Killings Bring 200 year Terms for 2 Robbers," *Chicago Daily Tribune*, January 20, 1953, 4.

4. Christopher Wildeman, "Incarceration and Population Health in Wealthy Democracies," *Criminology* 54, no. 2 (2016): 360.

5. Losier, " . . . For Strictly Religious Reason[s]," 28.

6. Ibid.

7. Joseph T. Hallinan, *Going up the River: Travels in a Prison Nation*, (Random House Trade Paperbacks, 2003), 27.

8. James F. Anderson, Nancie J. Mangels, and Laronistine Dyson, *Significant Prisoner Rights Cases* (Carolina Academic Press, 2010), xiv.

9. Cooper v. Pate, 378 U.S. 546 (1964).

10. Archive of Muhammad Speaks, *Muhammad Speaks* 6, no. 48, August 18, 1967.

11. "Black Muslims in Prison: Of Muslim Rites and Constitutional Rights," *Columbia Law Review* 62, no. 8 (1962): 1490.

12. Cooper v. Pate, 324 F.2d 165 (1963).

13. Cooper v. Pate, 382 F.2d 518 (7th Cir. 1967).

14. Joseph Shapiro, "How One Inmate Changed the Prison System from the Inside," *NPR*, April 14, 2017, https://www.npr.org/sections/codeswitch/2017/04/14/507297469/how-one-inmate-changed-the-prison-system-from-the-inside.

15. Jacobs, *Stateville*, 9.

16. Kathleen M. Moore, *Al-Mughtaribun: American Law and the Transformation of Muslim Life in the United States* (State University of New York Press. 1995), 70.

17. Anderson, Mangels, and Dyson, *Significant Prisoner Rights Cases*, xiv.

18. James B. Jacobs, "The Prisoners' Rights Movement and its Impacts, 1960–80," *Crime & Justice* 2 (1980): 434.

19. John L. Fliter, *Prisoners' Rights: The Supreme Court and Evolving Standards of Decency* (Greenwood Press, 2001), 81.

20. Dan Berger and Toussaint Losier, *Rethinking the American Prison Movement* (Routledge, 2017), 67.

21. Hallinan, *Going up the River*, 28.

22. Fliter, *Prisoners' Rights*, 81 (this figure would be drastically reduced to twenty-two thousand by 2016 due to the enactment of the PLRA).

23. Dulcey A. Brown, "Black Muslim Prisoners and Religious Discrimination: The Developing Criteria for Judicial Review," *George Washington Law Review* 32, no. 5 (1964): 1130.

24. State of California Department of Corrections, *Special Procedures for Muslim Inmates*, Administrative Bulletin no. 58/16. (February 25, 1958).

25. Felber, *Those Who Know Don't Say*, 57.

26. Felecia Dix-Richardson and Billy R. Close, "Intersections of Race, Religion, and Inmate Culture: The Historical Development of Islam in American Corrections," *Journal of Offender Rehabilitation* 35, nos. 3–4 (2002), 90.

27. Jacobs, *Stateville*, 107.

28. Margaret Moore Jackson, "Confronting 'Unwelcomeness' from the Outside: Using Case Theory to Tell the Stories of Sexually-Harassed Women," *Cardozo Journal of Law and Gender* 14 (2007): 78–79.

29. Pierce v. La Vallee, 293 F.2d 233 (1961).

30. Adam Daniel Morrison, "Religious Legitimacy and the Nation of Islam: In Re Ferguson and Muslim Inmates' Religious Rights in the 1950s and 1960s" (master's thesis, University of California Santa Barbara, 2013): 3.

31. Morrison, "Religious Legitimacy and the Nation of Islam," 3.

32. Morrison, "Religious Legitimacy and the Nation of Islam," 4.

33. Sewell v. Pegelow, 291 F.2d 196 (4th Cir. 1961).

34. Muslim Advocates, "Fulfilling the Promise of Free Exercise for All."

35. Sewell v. Pegelow, 291 F.2d 196 (4th Cir. 1961).

36. Ibid.

37. Ibid.

38. Fulwood v. Clemmer, 206 F. Supp. 370, 374 (D.C. Cir. 1962).

39. Ibid.

40. Ibid.

41. Cruz v. Beto, 405 U.S. 319 (1972).

42. Crawford, *Black Muslims and the Law*, xi.

43. Ibid., 66, 91.

44. From individual in Florida State Prison, letter to author.

45. Garrett Felber, "'Shades of Mississippi': The Nation of Islam's Prison Organizing, the Carceral State, and the Black Freedom Struggle," *Journal of American History*, 105, no. 1 (2018): 81.

46. Lincoln, *The Black Muslims in America*, 26.

47. Coward v. Robinson, No. 1:2010cv00147—Document 248 (E.D. Va. 2017).

48. Warren L. Schaich and Diane S. Hope, "The Prison Letters of Martin Sostre: Documents of Resistance," *Journal of Black Studies* 7, no. 3 (1977): 290.

49. Shapiro, "How One Inmate Changed the Prison System from the Inside."

50. Berger and Losier, *Rethinking the American Prison Movement*, 63.

51. Copeland, *The Crime of Martin Sostre*, 125.

52. "Black Muslims in Prison," *Columbia Law Review*, 1492.

53. Lincoln, *The Black Muslims in America*, 193.

54. Pierce v. LaVallee, 212 F. Supp. 865 (N.D.N.Y. 1962).

55. Shapiro, "How One Inmate Changed the Prison System from the Inside."

56. Malcolm McLaughlin, "Storefront Revolutionary: Martin Sostre's Afro-Asian Bookshop, Black Liberation Culture, and the New Left, 1964–75," *The Sixties: A Journal of History, Politics, and Culture* 7, no. 1 (2014): 1.

57. Ibid.

58. Martin Sostre, "The New Prisoner," *North Carolina Central Law Review* 4, no. 2 (1973): 251.

59. Berger and Losier, *Rethinking the American Prison Movement*, 63.

60. Shapiro, "How One Inmate Changed the Prison System from the Inside."

61. Sostre v. Rockefeller, 312 F. Supp. 863 (S.D. N.Y. 1970).

62. Sostre v. Otis, 330 F. Supp. 941 (S.D. N.Y. 1971).

63. Gerald J. Gross, "The Case of Martin Sostre," *New York Review*. March 23, 1972,http://www.nybooks.com/articles/archives/1972/mar/23/the-case-of-martin-sostre/.

64. Shapiro, "How One Inmate Changed the Prison System from the Inside."

65. Copeland, *The Crime of Martin Sostre*, 127.

66. Jacobs, *Stateville*, 59.

67. This push for civil rights was another major wave in the history of civil rights advocacy. Thttps://www.npr.org/sections/codeswitch/2017/04/14/507297469/how-one-inmate-changed-the-prison-system-from-the-insidehe first wave of civil rights victories resulted from the Civil War and the postwar implementation of the Thirteenth, Fourteenth, and Fifteenth Amendments.

68. Berger and Losier, *Rethinking the American Prison Movement*, 59.

69. Jacobs, *Stateville*, 59.

70. Davis v. Beason, 133 U.S. 333 (1890).

71. Church of the Holy Trinity v. United States, 143 U.S. 457, 471 (1892).

72. Davis v. Beason, 133 U.S. 333, 345–48 (1890); United States v. Macintosh, 283 U.S. 605, 633–34 (1931).

73. United States v. Ballard, 322 U.S. 69–70, 78, 86–87 (1944); Witmer v. United States, 75 S.Ct. 392 (1955).

74. United States v. Kauten, 133 F.2d 703 (2d Cir. 1943).

75. United States v. Ballard, 322 U.S. 78 (1944).

76. Toracaso v. Watkins, 367 U.S. 488 (1961).

77. United States v. Seeger, 380 U.S. 163, 165–166 (1965).

78. Lee v. Crouse, 284 F. Supp. 541 (D.KA. 1967).

4. FIGHTING FOR RELIGIOUS RIGHTS

Epigraph 1: Jami' at-Tirmidhi, *Book of Tafsir of the Quran*, vol. 5, Hadith 2763.
Epigraph 2: Holt v. Hobbs, 135 S. Ct. 853 (2015), Joint appendix.

1. A number of cases in federal and state courts addressed the religious right to grow a beard, which involved Muslims and non-Muslims alike. Moskowitz v. Wilkinson, 432 F. Supp. 947 (1977).

2. Mayweathers v. Terhune, 328 F. Supp. 2d 1086 (E.D. Cal. 2004).

3. Heather MacKay and the Prison Law Office, *The California Prison and Parole Law Handbook* (Prison Law Office, 2019), https://prisonlaw.com/wp-content/uploads/2019/01/Handbook-Chapter-2.pdf.

4. Holt v. Hobbs, 135 S. Ct. 853 (2015).

5. Jonathan J. Sheffield, Alex S. Moe, and Spencer K. Lickteig, "Holt v. Hobbs: RLUIPA Requires Religious Exception to Prison's Beard Ban," *Loyola University Chicago Law Journal* 46, no. 4 (2015): 1085.

6. Holt v. Hobbs, 135 S. Ct. 853 (2015), declaration of Robert Hawk, Joint Appendix, 24.

7. William Bennett Turner, "Establishing the Rule of Law in Prisons: A Manual for Prisoners' Rights Litigation," *Stanford Law Review* 23, no. 3 (1971).

8. Muslim Advocates, "Fulfilling the Promise of Free Exercise for All."

9. Kathleen M. Moore, *Al-Mughtaribun*, 83.

10. Shelly S. Rachanow, "The Effect of O'Lone v. Estate of Shabazz on the Free Exercise Rights of Prisoners," *Journal of Church and State* 40, no. 1 (1998): 131.

11. Woods v. Evatt, 876 F. Supp. 756 (D.S.C. 1995).

12. Jennifer K. Beaudry, "Islamic Sectarianism in United States Prisons: The Religious Right of Shi'a Inmates to Worship Separately from Their Fellow Sunni Inmates," *Hofstra Law Review* 35, no. 4 (2007): 1833.

13. Holt et al. v. Kelley (E.D.AK. filed March 1, 2019).

14. Ibid. Verified Complaint for Declaratory, Injunctive, and Monetary Relief.

15. Ibid.

16. Ibid.

17. Ali v. Stephens, 822 F.3d 776, 794–797 (5th Cir. 2016).

18. Smith v. Owens, 848 F.3d 975 (11th Cir. 2017).

19. Lewis M. Wasserman, John P. Connolly, and Kent R. Kerley, "Religious Liberty in Prisons under the Religious Land Use and Institutionalized Persons Act Following *Holt v. Hobbs*: An Empirical Analysis," *Religions* 9, no. 7 (2018): 210.

20. Maye v. Klee, 915 F.3d 1076 (6th Cir. 2019).

21. Dowdy-El v. Caruso, No. 06–11765, 2013 U.S. Dist. Lexis 73612 (E.D. Mich. Nov. 20, 2013).

22. Salahuddin v. Goord, 467 F.3d 263 (2d Cir. 2006); Orafan v. Goord, 411 F. Supp. 2d 153 (N.D. NY 2006).

23. Pugh v. Goord, 571 F. Supp. 2d 477 (S.D. N.Y. 2008).

24. Totten v. Caldwell, 2012 U.S. Dist. Lexis 129124 (E.D. Mich. July 31, 2012); Aziyz v. Tremble, No. 5:03-cv-412, 2008 WL 282738 (M.D. Ga. Jan. 31, 2008); Malik v. Ozmint, No. 8:06–3060-RBH-BHH, 2008 U.S. Dist. LEXIS 33904 (D.S.C. Feb. 13, 2008).

25. Ajala v. West, 106 F. Supp. 3d 976 (W.D. W.I. 2015).

26. Charles v. Frank, 101 Fed. Appx. 634 (7th Cir. 2004).

27. Abdullah v. Frank, 2007 U.S. Dist. LEXIS 13215 (E.D. Wisc. Feb. 26, 2007).

28. Barnett v. Rodgers, 410 F.2d 995 (D.C. Cir. 1969).

29. Finney v. Hutto, 410 F. Supp. 251 (E.D. Ark. 1976).

30. Walker v. Blackwell, 411 F.2d 23 (5th Cir. 1969).

31. Ibid.

32. Pratt v. Corr. Corp. of Am., 124 F. App'x 465, 466–67 (8th Cir. 2005); Spruel v. Clarke, No. C06–5021 (RJB), 2007 WL 15577729, at *3 (W.D. Wash. May 31, 2007); Bilal v. Lehman, No. C04–2507-JLR-JPD, 2006 WL 3626781, at *19 (W.D. Wash. Oct. 2, 2006); Bilal v. Lehman, No. C04–2507-JLR, 2006 WL 3626808, at *19–21 (W.D. Wash. Dec. 8, 2006); Ghashiyah v. Wis. Dep't of Corr., No. 01-C-10, 2006 WL 2845701, at *14 (E.D. Wis. Sept. 29, 2006); Phipps v. Morgan, No. CV-04–5108-MWL, 2006 WL 543896, at *2 (E.D. Wash. Mar. 6, 2006).

33. Allah v. Jordan-Luster, No. 04–1083, 2007 WL 2582199, at *9 (W.D. Ill. Aug. 3, 2007); Mayweathers v. Hickman, No. 05-CV-713 WGH (CAB), 2006 WL

4395859, at *7 (S.D. Cal. Dec. 26, 2006); Holiday v. Giusto, No. Civ. 03–1385–AS, 2004 WL 1792466, at *5 (D. Or. Oct. 26, 2004).

34. Ali v. Dewberry, No. 6:10cv454, 2011 U.S. Dist. LEXIS 52766 (E.D.T.X. May 17, 2011).

35. Abdul-Aziz v. Lanigan, No. 14–2026, 2016 U.S. Dist. LEXIS 38884 (D.N.J. March 24, 2016).

36. Abdul-Malik v. Goord, No. 1021 (DLC), 1997 U.S. Dist. LEXIS 2047 (S.D. N.Y. Feb. 27, 1997).

37. Abdulhaseeb v. Calbone, 600 F.3d 1301 (10th Cir. 2010).

38. Ibid.

39. Ibid.

40. Equal Justice Initiative, "Banning Books in Prisons," *Equal Justice Initiative*, January 7, 2020, https://eji.org/news/banning-books-in-prisons/.

41. Office of the Inspector General, "A Review of the Federal Bureau of Prisons' Selection of Muslim Religious Services Providers," *Department of Justice*, April 2004.

42. Office of the Inspector General, "Audit of the Federal Bureau of Prisons' Management and Oversight of its Chaplaincy Services Program," *Department of Justice*, July 7, 2021, https://oig.justice.gov/sites/default/files/ reports /21-091.pdf.

43. Hampton v. Ayers, Np. CV 07–8130-RSWL (MAN), 2011 U.S. Dist. Lexis 69742 (C.D.C.A. 2011).

44. US Congress, House, Committee on Homeland Security, *The Threat of Muslim-American Radicalization in US. Prisons*, 112th Cong., 2011.

45. Coleman v. Jabe, No. 7:11cv00518, 2012 U.S. Dist. Lexis 187385 (W.D. V.A. Dec. 26, 2012).

46. Brown v. Livingston, 17 F. Supp. 3d 616 (S.D. Tex. 2014).

47. Young v. Newton, No. 1:18-cv-851 (E.D.VA. Oct. 16, 2020), https://www .cair.com/wp-content/uploads/2020/10/GodPodDecision.pdf.

48. Maye v. Klee, No. 18–1460, 2019 WL 613732, at *5 (6th Cir. Feb. 14, 2019).

49. Complaint, Holt et al. v. Kelley (E.D.AK. filed Mar. 1, 2019).

50. Al-Fuyudi v. Corr. Corp. of Am., No. CIV-12–1170-D, 2016 WL 800194 (W.D. OK. 2016).

51. Blagman v. White, 112 F. Supp. 2d 534, 538 (E.D. Va. 2000).

52. Ali v. Quarterman, 607 F.3d 1046 (E.D. TX. 2010).

5. HOLDING PRISONS ACCOUNTABLE

Epigraph: *O'Lone v. Estate of Shabazz*, 482 U.S. 342, 355 (1987) (Brennan, J., dissenting).

1. Johanna Fernandez, "Justice on Trial: The Case of Mumia Abu-Jamal," *Aljazeera,* November 8, 2012, https://www.aljazeera.com/opinions/2012/11/8/justice-on-trial-the-case-of-mumia-abu-jamal/.

2. Unbound Allstars, "Mumia 9/11," *Genius,* https://genius.com/Unbound-allstars-mumia-911-lyrics.

3. Immortal Technique, "Homeland Security and Hip Hop," *Genius,* https://genius.com/Immortal-technique-homeland-and-hip-hop-lyrics.

4. Smith, "Black Muslims and the Development of Prisoners' Rights," 143.

5. Margo Schlanger, "Trends in Prisoner Litigation, as the PLRA Enters Adulthood," *University of California Irving Law Review* 5, no. 1 (2015).

6. Jackson v. Dep't of Corr., 2006 Mass. Super. Lexis 389 (2006).

7. Ibid.

8. Mumia Abu-Jamal, *Jailhouse Lawyers: Prisoners Defending Prisoner v. the USA* (City Lights, 2009).

9. Mark S. Hamm et al., "The Myth of Humane Imprisonment: A Critical Analysis of Severe Discipline in Maximum Security Prisons, 1945–1990," in *Prison Violence in America*, 2nd ed., ed. Michael C. Braswell, Reid H. Montgomery Jr., and Lucien X. Lombardo (Anderson, 1994).

10. SpearIt, "Muslim Radicalization in Prison: Responding with Sound Penal Policy or the Sound of Alarm?," *Gonzaga Law Review* 49 (2014).

11. Sostre v. Rockefeller, 312 F. Supp. 863 (S.D.NY. 1971). On appeal, the Second Circuit upheld the district court's ruling that Sostre was denied due process of law when he was placed in solitary confinement without any administrative proceeding, but did not find this was cruel and unusual punishment.

12. Allah v. Al-Hafeez, 226 F.3d 247, 252 (3d Cir. 2000).

13. Salahuddin v. Goord, 467 F.3d 263 (2d Cir. 2006).

14. Cancel v. Mazzuca, 2003 U.S. Dist. Lexis 4888 (S.D.NY. 2003).

15. Green, *The Fear of Islam*, 113.

16. Aziz, "'Whosoever Sees an Evil.'"

17. Mark S. Hamm, *The Spectacular Few: Prisoner Radicalization and the Evolving Terrorist Threat* (New York University Press, 2013).

18. US Congress, Senate, Committee on the Judiciary, *Terrorism: Radical Islamic Influence of Chaplaincy of the U.S. Military and Prisons,* 108th Cong., 2003, 1; US Congress, Senate, Committee on Homeland Security and Governmental Affairs, *Prison Radicalization: Are Terrorist Cells Forming in U.S. Cell Blocks?,* 109th Cong., 2006, 2; US Congress, House, Committee on Homeland Security, *The Threat of Muslim-American Radicalization in US. Prisons,* 112th Cong., 2011.

19. "Black Muslims in Prison," *Columbia Law Review.*

20. Mary Beth Sheridan, "U.S. Muslim Groups Cleared," *Washington Post,* November 19, 2005.

21. Stephen Seymour, "The Silence of Prayer: An Examination of the Federal Bureau of Prisons' Moratorium on the Hiring of Muslim Chaplains," *Columbia Human Rights Law Review* 37, no. 2 (2006): 523.

22. US Congress, *Prison Radicalization*.

23. SpearIt, "Facts and Fictions about Islam in Prison: Assessing Prisoner Radicalization in Post-9/11 America," *Institute for Social Policy and Understanding* (2013): 24.

24. Federal Bureau of Prisons, "Program Statement 5214.02 Communications Management Units," April 1, 2015, 2.

25. Carrie Johnson and Margot Williams, "'Guantanamo North': Inside Secretive U.S. Prisons," *NPR*, March 3, 2011, https://www.npr.org/2011/03/03/134168714/guantanamo-north-inside-u-s-secretive-prisons.

26. David Holthouse, "Leaders of Racist Prison Gang Aryan Brotherhood Face Federal Indictment," *Southern Poverty Law Center*, October 14, 2005.

27. Mark S. Hamm, "Terrorist Recruitment in American Correctional Institutions: An Exploratory Study of Non-Traditional Faith Groups," unpublished federally commissioned report, *National Institute of Justice*, 2007, https://www.ncjrs.gov/pdffiles1/nij/grants/220957.pdf.

28. Doyle v. United States, Nos. 18–6282, 18–6324 (6th Cir. 2019), https://muslimadvocates.org/wp-content/uploads/2019/06/Court-Case_2019.03.11_Doyle-v.-USA_Opening-Brief-of-Plaintiff-Appellant.pdf.

29. Ibid.

30. Dowl v. Williams, complaint, case No. 3:15-cv-00119-JWS (D. Ak. 2018).

31. Ibid.

32. Tom Perkins, "Muslim Prisoners Are Suing Michigan for Staving Them during Ramadan," *Vice*, November 6, 2015, https://www.vice.com/en/article/ypxn9v/muslim-prisoners-are-suing-michigan-for-starving-them-during-ramadan.

33. American Civil Liberties Union, "Muslim Woman Sues Prison for Forcing Her to Remove Headscarf in Front of Male Guards and Prisoners," *ACLU*, May 25, 2005, https://www.aclu.org/press-releases/muslim-woman-sues-prison-forcing-her-remove-headscarf-front-male-guards-and-prisoners.

34. Sarah Ladd, "Muslim Woman Sues Louisville Over Jail Photo Taken Without Her Hijab," *USA Today*, July 31, 2019, https://www.usatoday.com/story/news/nation/2019/07/31/muslim-woman-sues-over-louisville-jail-photo-taken-without-her-hijab/1885131001/.

35. Ibrahim Hooper, "CAIR-Michigan Announces Federal Civil Rights Lawsuit Against City of Detroit, Michigan Department of Corrections for Woman Who Had Hijab Forcibly Removed for Booking Photo," *CAIR*, October 6, 2020, https://www.cair.com/press_releases/cair-michigan-announces-federal-civil-rights-lawsuit-against-city-of-detroit-michigan-department-of-corrections-for-woman-who-had-hijab-forcibly-removed-for-booking-photo/.

36. Tim Nelson, "Ramsey County Settles Lawsuit Over Hijab Removal," *MPR News,* December 17, 2019, https://www.mprnews.org/story/2019/12/17/ramsey-county-settles-lawsuit-over-hijab-removal.

37. Paige St. John, "29,000 California Prison Inmates Refuse Meals in 2nd Day of Protest," *Los Angeles Times,* July 9, 2013, https://www.latimes.com/local/la-xpm-2013-jul-09-la-me-ff-prison-strike-20130710-story.html.

38. Abdulmutallab v. Sessions, complaint, No. 1:17-cv-02493 (U.S.D.C. Colorado, 2017), https://www.documentcloud.org/documents/4113423-Abdulmutallab-hunger-strike-complaint.html.

6. MUSLIM LITIGIOSITY

1. Mot., Ray v. Comm'r, Ala. Dep't of Corr., No. 2:19-cv-00088-WKW-CSC (11th Cir. 2019), https://media.ca11.uscourts.gov/opinions/pub/files/201910405.ord.pdf.

2. Dunn v. Ray, 586 U.S. ___ (2019).

3. Ibid.

4. Murphy v. Collier, 587 U.S. ___ (2019).

5. Ibid.

6. Smith, "Black Muslims and the Development of Prisoners' Rights," 139.

7. Archive of Muhammad Speaks, *Muhammad Speaks,* 7, no. 5, October 20, 1967.

8. From individual in Texas State Prison, letter to author.

9. Letter from Abdul Maalik Muhammad, Pet'r in Holt v. Hobbs (2015) (Jan. 16, 2022) (on file with author).

10. From individual in Florida State Prison, letter to author.

11. From individual in Georgia State Prison, letter to author.

12. This observation builds from ideas articulated in the author's previous work: SpearIt, "Muslims in American Prisons: Advancing the Rule of Law through Litigation Praxis," *Journal of Islamic Law* 3 (2022).

13. Justice Stephen Brennan in a Clinton, New York, prison case, quoted in the *New York Times*: Lawrence O'Kane, "Muslim Negroes Suing the State," *New York Times,* March 19, 1961.

14. From individual in Tennessee State Prison, letter to author.

15. Archive of Muhammad Speaks, *Muhammad Speaks,* 6, no. 17, January 13, 1967.

16. Al-Amin v. Warden Hugh Smith, 511 F.3d 1317 (11th Cir. 2008).

17. Sharon Dolovich, "Teaching Prison Law," *Journal of Legal Education* 62, no. 2 (2012).

18. See Richard H. Fallon Jr., "'The Rule of Law' as a Concept in Constitutional Discourse," *Columbia Law Review* (1997).

19. Peter Rijpkema, "The Rule of Law Beyond Thick and Thin," *Law and Philosophy* 32, no. 6 (2012).

20. Peter Ingram, "Maintaining the Rule of Law," *Philosophical Quarterly* 35, no. 141 (1985): 359.

21. Fallon Jr., "'The Rule of Law,'" 7–8.

22. Timothy A. O. Endicott, "The Impossibility of the Rule of Law," *Oxford Journal of Legal Studies* 19, no. 1 (1999).

23. Crawford, *Black Muslims and the Law*, 66.

24. Basia Spalek and Salah El-Hassan, "Muslim Converts in Prison," *Howard Journal of Criminal Justice* 46, no. 2 (2007).

25. Elijah Muhammad, *Message to the Blackman in America* (Secretarius MEMPS, 2009), 63.

26. Jacobs, "The Prisoners' Rights Movement," 4585.

27. Ibid.

28. Ibid.

29. From individual in Tennessee State Prison, letter to author.

30. From individual in Florida State Prison, letter to author.

7. CONCLUSIONS AND FINAL THOUGHTS

Epigraph: Garrett Felber, *Those Who Know Don't Say: The Nation of Islam, the Black Freedom Movement, and the Carceral State* (University of North Carolina Press, 2019), 77.

1. Mari J. Matsuda, "Public Response to Racist Speech: Considering the Victim's Story," *Michigan Law Review* 87, no. 8. (1989): 2324.

2. William J. Aceves, "Critical Jurisprudence and International Legal Scholarship: A Study of Equitable Distribution," *Columbia Journal of Transnational Law* 39, no. 2 (2001): 299–394.

3. Houchins v. KQED, Inc., 438 U.S. 1 (1978).

4. Hudson v. Palmer, 468 U.S. 517 (1984).

5. Cyra Akila Choudhury and Khaled A. Beydoun, eds., *Islamophobia and the Law* (Cambridge University Press, 2020), 36.

6. Eldridge Cleaver and Robert Scheer, *Post-prison Writings and Speeches* (Random House, 1969), 14.

7. Moore, *Al-Mughtaribun*, 100.

8. Meachum v. Fano, 427 U.S. 215 (1976); Montanye v. Haymes, 427 U.S. 236 (1976).

9. Holt v. Hobbs, On Writ of Certiorari to the Eighth Circuit Court of Appeals, Joint Appendix (April 23, 2014).

10. Jacobs, *Stateville*, 117.

11. Turner, "Establishing the Rule of Law in Prisons."

12. Smith, "Black Muslims and the Development of Prisoners' Rights," 143–44.

13. Green v. Caruso, 2011 U.S. Dist. Lexis 30520 (W.D. MI. 2011).

14. Abdullah v. Wis. Dep't of Corr., 2005 U.S. Dist. LEXIS 27999 (E.D. Wis 2005).

15. Lester Smith, survey on file with author.

16. Archive of Muhammad Speaks, *Muhammad Speaks* 9, no. 52 (September 11, 1970).

17. Seymour, "The Silence of Prayer," 532 (finding the recidivism rate for Muslims was about 8 percent compared to 40 percent for Catholics and Protestants).

18. Howard v. Foster, 208 F. Supp. 3d 1152 (D. Nevada 2016).

19. Eliade, "Symbolism of the Center," 54.

20. Hecht, "The Study of Religions in America," 17.

21. Ibid.

22. Richard Child, "Concepts of Political Prisonerhood," *New England Journal on Prison Law* 1, no. 1 (1974): 25–26.

23. Hecht, "The Study of Religions in America," 17.

24. Marcellus Williams, email message to author, February 22, 2021.

25. Verified Complaint for Declaratory, Injunctive, and Monetary Relief, Holt v. Kelley, (E.D.A.K).

26. Moore, *Al-Mughtaribun,* 102.

27. James B. Jacobs, *New Perspectives on Prisons and Imprisonment* (Cornell University Press, 1983), 67.

28. Brian M. Drinkwine, "The Serpent in Our Garden: Al-Qa'ida and the Long War. Report," Strategic Studies Institute, US Army War College, 2009, 56, https:// www.jstor.org/stable/resrep11926.23?seq = 1#metadata_info_tab_contents.

29. Pamela Geller, *Stop the Islamization of America: A Practical Guide to the Resistance* (WND Books, 2017).

30. American Bar Association, "Resolution 100A" (2018).

31. Michele C. Nielson, "Mute and Moot: How Class Action Mootness Procedure Silences Inmates," *UCLA Law Review* 63, no. 3 (2016): 760.

32. Schlanger, "Trends in Prisoner Litigation," 159.

33. Shahid W. Muhammad, survey on file with author.

34. Smith, "Black Muslims and the Development of Prisoners' Rights," 140.

Bibliography

Abu-Jamal, Mumia. *Jailhouse Lawyers: Prisoners Defending Prisoners v. the U.S.A.* San Francisco: City Lights Publishers, 2009.

Aceves, William J. "Critical Jurisprudence and International Legal Scholarship: A Study of Equitable Distribution." *Columbia Journal of Transnational Law* 39, no. 2 (2001).

Ackerman, Spencer. "Peter King Pioneered the Persecution of American Muslims." *Daily Beast,* November 12, 2019. https://www.thedailybeast.com/peter-king-pioneered-the-persecution-of-american-muslims.

Almog, Shulamit. "As I Read, I Weep: In Praise of Judicial Narrative." *Oklahoma City University Law Review* 26, no. 2 (2001).

American Bar Association. "Resolution 100A." 2018.

American Civil Liberties Union. "Muslim Woman Sues Prison for Forcing Her to Remove Headscarf in Front of Male Guards and Prisoners." *ACLU,* May 25, 2005. https://www.aclu.org/press-releases/muslim-woman-sues-prison-forcing-her-remove-headscarf-front-male-guards-and-prisoners.

Anderson, James F., Nancie J. Mangel, and Laronistine Dyson. *Significant Prisoner Rights Cases.* Durham, NC: Carolina Academic Press, 2010.

Archive of Muhammad Speaks. *Mr. Muhammad Speaks* 1, no. 1 (May 1960).

———. *Muhammad Speaks* 1, no. 3 (January 1961).

———. *Muhammad Speaks* 1, no. 3 (January 1962).

———. *Muhammad Speaks* 1, no. 22 (December 1961).

———. *Muhammad Speaks* 5, no. 23 (February 12, 1971).

———. *Muhammad Speaks* 5, no. 23 (February 25, 1966).

———. *Muhammad Speaks* 6, no. 16 (January 6, 1967).

———. *Muhammad Speaks* 6, no. 17 (January 13, 1967).

———. *Muhammad Speaks* 6, no. 26 (March 17, 1967).

———. *Muhammad Speaks* 6, no. 30 (April 14, 1967).

———. *Muhammad Speaks* 6, no. 48 (August 18, 1967).

———. *Muhammad Speaks* 7, no. 5 (October 20, 1967).

———. *Muhammad Speaks* 9, no. 52 (September 11, 1970).

———. *Muhammad Speaks* 11, no. 28 (March 24, 1972).

Arzi, Donna E. "The Role of Compulsion in Islamic Conversion: Jihad, Dhimma, and Ridda." *Buffalo Human Rights Review* 8, no. 15 (2002).

Aziz, Sahar. "'Whosoever Sees an Evil:' Muslim Americans' Human Rights Advocacy." *Oxford Encyclopedia on Religion* (2020).

Baldwin, James. *The Fire Next Time.* Cologne, Germany: Taschen 1963.

Beaudry, Jennifer K. "Islamic Sectarianism in United States Prisons: The Religious Right of Shi'a Inmates to Worship Separately from Their Fellow Sunni Inmates." *Hofstra Law Review* 35, no. 4 (2007).

Berg, Herbert. *Elijah Muhamad and Islam.* New York: New York University Press, 2009.

Berger, Dan. *Captive Nation: Black Prison Organizing in the Civil Rights Era.* Chapel Hill: University of North Carolina Press, 2014.

Berger, Dan, and Toussaint Losier. *Rethinking the American Prison Movement.* London: Taylor & Francis Group, 2017.

Beydoun, Khaled. *American Islamophobia: Understanding the Roots and Rise of Fear.* Oakland: University of California Press, 2018.

———. "Islam Incarcerated: Religious Accommodation of Muslim Prisoners before Holt v. Hobbs." *University of Cincinnati Law Review* 84, no. 1 (2018).

"Black Muslims in Prison: Of Muslim Rites and Constitutional Rights." *Columbia Law Review* 62, no. 8 (1962).

Brown, Dulcey A. "Black Muslim Prisoners and Religious Discrimination: The Developing Criteria for Judicial Review." *George Washington Law Review* 32, no. 2 (1964).

Child, Richard. "Concepts of Political Prisonerhood." *New England Journal on Prison Law* 1, no. 1 (1974).

Choudhury, Cyra Akila, and Khaled A. Beydoun, eds. *Islamophobia and the Law.* Cambridge, UK: Cambridge University Press, 2020.

Clark, Kenneth B. "Malcolm X Talks with Kenneth B. Clark." In *The Negro Protest: James Baldwin, Malcolm X and Martin Luther King Talk with Kenneth B. Clark,* 22. Boston: Beacon Press, 1963.

Clear, Todd R., Patricia L. Hardyman, Bruce Stout, Karol Lucken, and Harry R. Dammer. "The Value of Religion in Prison." *Journal of Contemporary Criminal Justice* 16, no. 1. (2000).

Cleaver, Eldridge, and Robert Scheer. *Post-prison Writings and Speeches*. New York: Random House, 1969.

Clegg, Claude Andrew, III. *An Original Man: The Life and Times of Elijah Muhammad*. Chapel Hill: University of North Carolina Press, 1997.

Colley, Zoe. "'All America Is a Prison': The Nation of Islam and the Politicization of African American Prisoners, 1955–65." *Journal of American Studies* 48, no. 2 (2014).

Copeland, Vincent. *The Crime of Martin Sostre*. New York: McGraw-Hill, 1970.

Crawford, Malachi D. *Black Muslims and the Law: From Civil Liberties from Elijah Muhammad to Muhammad Ali*. Lanham, MD: Lexington Books, 2015.

Cripe, Clair A. Proceedings of the 106th Annual Congress of Corrections, Denver, August 22–26, 1976. College Park, MD: American Corrections Association, 1977.

Curtis, Edward E. IV. *Islam in Black America: Identity, Liberation, and Difference in African-American Islamic Thought*. Albany: State University of New York Press, 2002.

Dammer, Harry R. "Piety in Prison: An Ethnography of Religion in the Correctional Environment." PhD diss., Rutgers University, 1992.

Dannin, Robert. *Black Pilgrimage to Islam*. New York: Oxford University Press, 2002.

———. "Island in a Sea of Ignorance: Dimensions of the Prison Mosque." In *Making Muslim Space in North America and Europe*, edited by Barbara Daly Metcalf, 139–140. Berkeley: University of California Press, 1996.

Delgado, Richard. "The Inward Turn in Outsider Jurisprudence." *William and Mary Law Review* 34, no. 3 (1993).

———. "Storytelling for Oppositionists and Others: A Plea for Narrative." *Michigan Law Review* 87, no. 8 (1989).

Diouf, Sylviane A. *Servants of Allah: African Muslims Enslaved in the Americas*. New York: New York University Press, 1998.

Dix-Richardson, Felecia, and Billy R. Close. "Intersections of Race, Religion, and Inmate Culture: The Historical Development of Islam in American Corrections." *Journal of Offender Rehabilitation* 35, nos. 3–4 (2002).

Dolovich, Sharon. "Teaching Prison Law." *Journal of Legal Education* 62, no. 2 (2012).

Dow, Steven B. "Navigating through the Problem of Mootness in Corrections Litigation." *Capital University Law Review* 43, no. 3 (2015).

Drinkwine, Brian M. "The Serpent in Our Garden: Al-Qa'ida and the Long War." Strategic Studies Institute US Army War College, January 1, 2009. https://www.jstor.org/stable/resrep11926.23?seq=1#metadata_info_tab_contents.

Duhart, Olympia. "Soldier Suicides and OutCrit Jurisprudence." *Creighton Law Review* 44, no. 4 (2011).

Eliade, Mircea. "Symbolism of the Center." In *Images and Symbols*. Princeton, NJ: Princeton University Press, 1991.

Endicott, Timothy A. O. "The Impossibility of the Rule of Law." *Oxford Journal of Legal Studies* 19, no. 1 (1999).

Enforcing Religious Freedom in Prison. Edited by Quentin Willems. Hauppauge, NY: Nova Science Publishers, 2010.

Equal Justice Initiative. "Banning Books in Prisons." *Equal Justice Initiative*, January 7, 2020. https://eji.org/news/banning-books-in-prisons/.

Fallon, Richard H., Jr. "'The Rule of Law' as a Concept in Constitutional Discourse." *Columbia Law Review* 97, no. 1 (1997).

Fathi, David C. "Prison Litigation Reform Act: A Threat to Civil Rights." *Federal Sentencing Reporter* 24, no. 4 (2012).

Federal Bureau of Prisons. "Program Statement 5214.02 Communications Management Units." April 1, 2015.

Felber, Garrett. "'Shades of Mississippi': The Nation of Islam's Prison Organizing, the Carceral State, and the Black Freedom Struggle." *Journal of American History* 105, no. 1 (2018).

———. *Those Who Know Don't Say: The Nation of Islam, the Black Freedom Movement, and the Carceral State*. Chapel Hill: University of North Carolina Press, 2019.

———. *A Continuous Struggle: The Revolutionary Life of Martin Sostre* (forthcoming).

Fernandez, Johanna. "Justice on Trial: The Case of Mumia Abu-Jamal." *Aljazeera*. November 8, 2012. https://www.aljazeera.com/opinions/2012/11/8/justice-on-trial-the-case-of-mumia-abu-jamal/.

Flinn, Frank K. "Criminalizing Conversion: The Legislative Assault on New Religions." In *Crime, Values, and Religion*, edited by James M. Day and William S. Laufer. Norwood, NJ: Ablex, 1987.

Fliter, John A. *Prisoners' Rights: The Supreme Court and Evolving Standards of Decency*. Westport, CT: Greenwood Press, 2001.

Geller, Pamela. *Stop the Islamization of America: A Practical Guide to the Resistance*. Chicago: WND Books, 2017.

Gidman, Jenn. "From 'Politicized Prisoner' to Inmate Hero." *Newser*, April 18, 2017. https://www.newser.com/story/241422/the-inmate-who-upended-the-us-prison-system.html.

Green, Todd H. *The Fear of Islam: An Introduction to Islamophobia in the West*. Minneapolis: Fortress Press, 2015.

Gross, Gerald J. "The Case of Martin Sostre." *New York Review*, March 23, 1972. http://www.nybooks.com/articles/archives/1972/mar/23/the-case-of-martin-sostre/.

Hallinan, Joseph T. *Going up the River: Travels in a Prison Nation*. New York: Random House Trade Paperbacks, 2003.

Hamm, Mark S. *The Spectacular Few: Prisoner Radicalization and the Evolving Terrorist Threat*. New York: NYU Press, 2013.

———. "Terrorist Recruitment in American Correctional Institutions: An Exploratory Study of Non-Traditional Faith Groups." Unpublished federally commissioned report. *National Institute of Justice*, 2007. https://www.ojp .gov/pdffiles1/nij/grants/220957.pdf.

Hamm, Mark S., Therese Coupez, Frances E. Hoze, and Corey Weinstein. The Myth of Humane Imprisonment: A Critical Analysis of Severe Discipline in Maximum Security Prisons, 1945–90 in *Prison Violence in America*, 2nd ed., edited by Michael C. Braswell, Reid H. Montgomery, Jr. and Lucien X. Cincinnati, OH: Anderson, 1990.

Hasan, Ahmad. "Social Justice in Islam." *Islamic Studies* 10, no. 3 (1971).

Hasan, Asma Gull. *American Muslims: The New Generation*. London: Bloomsbury Academic, 2000.

Hecht, Richard D. "The Study of Religions in America and the Department of Religious Studies at the University of California, Santa Barbara." *Pantheon* 8, no. 1 (2013). https://www.religion.ucsb.edu/wp-content/uploads/Hecht-in-Pantheon.pdf.

Holthouse, David. "Leaders of Racist Prison Gang Aryan Brotherhood Face Federal Indictment." *Southern Poverty Law Center*, 2005.

Hooper, Ibrahim. "CAIR-Michigan Announces Federal Civil Rights Lawsuit against City of Detroit, Michigan Department of Corrections for Woman Who Had Hijab Forcibly Removed for Booking Photo." *CAIR-Michigan*, October 6, 2020. https://www.cair.com/press_releases/cair-michigan-announces-federal-civil-rights-lawsuit-against-city-of-detroit-michigan-department-of-corrections-for-woman-who-had-hijab-forcibly-removed-for-booking-photo/.

Hunter, James Davison, Alan Wolfe, E. J. Dionne, and Michael Cromartie. *Is There a Culture War? A Dialogue on Values and American Public Life*. Washington, DC: Brookings Institution Press, 2006.

Immortal Technique. "Homeland Security and Hip Hop." *Genius*. https://genius .com/Immortal-technique-homeland-and-hip-hop-lyrics.

Ingram, Peter. "Maintaining the Rule of Law." *Philosophical Quarterly* 35, no. 141 (1985).

Islam in America. Boston: Christian Science Publications. 1991. Videocassette.

Ismail, Khalid Bin. "Islam and the Concept of Justice." *Centre for Islamic Thought and Understanding*. https://ir.uitm.edu.my/id/eprint/32047/1/32047.pdf.

Jackson, Margaret Moore. "Confronting 'Unwelcomeness' from the Outside: Using Case Theory to Tell the Stories of Sexually-Harassed Women." *Cardozo Journal of Law and Gender* 14 (2007).

Jacobs, James B. *New Perspectives on Prisons and Imprisonment*. Ithaca, NY: Cornell University Press, 1983.

———. "The Prisoners' Rights Movement and its Impacts, 1960–80." *Crime and Justice* 2 (1980).

———. *Stateville: The Penitentiary in Mass Society.* Chicago: University of Chicago Press, 2015.

———. "Stratification and Conflict among Prison Inmates." *Journal of Criminal Law and Criminology* 66, no. 4 (1976).

James, William. *The Varieties of Religious Experience.* New Hyde Park, NY: University Books, 1963.

Jami' at-Tirmidhi. Vol. 5, Book of Tafsir of the Qu'ran. Hadith 2763.

Johnson, Carrie, and Margot Williams. "'Guantanamo North': Inside Secretive U.S. Prisons." *NPR*, March 3, 2011. https://www.npr.org/2011/03/03 /134168714/guantanamo-north-inside-u-s-secretive-prisons.

Khadduri, Majid. *The Islamic Conception of Justice.* Baltimore, MD: Johns Hopkins University Press, 1984.

Kusha, Hamid Reza. *Islam in American Prisons: Black Muslims' Challenge to American Penology.* Milton Park, UK: Taylor & Francis, 2009.

Ladd, Sarah. "Muslim Woman Sues Louisville over Jail Photo Taken without Her Hijab." *USA Today*, July 31, 2019. https://www.usatoday.com/story /news/nation/2019/07/31/muslim-woman-sues-over-louisville-jail-photo- taken-without-her-hijab/1885131001/.

Leone, Massimo. *Religious Conversion and Identity: The Semiotic Analysis of Texts.* Milton Park, UK: Taylor & Francis, 2003.

Lincoln, C. Eric. *The Black Muslims in America.* Boston: Beacon Press, 1973.

Losier, Toussaint. ". . . For Strictly Religious Reason[s]: Cooper v. Pate and the Origins of the Prisoners' Rights Movement." *Souls* 15, nos. 1–2 (2013).

MacKay, Heather, and the Prison Law Office. "The California Prison and Parole Law Handbook." Prison Law Office, 2019. https://prisonlaw.com/wp-content /uploads/2019/01/Handbook-Chapter-2.pdf.

Marable, Manning. *Malcolm X: A Life of Reinvention.* London: Penguin Books, 2011.

Marr, Timothy. *The Cultural Roots of American Islamicism.* Cambridge, UK: Cambridge University Press, 2006.

Marx, Karl. "Introduction: A Contribution to the Critique of Hegel's Philosophy of Right." *Deutsch-Französische Jahrbücher* (1844).

Matsuda, Mari. "Public Response to Racist Speech: Considering the Victim's Story." *Michigan Law Review* 87, no. 8 (1989).

McCall, Nathan. *Makes Me Wanna Holler: A Young Black Man in America.* New York: Random House, 1994.

McLaughlin, Malcolm. "Storefront Revolutionary: Martin Sostre's Afro-Asian Bookshop, Black Liberation Culture, and the New Left, 1964–75." *A Journal of History, Politics, and Culture* 7, no. 1 (2014).

Miyakawa, Felicia. *Five Percenter Rap: God Hop's Music, Message, and Black Muslim's Mission*. Bloomington: Indiana University Press, 2005.

Moore, Kathleen M. *Al-Mughtaribun: American Law and the Transformation of Muslim Life in the United States*. Albany: State University of New York Press, 1995.

———. "The Case for Muslim Constitutional Interpretive Activity." *American Journal of Islamic Social Sciences* 7 (1990).

Morrison, Adam Daniel. "Religious Legitimacy and the Nation of Islam: In Re Ferguson and Muslim Inmates' Religious Rights in the 1950s and 1960s." Master's thesis, University of California Santa Barbara, 2013.

Morrison, Karl F. *Understanding Conversion*. Charlottesville: University Press of Virginia, 1992.

"The Most Remarkable Revelatory Letter Ever Written by Malcolm X." Moments in Time, accessed August 6, 2022. https://momentsintime.com/the-most-remarkable-revelatory-letter-ever-written-by-malcolm-x/#.YR0awy1hOTZ.

Muhammad, Elijah. *Message to the Blackman in America*. Goodyear: Secretarius MEMPS, 2009.

Mufti, Siraj Islam. "Islam in American Prisons." *Umma Forum*. December 14, 2006. http://www.ummah.com/forum/showthread.php?106570-Islam-in-American-Prisons.

Muslim Advocates. "Fulfilling The Promise of Free Exercise for All: Muslim Prisoner Accommodation in State Prisons," July 2019. https://muslimadvocates.org/wp-content/uploads/2019/07/FULFILLING-THE-PROMISE-OF-FREE-EXERCISE-FOR-ALL-Muslim-Prisoner-Accommodation-In-State-Prisons-for-distribution-7_23.pdf.

"Muslims in American Prisons Face Battles to Practice Religion: Courts Offer Insight for Peaceful Facilities." *Corrections Professional* 10 (2005).

Musnad Aḥmad. Vol. 5. Book of Tafsir of the Qu'ran. Hadith 2297.

Nawawi, Imam. *A Translation and Commentary of Riyad Al-Salihin*. Translated and edited by Moulana Afzal Ismail. Vol. 1, Hadith 1–601 (Heidelberg: Muslims at Work Publications, 2016).

Nelson, Tim. "Ramsey County Settles Lawsuit over Hijab Removal." *MPR News*, December 17, 2019. https://www.mprnews.org/story/2019/12/17/ramsey-county-settles-lawsuit-over-hijab-removal.

Nielsen, Michele C. "Mute and Moot: How Class Action Mootness Procedure Silences Inmates." *UCLA Law Review* 63, no. 3 (2016).

Nyang, Sulayman S. *Islam in the United States of America*. Chicago: ABC International Group, 1999.

Office of the Inspector General, Department of Justice. *A Review of the Federal Bureau of Prisons' Selection of Muslim Religious Services Providers*. April

2004, 55. https://oig.justice.gov/sites/default/files/legacy/special/0404/final
.pdf.

Office of the Inspector General, Department of Justice. *Audit of the Federal Bureau of Prisons' Management and Oversight of its Chaplaincy Services Program.* July 2021. https://oig.justice.gov/sites/default/files/reports /21-091.pdf.

O'Kane, Lawrence. "Muslim Negroes Suing the State." *New York Times,* March 19, 1961.

Otto, Rudolf. *The Idea of the Holy: An Inquiry in the Non-rational Factor in the Idea of the Divine and Its Relation to the Rational.* Translated by John W. Harvey. Oxford, UK: Oxford University Press, 1917.

Pedrioli, Carlo A. "Constructing the Other: U.S. Muslims, Anti-Sharia Law, and the Constitutional Consequences of Volatile Intercultural Rhetoric." *Southern California Interdisciplinary Law Journal* 22 (2012).

Perkins, Tom. "Muslim Prisoners Are Suing Michigan for Staving Them During Ramadan." *Vice,* November 6, 2015. https://www.vice.com/en/article/ypxn9v /muslim-prisoners-are-suing-michigan-for-starving-them-during-ramadan.

Peru, Farouk A. "A Muslim on the Idea of Protest." *Muslim Institute,* 2017. https://musliminstitute.org/freethinking/culture/muslim-idea-protest.

Quran 2:83.

———. 4:135.

———. 4:36.

———. 4:75–76.

———. 6:151.

———. 16:90.

———. 17:23.

———. 30:22.

———. 49:13.

Qureshi, Tufail Ahmad. "Justice In Islam." *Islamic Studies* 21, no. 2 (1982).

Qurtuby, Sumanto Al. "The Islamic Roots of Liberation, Justice, and Peace: An Anthropocentric Analysis of the Concept of Tawhid." *Islamic Studies* 52, no. 3–4 (2013).

Qutb, Amal, Nazir Khan, and Mahdi Qasqas. "Islam and Social Justice." In *Spirituality and Social Justice,* edited by Norma Jean Profitt and Cyndy Baskin. Toronto: Canadian Scholars' Press Inc, 2019.

Rachanow, Shelly S. "The Effect of O'Lone v. Estate of Shabazz on the Free Exercise Rights of Prisoners." *Journal of Church and State* 40, no. 1 (1998).

"Report 12 Bar Robberies and Murder Solved." *Chicago Daily Tribune,* August 29, 1952.

Rijpkema, Peter. "The Rule of Law beyond Thick and Thin." *Law and Philosophy* 32, no. 6 (2013).

Roman, Ediberto. "Afterword: LatCrit VI, Outsider Jurisprudence and Looking beyond Imagined Borders." *Florida Law Review* 55, no. 1 (2003).

Schaich, Warren L., and Diane S. Hope. "The Prison Letters of Martin Sostre: Documents of Resistance." *Journal of Black Studies* 7, no. 3 (1977).

Schlanger, Margo. "Trends in Prisoner Litigation, as the PLRA Enters Adulthood." *University of California Irving Law Review,* 5, no. 1 (2015).

Seymour, Stephen. "The Silence of Prayer: An Examination of the Federal Bureau of Prisons' Moratorium on the Hiring of Muslim Chaplains." *Columbia Human Rights Law Review* 37, no. 2 (2006).

Shakur, Tupac Amaru. "I Ain't Mad at Cha." Track 13 on *All Eyez on Me,* Death Row Records, 1996, compact disc.

Shapiro, Joseph. "How One Inmate Changed the Prison System from the Inside." *NPR,* April 14, 2017. https://www.npr.org/sections/codeswitch/2017/04/14/507297469/how-one-inmate-changed-the-prison-system-from-the-inside.

Sheffield, Jonathan J., Alex S. Moe, and Spencer K. Lickteig. "Holt v. Hobbs: RLUIPA Requires Religious Exception to Prison's Beard Ban." *Loyola University Chicago Law Journal* 46, no. 4 (2015).

Sheridan, Mary Beth. "U.S. Muslim Groups Cleared." *Washington Post,* November 19, 2005.

Smith, Christopher E. "Black Muslims and the Development of Prisoners' Rights." *Journal of Black Studies* 24, no. 2 (1993).

Smith, Jane I. *Islam in America.* New York: Columbia University Press 1999.

Sostre, Martin. "The New Prisoner." *North Carolina Central Law Review* 4, no. 2 (1973).

Spalek, Basia, and Salah El-Hassan. "Muslim Converts in Prison." *Howard Journal Criminal Justice* 46, no. 2 (2007).

SpearIt. *American Prisons: A Critical Primer on Culture and Conversion to Islam.* Sarasota, FL: First Edition Design eBook Publishing, 2017.

———. "Facts and Fictions about Islam in Prison: Assessing Prisoner Radicalization in Post-9/11 America." *Institute for Social Policy and Understanding* (2013).

———. "Muslims in American Prisons: Advancing the Rule of Law through Litigation Praxis." *Journal of Islamic Law* 3 (2022).

———. "Muslim Radicalization in Prison: Responding with Sound Penal Policy or the Sound of Alarm?" *Gonzaga Law Review* 49 (2014).

Stark, Rodney. "Why Religious Movements Succeed or Fail: A Revised General Model." *Journal of Contemporary Religion* 11, no. 2 (1996).

State of California Department of Corrections. *Special Procedures for Muslim Inmates.* Administrative Bulletin No. 58/16 (February 25, 1958).

Stefancic, Jean, and Richard Delgado. "Outsider Jurisprudence and the Electronic Revolution: Will Technology Help or Hinder the Cause of Law Reform?" *Ohio State Law Journal* 52 (1991).

St. John, Paige. "29,000 California Prison Inmates Refuse Meals in 2nd Day of Protest." *Los Angeles Times,* July 9, 2013. https://www.latimes.com/local /la-xpm-2013-jul-09-la-me-ff-prison-strike-20130710-story.html.

Suleiman, Imam Omar. "How Can We Make It Right? What the World's Religions Have to Say about Justice." Interview by Carol Juruvilla. *Vox,* 2021. https://www.vox.com/the-highlight/22419487/religion-justice-fairness.

Sunan al-Tirmidhi. Vol. 5. Book of Tafsir of the Qu'ran. Hadith 2955.

Surat al-Rum 30:22.

Terrorism: Radical Islamic Influence of Chaplaincy of the U.S. Military and Prisons. Hearing before the Senate Subcommittee on Terrorism, Technology, and Homeland Security, 108th Congress (2003).

Thomas, Jim, and Barbara H. Zaitzow. "Conning or Conversion? The Role of Religion in Prison Coping." *Prison Journal* 86, no. 2 (2004).

The Threat of Muslim-American Radicalization in U.S. Prisons. Hearing before the House Committee on Homeland Security, 112th Congress (2011).

Turner, William Bennett. "Establishing the Rule of Law in Prisons: A Manual for Prisoners' Rights Litigation." *Stanford Law Review* 23, no. 3 (1971).

"2 Killings Bring 200 year Terms for 2 Robbers." *Chicago Daily Tribune,* January 20, 1953.

Unbound Allstars. "Mumia 9/11." *Genius.* https://genius.com/Unbound-allstars-mumia-911-lyrics.

United States Commission on Civil Rights. "Prisoners' Free Exercise Claims," table 2.1. In *Enforcing Religious Freedom in Prison.* US Commission on Civil Rights, 2008.

United States Congress, Senate. *Committee on Intelligence of the United States Senate. Current and Projected National Security Threats to the United States.* 108th Congress, February 16, 2005.

United States Congress, House. Committee on Homeland Security. *The Threat of Muslim American Radicalization in U.S. Prisons.* 112th Congress, March 10, 2011.

United States Congress, Senate. Committee on Homeland Security and Governmental Affairs. *Prison radicalization: Are Terrorist Cells Forming in U.S. Cell Blocks?* 109th Congress, September 19, 2006.

Valdes, Francisco. "Outsider Jurisprudence, Critical Pedagogy, and Social Activism: Marking the Stirrings of Critical Legal Education." *Asian American Law Journal* 10 (2003).

———. "Outside Scholars, Legal Theory and OutCrit Perspectivity: Postsubordination Vision as Jurisprudential Method." *De Paul Law Review* 49 (2000).

Viswanathan, Gauri. *Outside the Fold: Conversion, Modernity, and Belief.* Princeton NJ: Princeton University Press, 1998.

Waller, Michael. *Terrorist Recruitment and Infiltration in the United States: Prisons and Military as an Operational Base, Testimony before the Subcom-*

mittee On Terrorism, Technology, and Homeland Security of the Senate Committee on the Judiciary, 108th Congress (2003).

Warfare History Network. "Vietnam War: Muhammad Ali's Draft Controversy." *National Interest,* January 12, 2021, https://web.archive.org /web/20210117132706/https://nationalinterest.org/blog/reboot/vietnam-war-muhammad-alis-draft-controversy-176177.

Wasserman, Lewis M., John P. Connolly, and Kent R. Kerley. "Religious Liberty in Prisons under the Religious Land Use and Institutionalized Persons Act Following *Holt v. Hobbs:* An Empirical Analysis." *Religions* 9, no. 7 (2018): 210.

Wildeman, Christopher. "Incarceration and Population Health in Wealthy Democracies." *Criminology* 54, no. 2 (2016).

Willingham, A. J. "By 2040, Islam Could Be the Second Biggest Religion in the US." *CNN,* January 10, 2018. https://www.cnn.com/2018/01/10/politics /muslim-population-growth-second-religious-group-trnd/index.html.

X, John. "Muhammad Subject of Wide Press Coverage." *Muhammad Speaks* (1960).

X, Malcolm. *The Autobiography of Malcolm X.* New York: Grove Press, 1965.

X, Malcom, and Alex Haley. *The Autobiography of Malcolm X (As Told to Alex Haley).* New York: Ballantine Books, 1992.

X, Malcolm, and Alex Haley. *The Autobiography of Malcolm X.* New York: Random House Publishing Group, 2015.

Yamani, Ahmad Zaki. "Social Justice in Islam." *Islamic Studies* 41, no. 1 (2002).

Index